Language Ideologies and L2 Speaker Legitimacy

MULTILINGUAL MATTERS

Series Editors: Leigh Oakes, *Queen Mary, University of London, UK* and Jeroen Darquennes, *Université de Namur, Belgium.*

Multilingual Matters series publishes books on bilingualism, bilingual education, immersion education, second language learning, language policy, multiculturalism. The editors are particularly interested in 'macro' level studies of language policies, language maintenance, language shift, language revival and language planning. Books in the series discuss the relationship between language in a broad sense and larger cultural issues, particularly identity related ones.

All books in this series are externally peer-reviewed.

Full details of all the books in this series and of all our other publications can be found on http://www.multilingual-matters.com, or by writing to Multilingual Matters, St Nicholas House, 31-34 High Street, Bristol, BS1 2AW, UK.

MULTILINGUAL MATTERS: 172

Language Ideologies and L2 Speaker Legitimacy

Native Speaker Bias in Japan

Jae DiBello Takeuchi

MULTILINGUAL MATTERS
Bristol • Jackson

DOI https://doi.org/10.21832/TAKEUC4648
Library of Congress Cataloging in Publication Data
A catalog record for this book is available from the Library of Congress.
Names: Takeuchi, Jae DiBello, author.
Title: Language Ideologies and L2 Speaker Legitimacy: Native Speaker Bias in Japan/Jae DiBello Takeuchi.
Description: Bristol; Jackson: Multilingual Matters, [2023] | Series: Multilingual Matters: 172 | Includes bibliographical references and index. | Summary: "This book examines dilemmas faced by second language Japanese speakers as a result of persistent challenges to their legitimacy as speakers of Japanese. It explores ideologies linked to three core speech styles of Japanese - keigo or polite language, gendered language and regional dialects - to show how such ideologies impact L2-Japanese speakers"— Provided by publisher.
Identifiers: LCCN 2022050554 (print) | LCCN 2022050555 (ebook) | ISBN 9781800414648 (hardback) | ISBN 9781800414662 (epub) | ISBN 9781800414655 (pdf)
Subjects: LCSH: Japanese language—Acquisition. | Japanese language—Study and teaching—Foreign speakers. | Second language acquisition. | Language awareness.
Classification: LCC PL524.85 .T35 2023 (print) | LCC PL524.85 (ebook) | DDC 306.442/956052—dc23/eng/20221223
LC record available at https://lccn.loc.gov/2022050554
LC ebook record available at https://lccn.loc.gov/2022050555

British Library Cataloguing in Publication Data
A catalogue entry for this book is available from the British Library.

ISBN-13: 978-1-80041-464-8 (hbk)
ISBN-13: 978-1-80041-463-1 (pbk)

Multilingual Matters
UK: St Nicholas House, 31-34 High Street, Bristol, BS1 2AW, UK.
USA: Ingram, Jackson, TN, USA.
Authorised Representative: Easy Access System Europe – Mustamäe tee 50, 10621 Tallinn, Estonia gpsr.requests@easproject.com.

Website: www.multilingual-matters.com
Bluesky: https://bsky.app/profile/multi-ling-mat.bsky.social
Twitter: Multi_Ling_Mat
Facebook: https://www.facebook.com/multilingualmatters
Blog: www.channelviewpublications.wordpress.com

Copyright © 2023 Jae DiBello Takeuchi.

All rights reserved. No part of this work may be reproduced in any form or by any means without permission in writing from the publisher.

The policy of Multilingual Matters/Channel View Publications is to use papers that are natural, renewable and recyclable products, made from wood grown in sustainable forests. In the manufacturing process of our books, and to further support our policy, preference is given to printers that have FSC and PEFC Chain of Custody certification. The FSC and/or PEFC logos will appear on those books where full certification has been granted to the printer concerned.

Typeset by Deanta Global Publishing Services, Chennai, India.

Contents

Acknowledgements	viii
1 Introduction	**1**
Why Speaker Legitimacy Matters: Foreign Residents in Japan	3
Japanese Speech Styles	15
Researcher Positionality	18
Outline of the Book	20
2 This Study: L2 Speakers in Japan	**24**
Study Background	24
Data and Procedures	25
Participants	29
Where Participants Lived and Worked	35
3 'Foreigners Don't Need *Keigo*': Excusing L2 Speakers from *Keigo*	**38**
Introduction	38
Previous Studies of *Keigo*	39
Study Participants: *Keigo's* Relevance for L2 Speakers	45
Beliefs about *Keigo*	46
Discussion	57
Conclusion	58
4 Trying (Not) to Sound Like a 'Girly-Girl' or a 'Manly-Man'	**60**
Introduction	60
Previous Studies of Japanese Gendered Language	61
Study Participants and Japanese Gendered Language	69
Discussion	86
Conclusion	88
5 'You're Speaking Dialect, That's Funny Cuz You're a Foreigner'	**90**
Introduction	90
Previous Studies of Japanese Dialect	91

Case Study: Ehime Dialect	99
L1 Study Participants' Views about Dialect and L2 Speakers	102
L2 Study Participants: Encountering and Negotiating Dialect	104
Discussion	124
Conclusion	125

6 'His Japanese Makes No Sense' 126
Introduction 126
Previous Studies of Native Speaker Bias 127
Study Participants and Depictions of L2 Speakers 134
Discussion 149
Conclusion 151

7 Conclusion 152
To Be an L2 Speaker in Japan 152

Appendix A: Sample L2 Interview Protocol 160
Appendix B: Sample L1 Interview Protocol 163
Appendix C: Transcription Conventions 167
Appendix D: Sample Questionnaires 168
References 173
Index 184

Acknowledgements

This book has occupied a huge space in my mind for a long time and now that it is done, I am overwhelmed when I think about everyone who has helped me as the book went from being an idea to a reality.

I would like to thank Junko Mori for her continuing guidance and thoughtful advice about all facets of research and publishing.

I have benefitted from sharing ideas with colleagues and participating in writing accountability groups. I would like to thank Amy Clay, Jason Kemp and Tiffany Creegan Miller for your friendship, ideas and writing encouragement. Also many thanks to Clemson University's Faculty Writing Group, organized by Cameron Bushnell, director of the Pearce Center for Professional Communication. I also want to give a shout out to the wonderful women in my FSP group, organized by the National Center for Faculty Development and Diversity.

I want to thank John Morgenstern, director of the Clemson University Press, for advice and guidance about book proposals and for making the process of contacting publishers less scary. I am forever indebted to everyone in Clemson University's Cooper Library Interlibrary Loan Department, especially Edward Rock and Jamal Williams, for their Herculean efforts to help me access the books and articles I needed. I would also like to thank Nalinee Patin, program administrator of Clemson's Institutional Review Board for her excellent (and patient!) guidance.

I am grateful to Salvador Oropesa, for his advice and support in the early stages of writing my book proposal. I am also grateful to the Clemson University Department of Languages and the College of Architecture, Arts and Humanities' Faculty Research Development Program for financial support for fieldwork in Japan.

Many thanks to Anna Roderick, editorial director at Multilingual Matters Press; the editors of the Multilingual Matters Series; and the anonymous reviewers: each of you helped me make my book better.

I am especially grateful for the support and encouragement of my family. Words cannot express my gratitude to my husband, Kenji Takeuchi, who kept me fed and never complained about being left alone while I worked through another weekend.

I want to thank my mother, Nan DiBello, for always being more interested in my research than anyone else, for offering excellent advice and for being the best role model anyone could hope for in terms of seeing and valuing the inherent legitimacy in others.

Lastly, I want to thank all the people in Japan who agreed to be study participants, made time to meet with me and generously shared some of their lives with me. I cannot thank each of you by name, but that does not diminish my gratitude. Without all of you, this book would not exist.

1 Introduction

Second language (L2) speakers have diverse experiences when they interact with first language (L1) speakers. Responses from their interlocutors run the gamut from positive affirmations that recognize them as speakers to messages that call into question their right to speak the L2. The legitimacy of L2 speakers, their 'speaker legitimacy', affects how they make choices about their L2 and how they use their L2, whether in social interactions or workplace contexts. The speaker legitimacy of L2 speakers refers to beliefs and opinions about who has the right to speak and have the content of their speech heard, and the absence of speaker legitimacy is a barrier to successful interactions in an L2. A central element in exploring L2 speaker legitimacy is 'native speaker bias', assumptions that posit L1 speakers as the standard for language use, which often take on a normative role in assessments of L2 speakers, both in terms of how L1 speakers assess L2 speakers and also how L2 speakers assess themselves.

Studies of second language acquisition (SLA), L2 speakers and L2 speaker legitimacy, while extensive, include a significant body of research that focuses exclusively on L2-English speakers and especially on L2-English speakers teaching English as an L2. To contribute to a broader understanding of L2 speakers with regard to whether and how they enjoy legitimacy as speakers of a language, my research focuses on L2-Japanese speakers. I analyze the kinds of dilemmas and challenges L2-Japanese speakers experience in Japan and the choices they make about Japanese use as a result of their experiences. Whether they are in workplaces or neighborhoods or chatting with acquaintances, L2-Japanese speakers in Japan have experiences that explicitly, or implicitly, diminish their legitimacy as speakers of Japanese. Thus, in my research, I seek a better understanding of speaker legitimacy by analyzing the impact of challenges to L2 speaker legitimacy in Japanese as an L2, with the goal of enhancing the legitimacy of L2-Japanese speakers and, by extension, L2 speakers more generally. My findings underscore the need for consideration of how L2 speakers can be, simultaneously, not Japanese *and* legitimate speakers of Japanese.

In order to understand the experience of L2 speakers, I focus on L2 speakers who live and work in Japan and are neither students nor in study abroad contexts. In addition, I include L1-speaker participants who are laypeople rather than Japanese language educators or linguists. While most studies focus on an individual aspect of Japanese, in this study I examine three speech styles that make up a core part of the Japanese linguistic repertoire: *keigo*, the complex and highly codified system of honorific and polite language; gendered language and ideas about how one should speak depending on one's gender; and regional dialects. L2 speakers living in Japan must not only learn and develop communication skills in these speech styles, but they must also reconcile these speech styles with language ideologies surrounding their use. I use the term 'language ideologies' to refer to beliefs, perceptions, constraints and tacit assumptions about language (e.g. Blackledge & Pavlenko, 2002; Kroskrity, 2004) that impact all speakers, whether L1 or L2.[1]

Through an ethnographic analysis of beliefs and perceptions of both L1 and L2 speakers, and my focus on L2 speakers who live and work in Japan, I offer insight into language ideologies and native speaker bias as experienced in daily life workplace and social settings. I detail how such ideologies serve to deny speaker legitimacy to L2 speakers, regardless of advanced language abilities or long-term residence in Japan. My findings contribute to the body of work examining language ideologies in applied linguistics and SLA and underscore the importance of speaker legitimacy for L2 speakers in general. At the same time, my focus on Japanese speech styles demonstrates how speaker legitimacy emerges in language-specific ways, in this case, in L2-Japanese. My findings affirm that legitimacy is often tenuous for L2-Japanese speakers and that native speaker bias is a persistent issue for L2 speakers in Japan.

This chapter begins with a discussion of the current situation for L2 speakers in Japan. In addition to adding depth to understanding the impacts of language ideologies that L2 speakers experience in Japan, this discussion is timely and important in light of Japan's current policies and practices toward immigrants and foreign workers. I also offer a brief introduction to the following concepts that are all aspects of language ideologies: speaker legitimacy, native speaker bias (along with a Japanese-specific version of this, *nihonjinron* or 'theories about the Japanese people') and language ownership. After consideration of language ideologies, I present a brief introduction to the three Japanese speech styles that will be the focus of the book. I conclude the chapter with a discussion of my researcher positionality and an overview of the chapters that present my research and analysis of L2-Japanese speakers in Japan.

Why Speaker Legitimacy Matters: Foreign Residents in Japan

Japan is known for having a small number of foreign residents. In 2012, Carroll (2012: 193) reported that 'Japan has the smallest number of foreign residents among the developed nations' and this remains accurate. Nevertheless, numbers have been increasing and, in 2020, the number of foreign residents increased to over 2.25% of the population, a number that is approximately three times larger than it was in the 1990s (eStat.go .jp, 2020).[2] As Japan's population declines, discussions about the need to rely on foreign workers have increased, especially in the popular media (e.g. Itabashi, 2020). Efforts to counter societal resistance to immigration have become a common topic (e.g. Facchini *et al.*, 2016) and some claim that Japan has been able to avoid the explicit opposition to immigration often seen in other countries (Gelin, 2020). Despite progress, researchers have identified subtle but persistent problems experienced by foreign nationals in Japan, and they are critical of Japan's reluctance to take an active role in helping foreign residents become connected and valued members of society (e.g. Burgess, 2020). Although the number of both foreign residents and foreign visitors to Japan has steadily increased, numerous criticisms highlight ways that both Japanese government policies and Japanese society are unwelcoming to foreigners. For example, Strausz (2019: xii) calls Japan's immigration policies 'extremely restrictive'. Kamiyoshi (2020) cites instances of xenophobia and points to increasing incidents of hate speech directed at foreign residents. Carlson (2018) describes the impacts on foreign residents' experience as a result of limited employment options in general and limited opportunities for long-term employment in particular. In addition, it is common for foreign residents to describe feeling like, and being treated as, perpetual guests in the country, despite being long-term residents (e.g. Arudou, 2012; Carlson, 2018).

That foreign residents feel like guests who are expected to eventually leave is not surprising given the official stance that Japan's visa categories and border control laws should not be interpreted as immigration policies. Even the name of the government agency responsible for border control belies the government's position: the Japanese name of the agency is *Shutsu-nyūkoku Zairyū Kanrikyoku*, which directly translated is 'bureau for entering, departing, and residing in the country'. However, the official English name, which appears on the agency website, is the Immigration Services Agency. What stands out here is that the Japanese name does not include the Japanese word for immigration, *imin*. This practice can also be seen in official documents and government statements, and Burgess (2020: 19) criticizes the consistent avoidance of *imin* 'in favor of euphemisms like "entrant" or "worker"'. Burgess observes that, despite new laws designed to facilitate visas for a wider range of occupations, including so-called low-skills occupations, public sentiment remains strongly anti-immigration, which can be seen in social practices, official policies and in the language used by politicians. Burgess (2020) reports that former Prime Minister Abe 'repeatedly emphasized that any kind of immigration policy is taboo', explaining:

> For example, in April 2014, during discussions on utilizing foreign workers in nursing care and house-keeping, Abe emphasized that such measures should not be misunderstood as immigration policies (*imin seisaku to gokai sarenai yo ni*) (Prime Minister of Japan and his Cabinet 2014). Similarly, in October of the same year he declared that his administration was not thinking of adopting a 'so-called immigration policy' (*iwayuru imin seisaku o toru koto o kangaeteinai*) (Sankei Shimbun, Oct. 1, 2014). This stance of not adopting an immigration policy (*imin seisaku wa toranai*) has remained consistent even during the latest 'immigration' debate. (Hashimoto, 2018, cited in Burgess, 2020: 9)

Kamiyoshi (2022: 170) argues that the word *imin* is so carefully avoided because it is seen as 'signifying migrants obtaining permanent residence, a situation they [the government] have been clear that they wish to avoid'. Indeed, the tendency to avoid the word '*imin*' in policy language reflects practices intended to discourage long-term residence by foreign workers. Strausz (2019) examines how Japan's border control policies align with public and political discourse about the role of immigration in Japan and he argues that deep-seated notions about what it means to be Japanese are responsible for the widespread belief that an increase in the number of immigrants is a threat to Japanese identity. As a result, although Japanese companies have lobbied for immigration laws that would allow them to hire larger numbers of foreign workers, especially so-called low-skills workers, Japanese lawmakers have 'concluded that foreign laborers threaten social stability, so they have resolved to limit their entry, even if that meant hurting Japanese industry and the Japanese economy' (Strausz, 2019: 28).

Nevertheless, the number of foreign residents in Japan continues to increase, and the number of foreign residents who call Japan home and intend to remain indefinitely is also increasing. Most foreign residents not only live their lives in Japan, but they also live their lives *in Japanese*, as speakers of Japanese. Most often, Japanese is an L2 for foreign residents, and Japanese is their primary resource for workplace and social interactions, and often is the language of some of their most important personal relationships. Japanese language is inseparable from the practical and affective needs of L2-Japanese speakers who reside in Japan, and Japanese language skills are essential for their success in a variety of contexts. In particular, Kamiyoshi (2022) points out that a foreign resident's Japanese language ability often plays a role in finding long-term employment. However, Japanese is not merely an instrumental resource. When the language skills of L2-Japanese speakers are considered, the role of language in building and maintaining community memberships, connecting to others and expressing a sense of self and identity is often overlooked, but language meets many needs and those needs do not change simply because one is speaking an L2.

Today, interest in the Japanese language abilities of non-native speakers in Japan is at an all-time high, as can be seen in some recent developments that illustrate the increased attention to non-native Japanese speakers. For example, visa categories in Japan have been revised in order to better attract foreign workers who can augment Japan's workforce, which is shrinking in the face of population decline (Ebuchi, 2019; Strausz, 2019). Policy changes relaxed visa restrictions and implemented a point-based system that actively rewards foreign professionals for advanced Japanese language competence (Japan Ministry of Justice, 2017; also see Burgess, 2020). Another example is the Promotion of Japanese Language Education Act (PJLEA) of 2019, which was passed after language educators in Japan petitioned the government to formalize education for Japanese as a foreign language (JFL) (Bunkacho, 2019; Kamiyoshi, 2020). While such developments attest to the widely held belief that Japanese language ability will facilitate the participation and integration of L2-Japanese speakers in workplaces and communities, problems remain. Kamiyoshi (2022) criticizes the use of Japanese language proficiency requirements as a gatekeeping method. He cites the arbitrary use of language tests for foreign migrants not only as a selection tool (e.g. when Japanese proficiency is an employment requirement), but also as an exclusion tool, as seen when language requirements are applied to some migrant workers but not others. Similarly, Otomo (2019, 2020) argues that there are hidden ideologies in language training for foreign workers, who are often expected to develop Japanese language skills based on a monolingual, native-speaker standard.

Another recent development is a renewed push to encourage L1-Japanese speakers to use *yasashii nihongo*, which is Japanese that has been modified to be easy to understand for L2 speakers. *Yasashii nihongo* is generally translated as 'easy Japanese' or 'plain Japanese', but the word can also be used to mean kind or considerate. Because neither 'easy' nor 'plain' captures the full range of meanings of *yasashii*, I will use *yasashii nihongo* rather than an English translation (following Burgess, 2012, 2021; Iori, 2016; Kimura, 2022; Kusunoki & Hashimoto, 2022).

Yasashii nihongo is generally described as Japanese that uses simple structures, avoids ambiguous expressions and difficult vocabulary and, when written, uses minimal kanji (characters) and includes pronunciation aids to facilitate reading (Hasegawa, 2022). *Yasashii nihongo* was originally introduced after the 1995 Great Hanshin-Awaji Earthquake as a way to provide emergency information in Japanese using simplified language to make it more accessible and understandable for foreign residents (Gottlieb, 2012; Iori, 2016). Calls to use *yasashii nihongo* increased as Japan prepared to host the 2020 Tokyo Olympics (Nakao, 2020), and Iori (e.g. 2019, 2021) has been a vocal advocate not only for the use of *yasashii nihongo* in emergency situations but also *yasashii nihongo* as a way to facilitate daily interactions between Japanese and foreign residents. Iori argues that *yasashii nihongo* should also be used in Japanese textbooks for adult foreign residents and for children of foreign residents who may not use Japanese at home. There has also been increased interest in implementing *yasashii nihongo* as a better way to communicate with tourists (Yamada, 2021).

Yasashii nihongo is promoted in pamphlets and training sessions geared toward government workers, businesses and companies that hire foreign workers, and shopkeepers and restaurants in tourist areas (e.g. Ito & Tokarev, 2021; Kimura, 2022) but questions have been raised regarding its implementation. Kusunoki and Hashimoto (2022) reviewed government websites and interviewed government workers and found numerous problems. For example, they found that different entities had different definitions for what counted as *yasashii nihongo* and used inconsistent and confusing definitions of *yasashii nihongo*. The target audience for *yasashii nihongo* was also unclear and inconsistent from one entity to another. Kusunoki and Hashimoto (2022: 3) conclude that there was 'a lack of systematic coordination within municipalities and an absence of any initiative by the central government to implement YN [*yasashii nihongo*], which has resulted in the inconsistent use of YN in local communities'. They also criticize the tendency to rely on volunteers for *yasashii nihongo* training and other language support for foreign residents, especially because the volunteers generally are not language teachers or language specialists. Kusunoki and Hashimoto also note the lack of input from the L2-Japanese-speaking residents for whom *yasashii nihongo* is intended. Hasegawa (2022) points out an additional problem, namely that while numerous publications offer instructional guidance for *yasashii nihongo*, there has been little to no research examining the effectiveness of *yasashii nihongo* in facilitating the interaction and social integration of L2-Japanese speakers.

In addition to the above logistical issues, there are also more substantial concerns. Yamada (2021) notes that *yasashii nihongo* was developed by Japanese language teachers who have the ability to adjust their speech based on years of teaching and interacting with L2-Japanese speakers. However, L1 speakers with little experience interacting with L2 speakers may find it more difficult to know when and how to adjust their speech. An additional concern relates to the potential for unintended consequences of relying on *yasashii nihongo* to interact with L2 speakers. Although the goal of making important information more accessible is a positive one, Burgess (2012) argues that the *yasashii nihongo* movement is based on the belief that Japanese language is too difficult for non-Japanese. More recent work reaches similar conclusions. Ito and Tokarev (2021) point out that overemphasis on using *yasashii nihongo* with L2-Japanese speakers could be patronizing and lead to discrimination against members of language minorities in Japan. They argue that emphasis on *yasashii nihongo* is based on a hidden 'Japanese language only' ideology. Similarly, Kusunoki (2018) argues that beliefs about the necessity of *yasashii nihongo* reveal both native speaker bias and ideologies of L1-Japanese speakers' ownership of Japanese. Kusunoki and Hashimoto (2022) also argue that advocating for the use of *yasashii nihongo* when interacting with foreign residents in daily life situations reinforces divisions between Japanese and non-Japanese people. Similar concerns were raised by Kimura (2022) and Inoue and Kurata (2020), who argue that reliance on *yasashii nihongo* will have a negative influence on the language development of foreign workers, trapping them in low-wage jobs and relegating them to the status of second-class citizens.

Recent attention to Japanese language education for foreign residents and the movement for *yasashii nihongo* reflect the belief that if the Japanese language abilities of foreign residents improve, Japanese people and foreigners will be better able to 'coexist' happily – as seen in the increasingly common use of the words *kyōsei* (coexisting) and *tabunka-kyōsei* (multicultural coexisting) on government websites and in the popular media (e.g. *Yasashii Nihongo ni tsuite*, 2020; also see Taniguchi & MacMahill, 2015). Kamiyoshi (2022) argues that the use of the word *kyōsei* in the 2019 PJLEA demonstrates the expectation that Japanese language ability will play a positive role in the social inclusion of foreign residents. However, numerous criticisms have been raised that call into question the degree to which attention to *kyōsei* is actually concerned with integrating foreign residents into Japanese society (e.g. Ueda & Yamashita, 2006). Taniguchi and MacMahill (2015: 168) argue that '"*tabunka-kyōsei*" has mainly been used to implement policies and programs that do not support multiculturalism or multilingualism but in fact are coercive and assimilative' for speakers of minority languages in Japan, and they observe that the idea of diversifying Japan is conspicuously missing from policy documents. Kamiyoshi (2022) comes to a similar conclusion, arguing that Japanese language activities and other *kyōsei* initiatives are centrally concerned with assimilating foreign residents to Japanese norms and do not entertain the possibility that Japanese society may need to change as well. Finally, Burgess (2021) calls *tabunka-kyōsei* 'Japanese-style multiculturalism' and argues that it is built upon *nihonjinron* ideology of a homogeneous and monolingual Japan which posits a binary between Japanese and non-Japanese and is othering to foreign residents:

> Unfortunately, equating *tabunka-kyōsei* with integration represents a grave misunderstanding of the term. Previously, I (2004a) have argued that *tabunka-kyōsei* is a particularly sophisticated discourse that defines,

contains, reifies, locks in, and reinforces difference thereby limiting access to social resources and maintaining the power of the dominant group – 'Othering' not by exclusion but by inclusion. Many others have also argued that the Japanese brand of multiculturalism is exclusionary and essentialising rather than accepting of difference, an ideology used by the dominant group to affirm its own distinctness and separateness and maintain the sharp Japanese/foreigner distinction. (Burgess, 2021: 17)

The above researchers agree that social integration must be a two-way process; however, the discourse of *kyōsei* seeks only a one-way assimilation of foreign residents into a normative Japanese society.

While greater attention to Japanese language education and calls for increased mutual understanding are all positive developments, it is clear that without addressing problems such as native speaker bias, improved Japanese ability alone will be insufficient to bring about mutual understanding. Japan's current interest in augmenting its workforce by attracting foreign workers has created more opportunities than ever before for foreign nationals to live in Japan. Recent policies supporting Japanese language instruction for foreign workers and greater awareness of the importance of promoting mutual understanding between Japanese citizens and foreign nationals are also welcome developments. Nevertheless, the findings I present in the following chapters underscore an important and necessary further step, namely, promoting L2-Japanese speakers as legitimate speakers and encouraging communities and businesses to reduce bias against those who speak Japanese as their L2.

Language ideologies and L2 speakers

The study of language ideologies is well developed as an area in applied linguistics. Silverstein's (1979) early work is foundational in how researchers approach and explain language ideologies. Silverstein (1979: 193) defined language ideologies as 'any sets of beliefs about language articulated by users as a rationalization or justification' for language use. In other words, language ideologies are best understood as how speakers understand and justify why they speak the way they do. Studies of language ideologies have described the use of language ideologies to rationalize or justify beliefs about language use and depictions of language users. Another important feature of language ideologies is that the ideas they represent are often viewed as common sense or taken for granted. According to Rumsey (1990: 346), language ideologies are 'shared bodies of commonsense notions about the nature of language'. Woolard (1992: 237) points out that language ideologies tend to be 'presented as universally true'. At the same time, language ideologies are often so ubiquitous that they evade awareness, which contributes to the impression that linguistic choices and the ideas that inform them are 'natural' (Heinrich, 2012: 1).

Consequently, language ideologies often go unnoticed, with the result that their impact on speakers is difficult to recognize. The pervasiveness of language ideologies is particularly apparent when even speakers who do not benefit from language ideologies subscribe to them, despite their detrimental impacts (Heinrich, 2012). An example can be seen when speakers ascribe to ideologies that position one form of language (e.g. an accent or dialect) as being superior to another, even when the form depicted as being worse is the form they themselves are using.

Nakamura (2011: 8) describes language ideologies as belief systems, rather than simply as ways of speaking or examples of speech, in which language and language forms are hierarchically ordered as 'good/bad' and 'correct/incorrect' forms. Depictions of accents, dialects and other aspects of language as good or bad, correct or incorrect, are then influenced by sociocultural contexts and vary with political, economic and academic circumstances. Nakamura also explained that ideologies can focus on languages themselves, such as a hierarchical ranking of, for instance, English as compared to French. Language ideologies can also focus on details within a language – in the case of Japanese, a hierarchical ranking could be applied to Standard Japanese in comparison to a regional dialect or to different speech styles, such as plain versus honorific speech. Nakamura's definition underscores the hierarchical nature of language ideologies, in which a way of speaking or a particular speaker is evaluated as better than another – more correct, more appropriate and, therefore, more legitimate.

Bourdieu's (1991) notion of 'linguistic capital' offers a useful way to describe hierarchical rankings of languages or language varieties. Linguistic capital, a form of symbolic capital, refers to the greater value that some languages or varieties have compared to others. According to Bourdieu (1991: 37), symbolic power is unevenly distributed, and linguistic exchanges are not merely exchanges of discrete referential information, but are also 'relations of symbolic power in which the power relations between speakers or their respective groups are actualized'. In general, standard languages and prestige dialects tend to afford speakers more linguistic capital; however, which language or variety of language has more linguistic capital depends on the context, the interlocutors, the topic and other features of the interaction. A crucial characteristic of linguistic capital is that it functions as a resource for speakers, for example, by facilitating access to educational or occupational contexts (e.g. Harrison, 2009; Silver, 2005; Vaish & Tan, 2008). Further, speakers' beliefs and perceptions about languages and speech styles – their language ideologies – inform their linguistic choices, and this underscores how language ideologies result in the unequal distribution of linguistic capital.

An additional role of language ideologies is their use in evaluating language and speakers, especially in terms of evaluating speakers as superior or inferior (e.g. Kroskrity, 2004). The impact of such judgments are seen when native speakers are evaluated as 'better than' non-native speakers. Language ideologies have particular relevance for L2 speakers because they serve a gatekeeping function, for example, when acceptable or appropriate language use is treated as a prerequisite for membership in particular realms or communities (Kubota, 2014). Language ideologies also include feelings that come from aesthetic reactions to language (Kroskrity, 2004). A common example of an aesthetic reaction can be seen when L1 speakers are critical of L2 speakers' accents, which is suggestive of the ways that language ideologies can and do undermine speakers of any language.

Speaker legitimacy

Language ideologies form the underpinnings of ideas about linguistic legitimacy, as introduced by Bourdieu (1991) and expanded upon by researchers in applied linguistics and SLA, including Grenfell (2011), Higgins (2003), Smith (2015) and Wee (2002). 'Legitimate language' refers to the language or language variety that is valued in a particular context, and thus is the 'socially dominant linguistic form' (Grenfell, 2011: 51). By definition, a legitimate language is the language used by those in positions of social, political or economic power, and which language or language variety is legitimate is highly context dependent (e.g. Reagan, 2019; Stroud, 2002). In addition to a focus on correct forms of language use, linguistic legitimacy also entails ideas and beliefs about speakers' rights and privileges, that is, which kinds of speakers have the 'right' to use which kinds of language. In his work examining the role of symbolic capital in linguistic exchanges, Bourdieu (1991) developed the concept of 'speaker legitimacy' and argued that it is the legitimate language which has the most linguistic capital. For Bourdieu, being a legitimate speaker is inherent in language ideologies of correctness and appropriateness, which position some forms of language as more correct or appropriate than others. Bourdieu also described how some speakers have more rights to a certain language or speech style than other speakers.

When speakers have both access to and competence in the legitimate language or language variety, Bourdieu found, they gain access to contexts and interlocutors, which affords them symbolic benefits and facilitates their membership in workplaces and local communities. Conversely, the absence of speaker legitimacy will have negative consequences, because 'speakers lacking the legitimate competence are de facto excluded from the social domains in which this competence is required, or are condemned to silence' (Bourdieu, 1991: 55). More specifically, Bourdieu suggested that speakers without competence in the legitimate language or legitimate variety may find that their access to communities and other speakers is restricted. Other researchers have found that those who seek long-term residence in a country where they are L2 speakers are especially impacted by the absence of speaker legitimacy. Both Kramsch and Zhang (2018) and O'Rourke and Ramallo (2011) have examined these consequences with regard to language teachers and learners of minority languages and their findings are consistent with Bourdieu's analysis.

The absence of speaker legitimacy is most apparent when the form of speech, rather than the content, becomes the focus of attention. For example, when someone lacks speaker legitimacy, their speech is vulnerable to being critiqued or evaluated by those speakers who do enjoy speaker legitimacy (e.g. Liddicoat, 2016). Moreover, it is often a speaker's identity, as immediately evident in visible identity, such as race or gender, or legal identity, such as citizenship, that will determine speaker legitimacy, rather than some objective linguistic knowledge or competence (e.g. Kubota, 2009; Smith, 2015). Consequently, L1 or so-called 'native' speakers are by default regarded as legitimate speakers.

Native speaker bias

When native speakers are positioned as legitimate, non-native speakers are correspondingly positioned as not legitimate; legitimate versus non-legitimate positioning is thus at the center of native speaker bias (e.g. Davies, 2007; Holliday, 2006). Native speaker bias has been criticized for depicting the native speaker as an idealized, perfect speaker while overlooking the significant diversity and variation that can be seen when comparing one native speaker to another (e.g. Doerr, 2009a; Firth & Wagner, 1997, 2007; Houghton & Rivers, 2013; Rampton, 1990). When the native speaker is posited as an ideal, perfect speaker, the non-native speaker is correspondingly depicted as a 'deficient communicator' (Firth & Wagner, 1997, 2007). Researchers examining ideologies about native speakers have used terms such as 'native speaker concept' (e.g. Doerr, 2009a) or 'native speakerism' (e.g. Holliday, 2006; Houghton *et al.*, 2018; Houghton & Hashimoto, 2018). What all of these studies have in common is a critique of the bias that results from native speaker ideologies, and native speaker bias has direct and negative impacts on L2 speakers. Therefore, in this book, I will use the term 'native speaker bias' to convey those negative implications.

Language ideologies have significant negative impacts on the ability of L2-Japanese speakers to freely use Japanese. Native speaker bias is apparent when we examine ideologies about language, including what counts as correct or appropriate language, along with ideologies about which speakers count as legitimate speakers. Ideas about what counts as correct or appropriate Japanese can also be in conflict with a speaker's attempts to use language in ways that fit their own ideas about identity and voice. Such attempts are complicated for L2 speakers who may feel constrained by beliefs about how they are 'supposed' to speak in the L2.

L2 speakers in Japan are affected by ideologies of native speaker bias that complicate their ability to negotiate Japanese speech styles, forcing them to contend with issues that go beyond acquiring linguistic competence and instead involve identity, access and agency. Native speaker bias has been extensively studied with regard to L2-English speakers who teach English (e.g. Cook, 1999, 2016; Davies, 2003; Holliday, 2006, 2014). With regard to native speaker bias experienced by L2-Japanese speakers, the studies in Doerr's (2009a) edited volume offer important insights. For example, Okubo (2009) criticizes the institutional reproduction and reinforcement of ethnicized understandings of speakerhood, with the result that only those who are ethnically Japanese are seen as native and legitimate speakers of Japanese.

Linguistic competence is a central concern in SLA, and ideologies of non-native speaker deficiency are reinforced when native speaker competence is used as the criteria against which L2 speakers are judged and evaluated, as opposed to, for example, evaluating functionality or communicative competence in its own right (e.g. Cook, 2016; Firth & Wagner, 1997, 2007). L2 speakers are also impacted by the tendency to make ideological linkages between citizenship and native speaker status (cf. Doerr, 2009a; Pennycook, 1994), and by links between ethnicity and native speaker status (e.g. Okubo, 2009). In addition, the discourse of the native speaker also views language as homogeneous and fixed (cf. Doerr, 2009a; Pennycook, 1994), with a focus on one standard, correct version of the language. These ideologies become visible when L2 speakers' language use is defined as incorrect and not 'native-like'. Finally, native speaker bias assumes that native speakers have complete and perfect competence, which can be a burden on individual speakers who may not measure up to this imaginary 'native speaker' standard.

Research on native speaker bias also includes work examining Japanese teachers and learners of Japanese as an L2, and these studies include both classroom and non-classroom contexts (e.g. Kubota, 2009; Okubo, 2009; Sato, 2009). However, studies of Japanese instruction and L2-Japanese learners are in the minority – the vast majority of research on native speaker bias remains focused on English as an L2, and especially on non-native speakers who are teachers of English as an L2. There remains a need for more inquiry into how native speaker bias plays a role in languages other than English; moreover, few studies consider the experience of L2 speakers who are no longer involved in classroom or instructional contexts.

Language ownership

An additional consequence of restricted speaker legitimacy and native speaker bias is that L2 speakers lack ownership of their L2. Language ownership refers to the control that speakers have over the use and development of a language (Wee, 2002). In addition, language ownership also entails the right to evaluate or judge linguistic output, for example when one speaker explicitly comments on the appropriateness of the speech of another person (Takeuchi, 2020b). Language ownership is closely connected to ideologies about native speakers in that native speakers are the *de facto* owners of the language. Thus, ideologies that undermine L2 speakers' efforts to achieve and maintain language proficiency also diminish language ownership.

Japanese-specific ideologies of language ownership and native speaker bias can also be seen in *nihonjinron*, or 'theories about the Japanese people'. *Nihonjinron* rose to prominence in the 1960s and posited a harmonious and homogeneous society, with the Japanese language depicted as being an essential component (Gottlieb, 2005). A core concept in *nihonjinron* is a view of Japan and the Japanese language as unique, and *speaking* Japanese is seen as an essential component of *being* Japanese (Kubota, 2014; Kusaka, 2014; Miller, 2015). Consequently, someone who is not Japanese is believed to be unable to become completely proficient in the Japanese language (Menard-Warwick & Leung, 2017).

Researchers increasingly criticize and denounce *nihonjinron* theories (e.g. Gottlieb, 2005; Morris-Suzuki, 1998). Despite such criticisms, Kubota (2014) argues that there is ample evidence that *nihonjinron* ideas remain widespread, including beliefs about the uniqueness, and unique difficulty, of the Japanese language and the homogeneity of Japanese speakers. More recent works by Burgess (2020) and Fairbrother (2020) confirm the persistence of *nihonjinron* ideologies. These ideas impact L2 speakers in a variety of ways. For example, *nihonjinron* ideas are presented uncritically as factual information in JFL textbooks and other materials for L2 speakers (Gottlieb, 2005; Menard-Warwick & Leung, 2017). Cook (2006) also found that Japanese host families often invoked *nihonjinron* beliefs in conversations with L2-Japanese-speaking homestay students. Suzuki (2009) demonstrates how *nihonjinron* theories can be co-constructed in interaction between L1 and L2 speakers and she discussed the impact of *nihonjinron* on L2 speakers. Suzuki (2009: 105) observes that L2 speakers in Japan may find it necessary not only to acquire linguistic skills but also 'to negotiate their cultural membership [which] may occur irrespective of the learner's proficiency in the language'. Fairbrother (2020: 51) similarly argues that a core tenet of *nihonjinron* is the 'bifurcation of "Japanese" and "Others"', and she finds that hiring practices in Japan 'reflect these ideologies [and] then take native-speakerism into the realm of institutional racism, defined as systemic institutional inequality based on race' (Hardie & Tyson, 2013, cited in Fairbrother, 2020: 51).

Fukuda (2014: 55) argues that *nihonjinron* beliefs form the basis of Japanese language ownership in which L2 speakers are granted 'only partial ownership of Japanese'. She also argues that 'for many Japanese people, vernacular varieties such as regional dialects and slang are not considered to be part of the category-bound language of L2 speakers/ foreigners, but solely of L1 speakers or Japanese' (Fukuda, 2014: 54). These beliefs emerge in L1/L2 interaction when L1 speakers single out an L2 speaker's choice of words as strange or surprising, when the same words used by an L1 speaker would be treated as unremarkable. This practice leads to a type of linguistic marginalization (cf. Kroo & Satoh, 2021) in which the L2 speaker is treated as a *'henna gaijin*' or 'strange foreigner'. Nishizaka's (1999) work, along with Fukuda's and others, is particularly well known for examining how 'foreigners' – generally white, European foreigners – who excel at Japanese language or are knowledgeable about Japanese culture are treated as strange or surprising. Fukuda (2014), Iino (2006) and others have criticized *nihonjinron* for its depiction of an essentialized link between Japanese language fluency and being Japanese, and Fukuda, Iino and Nishizaka each point out ways that this practice forms the basis for the stereotype of the '*henna gaijin*' as someone who, despite being foreign and not of Japanese descent, is fluent in Japanese language. The '*henna gaijin*' stereotype is seen in television programing in which 'foreigners' (usually white, European foreigners) are invited on a program and their status as *henna gaijin* is not only highlighted, but also often the basis of the entire segment. Based on my own review, such television shows continue to be common, and they not only perpetuate the stereotype that it is strange for non-Japanese to be competent speakers of Japanese, but they also further contribute to the marginalization of L2 speakers by treating them as a source of entertainment.

In my study of L2 speakers' use of dialect (Takeuchi, 2020b), I examined language ownership of Japanese Dialect which emerged in the form of meta-talk about dialect, and I argued that meta-talk can have a negative impact on L2 speaker legitimacy. I found that language ownership can be explicit, as when one speaker describes a language (or variety) as 'my language' or 'our language' in ways that exclude the L2 speaker. These statements convey that the dialect does not belong to the L2 speaker. Other examples of less explicit assertions of language ownership include an L1 speaker giving advice to an L2 speaker about how to speak. Although not a direct claim of ownership by the L1 speaker, such practices are a way of exerting ownership over the language and control over how it is used. Crucially, the assertion of language ownership by an L1 speaker in an L1/L2 interaction can be othering for the L2 speaker. However, language ownership need not be restricted and can instead be implicitly shared between interlocutors, for example when an L2 speaker's language use is not the focus and talk proceeds unhindered. In such interactions, language ownership is shared between the L1 and the L2 speaker.

Ideally, all speakers of any language will exercise language ownership and experience a measure of control in using the language (Wee, 2002). From the standpoint of language learning, and drawing on Bourdieu (1991), Norton (1997) points out that when an L2 learner does not have ownership of the language they are learning, they are likely to feel that they are not legitimate speakers of that language. Further, as Fukuda (2014) argues, unrestricted access to a language should be seen as a linguistic human right (also see Phillipson *et al.*, 1995). However, as my book shows, L2-Japanese speakers, even those with advanced ability, encounter language ideologies that undermine their legitimacy and ownership as Japanese speakers.

Japanese Speech Styles

A major goal of my work is to examine ideologies of Japanese language with regard to speech styles. Japanese spoken language is well known for its rich variety of speech styles, which include *keigo* (polite and honorific language), gendered language (including men's and women's language) and regional dialects. Although there are other stylistic differences that could be considered (e.g. slang and casual speech, or written styles), these three styles, what Okamoto and Shibamoto-Smith (2016: 298) refer to as 'politeness, gender, and locality', tend to be the focus of Japanese sociolinguistic research and are also the most commonly described speech styles in materials designed for learners of JFL (e.g. Oka *et al.*, 2009). However, as Okamoto and Shibamoto-Smith (2016) point out with regard to sociolinguistic research on L1-Japanese speakers, most studies tend to only examine one of the three speech styles. The same can be said for studies of L2-Japanese: studies of L2-Japanese tend to examine either Japanese politeness or Japanese gendered language but not both; few studies examine Japanese Dialect as it pertains to L2-Japanese speakers; and there are no L2-Japanese studies that I am aware of in which these three speech styles are considered together. However, it can be argued that differences in politeness, gender and locality form the core of Japanese linguistic life, and L2-Japanese speakers who live in Japan quickly develop a degree of meta-linguistic awareness of these speech styles. This awareness also means that L2 speakers are likely to pick up on language ideologies about these speech styles, leading to a kind of reification of politeness, gender and locality that in turn facilitates scholarly examination of beliefs about the speech styles. An additional consideration is how these speech styles expand the expressive possibilities of Japanese and function as linguistic resources in a variety of contexts. Thus, in recognition of Okamoto and Shibamoto-Smith's point that these three speech styles are always interconnected for speakers, in this book, I examine each of the three speech styles as they pertain to L2-Japanese speakers.

Keigo: Polite and honorific language

Keigo is perhaps the most-studied Japanese speech style. It is a complex and highly codified system of honorific and polite language that includes grammatical forms, specialized vocabulary, polite prefixes and terms of address. Pedagogical texts and prescriptive approaches to language learning present a shopping list of factors that need to be taken into account in deciding when, with whom and how to use *keigo*. A common factor to consider is the relative ages of two speakers: a younger person would use humble forms to describe themselves and use honorific forms to describe an older person, while an older person could use plain or neutral forms. This is only one consideration, however. Additional factors include: the social standing of each speaker; their relationship to each other; the relationship of speakers to a referent (e.g. a person being discussed who may not be present at the interaction); group membership of the speakers; the topic at hand, the context and the aims of the interaction. These factors are sometimes described as 'distance', which includes vertical distance, such as social status, hierarchical positions in the workplace, and horizontal distance, such as degree of familiarity, and whether interlocutors are family members, friends or members of the same in-group versus out-group. An additional feature, about which there is much debate, is whether or to what degree the gender of a speaker influences the choice of *keigo* usage.

The different forms of *keigo* are sometimes described as being higher, or more polite, or lower, or less polite, than other forms. Researchers in Japanese linguistics have posited that *keigo* could be classified into three, four or more levels (e.g. Barešova, 2015; Barke, 2010; Coulmas, 2005; Okamoto & Shibamoto-Smith, 2016). The most common classification is as follows: plain speech, which could also be considered intimate speech; honorific speech, which elevates the interlocutor, the interlocutor's in-group or some other referent, including those not co-present; humble speech, which lowers the speaker or the speaker's in-group; and neutral polite speech, which neither elevates nor lowers any interlocutors or referents, but maintains a polite demeanor or sense of decorum. An additional category is *bikago*, or 'beautiful speech', which makes use of polite prefixes (*o-*, *go-*, *on-*) that attach to certain nouns. *Bikago* is not necessarily connected to interpersonal relationships but instead is used to make one's speech more 'beautiful', and includes examples such as *o-cha* (tea) and *o-sake* (sake), as well as nouns which we might see as connected to interpersonal relationships, such as *o-denwa* (phone) and *go-renraku* (contact). Research on *keigo* includes works that examine ideologies of *keigo* usage and *keigo* as a learning challenge for L2 speakers. These and other aspects of *keigo* are discussed in more detail in Chapter 3.

Gendered Japanese language

Gendered language in the case of Japanese refers not to grammatical gender (e.g. as is found in Romance languages) but to gendered linguistic forms, words and stylistic or speech habits that are normatively ascribed either to women as *joseigo* (women's language) or to men as *danseigo* (men's language). Examples of linguistic forms include the following: Japanese has numerous sentence-final particles, which do not have referential meaning but instead convey information such as emotive or affiliative stances (e.g. *ne* for seeking confirmation from an interlocutor) or epistemic stances (e.g. *deshō* for expressing lack of certainty about information). Some sentence-final particles are said to be used by women (e.g. *wa* or *kashira*) while others are said to be used by men (e.g. *ze or zo*). Examples of gendered words include the first-person singular pronouns, with *boku* and *ore* being part of men's language and *atashi* being part of women's language. Stylistic differences include a belief that women's language uses softer and more polite expressions while men's language uses rougher and less polite expressions. Gendered Japanese is discussed in Chapter 4.

Regional dialects

Japan has numerous regional dialects which are often discussed as a discrete speech style in contrast to Standard Japanese (*hyōjungo*) or common Japanese (*kyōtsūgo*). As such, while there are numerous dialects that can be considered individually, for ease of discussion, I will refer to dialect or Japanese Dialect in the singular when contrasting it to standard or Standard Japanese. Efforts to standardize Japanese began in the early 1900s and were so successful that it can now be said that standard or common Japanese can be understood anywhere in Japan. Standard Japanese is also the language of education and print and broadcast media. Despite efforts to the contrary, dialect use continues to be common, and some dialects are sufficiently different to be unintelligible to someone not familiar with them.

Japanese dialects can differ from Standard Japanese in a variety of ways, including differences at the phonological, morphological and lexical level. Phonological differences include differences in pitch accent as well as vowel shifts and lengthening, as in the standard *shimatta* (to do something regrettably) versus the dialect *shimōta* (Ehime Dialect). An example of a morphological difference can be seen in the conjugation of the present progressive, which in Standard Japanese is formed by combining the verb in the *te*-form with *iru*, while in Ehime Dialect, it is made by combining the verb stem with *yoru*. An example is the standard *yatte-iru* (am doing) which in Ehime Dialect becomes *yari-yoru*. Lexical differences include words that are only used in a dialect, like the Ehime Dialect word *gaina*, which is roughly equivalent to the standard *sugoi* (very, tremendous). Dialect tokens, or phonological, morphological or lexical features of dialect, can be used in conjunction with standard forms, resulting in a mixed style that nevertheless can be a comprehension challenge for someone unfamiliar with the dialect. Dialect will be discussed in Chapter 5.

As this brief introduction suggests, the variety of speech styles in Japanese can be challenging for Japanese language learners. At the same time, all three Japanese speech styles offer L2 speakers resources for richness of expression and linguistic interaction, and this is one of the reasons why many L2 speakers make active efforts to acquire not just general Japanese competence, but also competence in the various speech styles as well.

A recurring theme throughout the book is the need for L2 speakers to negotiate tensions between how they aspire to speak and the expectations they encounter for how L2 speakers 'should' speak. It is helpful to think of the three speech styles examined – *keigo*, gendered language and dialect – as a lens to reveal tensions about whether, how and when to use any one of them. As L2 participants contend with Japanese speech styles, they encounter language ideologies, or ideas about appropriate ways to speak. Sometimes, these ideologies dictate that L2 speakers should speak differently from their L1 counterparts. For example, L2 speakers may be discouraged from using *keigo* or be told that their Japanese speech is 'too feminine' or 'too masculine'. Also, when L2 speakers live in dialect-using regions and use dialect in their own speech, they sometimes learn that their dialect use is not always welcomed by local L1 speakers. Participants often struggled with contradictory messages and many described difficulties they had in reconciling competing ideologies of language use. Native speaker bias and a lack of speaker legitimacy and language ownership add to their struggles. Findings from the L1 participants add depth to the discussion and underscore the importance of including L1 speakers in research that seeks to understand the impact of language ideologies on L2 speakers' experiences.

Researcher Positionality

One issue that requires consideration is my positionality as the researcher – in other words, how various aspects of my identity may have impacted the study, including who I was able to recruit as participants, what spaces I was able to gain access to for observations and what kinds of data I was able to collect. From the standpoint of participants, I was both an 'insider' and an 'outsider'. First, I am a white woman and not of Asian descent. I originally went to Japan through the JET Program (described in Chapter 2) as an assistant language teacher (ALT). The JET Program is a common way for L1-English speakers to find work in Japan. In addition, the JET Program makes active efforts to encourage and maintain networking among current and former JET participants. As a result, when I recruited L2-Japanese speakers who were also connected to the JET Program, our shared connection likely made them more comfortable with participating in my study. Second, as an American who lived in Japan for 12 years, I found that other foreign residents often expressed curiosity about me and were interested in our common experiences. In addition to L2 speakers being happy to participate in the study, they also tended to agree to introduce me to other possible participants, both L2 and L1 speakers. When L2 speakers who lived in one of the four prefectures of Shikoku learned I had lived in Ehime, this was another commonality that helped people feel a connection to me and made them interested in participating.

Next, with regard to recruiting L1 participants, my ability to speak Japanese and to present my research materials in Japanese put them at ease and facilitated my access to various spaces for observations. My Japanese surname may have contributed to this and in some cases may have led L1 speakers to see me more as a 'cultural insider' than as a 'foreigner'. An additional factor here was the professional connections I had from my time living in Japan. After three years working in Ehime through the JET Program, I was hired directly by one of the local boards of education in Ehime, where I worked for another nine years until I left Japan. My connection to my former supervisors and coworkers was a resource for getting introductions and helped smooth the way to being admitted to L2 participants' workplaces. My background and connection to the board of education and city hall gave me important cultural capital, and my current position at an American university gave credibility to my project. I believe these aspects of my background encouraged people to trust me and not view my research project suspiciously. In addition, former L1-speaking colleagues helped with introductions to possible participants, both L1 and L2 speakers. In these ways, I think it was easy for both L1 and L2 participants to find something in me that they could easily connect with, which I believe had a positive impact and allowed me to recruit a large number of participants.

At the same time, there are ways in which I may have been perceived as more of an outsider. For example, unlike when I lived in Japan, I was now someone with higher educational credentials than most of my participants and, as a researcher from an overseas university, I may have been seen as someone coming from a position of authority. For L2 participants, I was usually older, and many asked about my Japanese skills, expressing surprise that I, as an L2-Japanese speaker, was teaching Japanese at a university in the United States. As a result, some L2 participants seemed self-conscious of their backgrounds and their Japanese language skills, and although it is impossible to know, this may have led them to be less open with me in their interviews. Lastly, I am visibly non-Japanese, and so whenever I was in public places with participants, I stood out in all of the same ways that any visibly non-Japanese person does in Japan. As such, my ability to 'fade into the background' during participant observations was sometimes limited.

I share all of these details not to suggest that they caused participants to respond to me in some predetermined way. Indeed, I do not believe there was a singular response to me that was similar across all participants. Further, I do not believe that it is possible to collect truly 'objective' data which is not influenced by the researcher. All interactions are the result of co-construction between interlocutors, and research interactions are no exception. Instead, I recognize that my identity, my background, my language skills and my appearance all influenced my interactions with participants, in ways that differed from one participant to the next and from one location to the next. See Chapter 2 for a discussion of the co-construction of talk and the use of interviews as data.

Outline of the Book

In Chapter 2, I present a discussion of beliefs and perceptions as a site of inquiry and consider why interviews are an effective way to study beliefs and perceptions with regard to language. Next, the L2 participants are introduced, and relevant aspects of their backgrounds are discussed. I highlight L2 participants' Japanese language abilities and discuss relevant details about their workplaces. Then I introduce the L1 participants and explain their connections to the L2 participants. The types of data gathered are detailed, along with a discussion of the approach to on-site observations. On-site observations were conducted in order to better understand participants' linguistic environments and the kinds of language use they encountered in their daily lives. An additional goal of observations was to observe the degree to which L2 participants were integrated into their workplaces and non-work communities. Finally, the benefits and drawbacks of this participant group are discussed and the differences in the relationships of some pairs of participants are considered. For example, some L1/L2 participant pairs are spouses or significant others, some are friends and others are coworkers. The implications of these relationships are discussed, in particular to consider how close friends and significant others may share similar views while simultaneously displaying beliefs that demonstrate the language ideologies examined in the book. Lastly, the strengths and weaknesses of the data types are considered.

Chapters 3–5 each focus on a specific speech style and introduce a subset of participants to consider issues related to speaker legitimacy with regard to the respective speech style. Chapter 3 focuses on *keigo*, the system of Japanese politeness language. The chapter begins with an introduction to some of the grammatical details of *keigo*, along with studies that demonstrate that *keigo* is one of the more challenging aspects of Japanese for L2 learners (e.g. Barešova, 2015; Carroll, 2005; Miyamoto Caltabiano, 2008). This is followed by an examination of ideologies of *keigo*, in particular, the way that the appropriate use of *keigo* is often viewed as an essential skill for L1-Japanese speakers to become full-fledged 'members of society' (e.g. Dunn, 2013; Inoue, 2006;

Niyekawa, 1991). Next, I discuss how L2 speakers approach or resist using *keigo* (e.g. Ishihara & Tarone, 2009; Siegal, 1996) and consider these findings in conjunction with my work examining the *keigo* ideologies of JFL teachers (Takeuchi, 2021). In order to examine the connection between (1) beliefs about the relevance of *keigo* for L2 speakers and (2) how ideologies impact those beliefs, Chapter 3 then presents findings from several participants along with an in-depth discussion of two participants, a married couple, 'David' and 'Megumi'. Examination of these participants demonstrates a disconnect between L1 and L2 speakers' beliefs about *keigo*. I analyze David's view of *keigo* as an important linguistic resource and the 'last, out-of-reach' skill to push his Japanese to the next level. This is then contrasted with Megumi's stance that L2 speakers should be 'excused' from social and linguistic norms that are applied to L1 speakers, a stance, I argue, that inadvertently infantilizes and exoticizes the speech of L2 speakers. The chapter concludes with a consideration of how ideologies which excuse or discourage L2 speakers from using honorifics inadvertently deny them status as legitimate speakers of Japanese. The case of David and Megumi underscores the fact that, even in the context of intimate interlocutors, legitimacy is tenuous for L2 speakers and highlights the need for a more nuanced understanding of how *keigo* interacts with what it means for L2 speakers to be legitimate speakers of Japanese.

Chapter 4 examines ideologies about Japanese gendered language and discusses how fears about inappropriate use of gendered language impact L2 participants' language ownership. Research in Japanese linguistics has found that gendered differences in spoken Japanese are decreasing (e.g. Matsumoto, 2002; Okamoto, 1995; Okamoto & Shibamoto-Smith, 2004). Despite changes in usage, ideologies about Japanese gendered language persist and are apparent in stereotypical depictions of masculine or feminine speech in various media (Inoue, 2006; Nakamura, 2008; Suzuki, 2020). L2-Japanese speakers also encounter these ideologies in pedagogical materials. Examples are found in textbooks in which male and female characters use stereotypically gendered speech patterns (e.g. the *Genki* textbook series by Banno *et al.*, 2011, 2020) or where Japanese is described as 'gendered' and learners are explicitly cautioned against using forms for the opposite gender (e.g. Oka *et al.*, 2009). Research findings attest to the impacts of such messages and describe how L2-Japanese learners attend to and often worry about when and how to incorporate Japanese gendered language forms in their own speech (e.g. Brown & Cheek, 2017; Ohara, 2001; Siegal, 1996).

The findings reported in Chapter 4 demonstrate that, for the L2 participants, concerns about gendered Japanese are magnified, and awareness of gendered norms of Japanese language complicates their efforts to 'sound like themselves'. I examine identity conceptions of both male and female L2 participants through their descriptions of the gendered nature of their spoken Japanese. Many participants struggled with how they wanted to sound, and they perceived gaps between how they wanted to sound and how they actually sounded. Focusing on a subset of participants, this chapter highlights the impact that gendered ideologies have on L2-Japanese speakers and points to L2 speakers' lack of ownership in their experiences as Japanese speakers.

Chapter 5 focuses on participants in less urban areas and discusses ideologies about standard language and dialects. I address concerns about whether L2 participants can be seen as legitimate speakers of Japanese Dialect and consider how dialect use or non-use impacts community membership. The chapter begins with a brief introduction to Japanese dialects (e.g. Ohuchi, 2014; Shibatani, 1990; Tanaka, 2014; Watanabe & Karasawa, 2013) and then focuses on the dialects of Ehime as an example of how dialects differ from Standard Japanese. I next introduce findings from L1 participants about their views of dialect in general and also with regard to the relevance of dialect for L2 speakers.

My findings show that all L2 participants who lived outside of major metro areas, and a few in metro areas, encountered dialects and negotiated complex linguistic choices about the use of dialect. I consider the important role that dialect plays in local communities, and I include research on L2 speaker identity and investment (Norton, 2006, 2013) to demonstrate the diversity and complexity of participants' stances toward dialect use. My analysis addresses questions about the role dialect plays for L2 speakers and how that may differ from L1 speakers. For the L2 participants introduced in Chapter 5, dialect matters for how they understand the speech used around them and for how they perform their identities in local communities.

In Chapter 6, the focus shifts from specific speech styles to Japanese language use in general to allow an exploration of how L1 speakers convey their opinions and judgments of L2 speakers' Japanese abilities. The findings introduced in this chapter show how native speaker bias impacts L1 depictions of L2 speakers' linguistic competence. Researchers have consistently criticized the practice of measuring L2 competence against biased and idealized conceptions of 'native speakers' (e.g. Cook, 1999; Firth & Wagner, 1997, 2007; Rampton, 1990). More recent research highlights the impacts of native speaker bias on non-native speaker teachers of Japanese (Nomura & Mochizuki, 2018). However, these discussions remain limited to research settings and educational contexts, which calls into question the degree to which L2 speakers in target language contexts will benefit from such advocacy. As Chapter 6 demonstrates, non-teacher L1 interlocutors often convey native speaker bias in their judgments of L2 speakers.

The first half of the chapter introduces findings from a subset of L2 and L1 participants to consider how L1 speakers express judgments about L2 speakers as Japanese speakers. The second half of the chapter focuses on two participants, an L2-Japanese speaker with advanced competency and his L1-Japanese spouse. Analysis details how L1 speakers' comments about L2 speakers can be simultaneously supportive and othering, stances which become visible in L1 depictions of L2 competence and present challenges to the acceptance of L2 speakers as legitimate speakers of Japanese.

Chapter 7 returns to the larger question of how L2 speakers encounter and negotiate language ideologies in Japan and reviews my contributions to existing studies in applied linguistics and SLA. Situating my work within the broader research literature on L2 speakers, I highlight contributions to studies that examine language ideologies, native speaker bias, language ownership and speaker legitimacy in a variety of L2s. In addition, I also present Japanese-specific considerations, the importance of which is underscored by the multiple ways that the Japanese speech styles discussed in this book function as linguistic and social resources. My participants' experiences demonstrate what is lost when access to the resources embedded within Japanese speech styles is denied.

I conclude with a discussion of how native speaker bias diminishes daily life interactions for L2 speakers living in Japan. The chapter ends with a reconsideration of what it means to be a legitimate speaker of Japanese in light of the findings I present. The relevance of speaker legitimacy for L2 speakers living and working in Japan will only become more urgent as the number of foreign residents and immigrants in Japan increases. Finally, I conclude with a discussion of implications for understanding speaker legitimacy with the goal of advocating for all L2 speakers to be, simply, speakers. While my book's findings are based on L2-Japanese speakers, these findings affirm the importance of advocating for speaker legitimacy for all L2 speakers.

Notes

(1) Because beliefs about language are complex and often competing, I follow Kroskrity (2004), Heinrich (2012) and others in using language ideologies in the plural.
(2) Although the number of foreign residents decreased during the Covid-19 pandemic, Kamiyoshi (2022) reports that it is expected that the pre-Covid trends of increasing numbers of foreign residents will continue once Covid-related restrictions are fully lifted.

2 This Study: L2 Speakers in Japan

Study Background

This study used ethnographic interviews and participant observations conducted with 54 participants between 2013 and 2017. I began participant recruitment in Ehime, Japan, and expanded to other areas in western and central Japan. Prior to the study, I had lived in Ehime for 12 years, and initial participant recruitment was conducted based on my previous professional connections. I then used snowball recruiting and asked study participants to share recruitment material with people they knew who might be interested in participating. Although I originally intended to prioritize second language (L2) speakers in a limited set of rural locations, snowball recruiting led me to participants living in multiple locations, including more urban areas. Snowball recruiting also led me to participants with differing lengths of residence in Japan. I decided to include all participants because the diversity of their backgrounds and residencies added depth to the data I was able to collect. Using a qualitative approach, my aim was not to arrive at a representative sample or achieve generalizable results, but rather, through triangulation (e.g. Duff, 2008; Hammersley & Gomm, 2008), make use of 'thick description' (Geertz, 1973) to examine the experiences of the L2 speakers in the study.

Study participants included both first language (L1) and L2 speakers of Japanese. The primary participant group was made up of 27 L2-Japanese speakers whose L1 was English. In selecting L2 participants for the study, my criteria were that (1) potential participants be residents of Japan, not tourists or exchange students; (2) they have some Japanese ability; and (3) their L1 was English, which gave me access to both their L1s and L2s. The L2 speakers lived and worked in a variety of locations in Japan, including semi-rural and rural locations in Ehime and Kagawa, on the island of Shikoku, and in urban and metropolitan locations including the Greater Tokyo Area and Osaka, on the island of Honshu. Reflecting the fact that English language teaching is a common occupation for English speakers in Japan, many of the L2 speakers were English teachers working in primary and secondary schools, universities or private, for-profit English conversation schools. Others worked in fields such as information technology (IT), tourism, fitness and entertainment.

One feature that distinguishes this study from previous studies is the length of residence in Japan of the L2 participants. Because many studies of L2 speakers examine students, their participants tend to have lived in Japan for a year or less. In my study, most participants had lived in Japan for much longer. Two participants had been in Japan for just over a year at the time of the study. Several participants had lived in Japan for two to four years, and a significant number of the participants were long-term residents, ranging from five to 25 years of residency. These varying lengths of residence made it possible to consider how length of residence impacted L2 speakers' beliefs and perspectives. The large number of long-term residents also resulted in participants with more advanced Japanese ability, which benefitted the study because these participants had more experiences with, and more complicated perspectives about, Japanese language encounters.

Another distinguishing feature of this study is the inclusion of L1 speakers of Japanese. The main criterion for L1-Japanese participants was that they have some professional and/or social connection to one or more of the L2 study participants. The study includes 27 L1 speakers who were coworkers, friends or significant others of one or more of the L2 study participants. Since many of the L2 speakers were English teachers, many of the L1 speakers also worked as English language teachers, mostly in primary and secondary schools. L1 study participants who were not teachers worked in the private sector, the public sector or were self-employed in the retail or fitness industry. Only six of the L1 participants were also L2-English speakers. As with the L2 participants, arriving at a representative sample of L1 speakers was not a goal of participant recruitment. Instead, L1 participants were included as a complement and counterpoint to L2 participants. The diversity of relationships between L1 and L2 participants included coworkers, friends as well as significant others. This gave me an opportunity to explore how language ideologies emerge in various types of interactions, including those in workplace and social settings. In addition, the inclusion of data from both L2 and L1 speakers facilitated triangulation, which strengthened the validity of the findings. Below, I describe the types of data I collected and the procedures for analysis. The chapter concludes with an introduction to the L2 participants, the L1 participants and information about the study context.

Data and Procedures

In order to understand the language ideologies that impact L2 speakers in Japan, I focused on participants' beliefs and perceptions. I used ethnographic interviews as the primary data collection method. Interviews were supplemented by on-site observations, background questionnaires completed by participants before the interviews and dialect artefacts, in particular, dialect used on signage and other aspects of the linguistic environment. I also made audio-recordings of conversational interactions with a few L2 participants.

Interviews

I conducted one-on-one ethnographic interviews in person with each participant, using an interview protocol that discussed participants' daily life, work-related experiences, beliefs about Japanese language and experiences with and opinions about learning and using Japanese. I conducted the interviews in each participant's L1 (either English or Japanese). Interviews with L2 participants tended to be long, lasting between one to three hours; interviews with L1 participants tended to be shorter, with most lasting between 30 minutes to an hour. Some L2 participants were interviewed only once, others were contacted soon after the interview for follow-up questions via email or online video-conferencing. Several L2 participants who were interviewed during the first round of data collection in 2013 were also interviewed during the final round of data collection in 2017. Follow-up interviews were conducted primarily based on participants' availability. For L2 participants interviewed in 2017, the interview ended with a short discussion in Japanese in order to have a record of the participants speaking Japanese. Almost all of the interviews were conducted with only the participant and myself present, but a small number of interviews include segments in which a participant's friend or significant other was present for a portion of the interview. During those interviews, there was some switching back and forth between English and Japanese during the interview.

All the interviews were conducted as semi-structured, open-ended interviews. The interview protocol for L2 participants included questions about their language background and how they became interested in Japanese, and I asked about their experiences living and working in Japan. Several questions were devoted to Japanese language. I first asked their opinions about learning Japanese and then I asked about their experiences using Japanese. (See Appendix A for the L2 interview protocol.) During the interview, I referred to the background questionnaires to guide some of the questions. I routinely asked follow-up questions throughout each interview, and I also allowed participants to discuss topics that they brought up. As a result, although I covered all of the same topics with each participant, there was variation from one interview to the next, especially in terms of the order in which topics were discussed. Some interviews were much longer than others, and this was determined by the participants themselves and how much they chose to share with me. As discussed in Chapter 1, my identity as an L2 speaker, a former resident of Japan and a former JET Program participant meant that I usually had a lot in common with the L2 participants. This led to some participants asking me questions, soliciting my agreement with reactions to common experiences and other interactions that pushed the discussion away from a 'research interview' and toward a chat between friends. Navigating these interactions was sometimes difficult but, at the same time, such interaction was not at odds with my approach since I view each interview to be a conversation between two interlocutors. Consequently, differences in the flow of the conversation contributed to variations seen across interviews in terms of length and content. Regardless of their duration and content, I treated all interviews as data and did not exclude any interview from my analysis. Although I cannot include every interview, I chose to include in the book excerpts from interviews that are representative examples, and I also include participants with whom I met multiple times.

The interview protocol for L1 participants started with background questions, including where they were from in Japan, whether they had experience using English or other languages, whether they had lived overseas and so on. I asked a series of questions about Japanese language, including specific questions about dialect. Interview questions asked L1 participants to share their beliefs and opinions about Japanese language in general and also with regard to L2 speakers. I asked about L1 participants' occupations and whether they interacted with L2 speakers in the workplace. I then focused on their experiences with L2 speakers and included questions about L1 participants' interactions with any specific L2 participants whom they knew. I asked follow-up questions as needed. (See Appendix B for the L1 interview protocol.) As with the L2 participant interviews, some L1 participants wanted to ask me questions and I tried to maintain a balance of accommodating questions while also keeping the interviews on track. In general, the L1 interviews tended to be shorter than the L2 interviews, with some only lasting 30 minutes. Of course, some interviews with L1 participants were much longer.

Other data sources

In addition to interviews with multiple participants and with both L1 and L2 participant groups, I also collected the following types of supplemental data sources which were used to inform my analysis and interpretation of interviews and helped facilitate triangulation.

Questionnaires: For the L2 participants, background questionnaires collected information about their experience in Japan, including length of residence and occupation, and their Japanese language ability. A series of items was designed to be a self-assessment of Japanese ability and other items were questions about experience with formal language instruction or language certification tests. For the L1 participants, background questionnaires focused on participants' connections to and experiences with

L2 speakers. L1 participants were also asked about their English language ability as well as general background questions, such as place of residence and occupation.

On-site observations: On-site observations took place in participants' workplaces and during leisure activities, including social events, community sports clubs or hobby activities, such as traditional music or dance lessons. The aim of observations was to consider the kinds of language to which L2 participants were exposed, and also to observe participants' language use during interactions with coworkers and friends. Field notes included information about the interactions, the physical environment, such as office layout and location of a participant's desk, as well as notes about the language and speech styles in use. I did not make audio- or video-recordings during observations because of the presence of people not enrolled as participants in the study.

Dialect artefacts: In addition to general observations about speech styles, I also collected artefacts, including objects or photographs of signage, related to Japanese Dialect use in order to get an idea of the dialect that participants encountered in the visible environment.

Conversational interactions: I asked a small group of L2 participants to record some Japanese language interactions. I gave participants a hand-held audio-recorder and asked them to record a conversation with a friend or coworker. I was only able to collect a few samples of this kind of data, so I do not include reference to it in my findings, but these recordings helped me consider the Japanese language ability of the L2 participants, as well as their linguistic environments.

Data analysis

Audio-recordings were made of all interviews. I transcribed all of the audio-recordings and used the transcripts for content and thematic analysis. My approach to qualitative interview data is based on a view of interview talk as being a 'joint production' (Mishler, 1991) between two speakers. Although speakers come to the interview as researcher and participant, their roles become 'co-constructors of knowledge' (Kvale & Brinkmann, 2009: 18). This co-constructed knowledge results in a representation of a participant's subjective understanding of their experience (cf. Seidman, 2006). I then use that representation to consider study participants' beliefs and perceptions about themselves and others as Japanese speakers.

My analysis of interview data was conducted within a qualitative research paradigm using content and thematic coding (Saldaña, 2013). I coded and categorized interview transcripts to examine beliefs and perceptions about L2 speakers of Japanese, ideas about who counts as a legitimate speaker of Japanese and beliefs about how Japanese should be spoken and by whom. I followed an iterative process of coding, making multiple coding passes which allowed me to refine my analysis with each additional coding pass. I also used holistic codes (Saldaña, 2013) which involves coding longer stretches of talk rather than line-by-line or phrase-level coding. I relied heavily on *in vivo* coding during initial coding passes, in which codes are derived from words used in the interviews. I then consolidated and renamed the *in vivo* codes to make it easier to do cross-participant comparisons. I did not count or quantify codes (cf. Creswell, 2007); instead, I relied on emotive and affective language to arrive at what was more important or relevant for participants.

Although analysis of conversations was not the primary analytical activity, recorded conversations were examined from an interactional sociolinguistic perspective (Gordon & Kraut, 2017; Gumperz, 2015), which combines the microanalysis of conversation (Erickson, 1992) with consideration of the sociocultural context through ethnographic observations (Kasper & Omori, 2010). Lastly, during coding and microanalysis activities, I drew on supplementary data sources to inform my analyses, to look for any errors and to ensure I was not overlooking important details or misinterpreting findings. Thus, I used data from both participant groups and multiple types of data drawn from questionnaires, interviews, observations, artefacts and interactional data, which supported triangulation to strengthen my findings and conclusions (e.g. Duff, 2007, 2008; Hammersley & Gomm, 2008).

Presentation of interview excerpts

In the chapters that follow, I include excerpts from selected interviews with L1 and L2 participants. Because my analysis focused on the content of participants' comments, I prioritized content analysis over interactional analysis. To keep excerpts in the book short and easy to read, I edited them in the following ways: First, when a participant was speaking and I was providing back-channel responses, e.g. 'uh huh', 'yeah', I deleted the back-channel responses from the excerpt. Second, if a participant repeated part of an utterance, I deleted the repeated part in the excerpt. For example, if an utterance included 'yeah, I think, hmm, I think so', the excerpt would be presented as 'yeah, I think so'. Third, if an utterance included a lot of fillers, e.g. 'um', 'uh', I deleted most of the fillers in the excerpt. Fourth, if a participant discussed one topic, mentioned a side topic and then returned to the first topic, I deleted the side topic in the excerpt, as shown by ellipses. Edited excerpts were not used for analysis and these edits were only conducted after analysis was complete. (For a full list of transcription conventions, see Appendix C.)

Participants

I had several goals when recruiting participants for this study. For L2 speakers of Japanese, I wanted to recruit participants whose L1 was

English, so that I would have access to both of their languages. This was especially important for conducting the thematic and content analysis. In terms of Japanese language ability, I aimed for L2-Japanese speakers who, at minimum, used Japanese regularly in their daily lives. An additional goal was to recruit participants who had lived in Japan for at least a year but preferably longer in order to recruit participants with ample experience living in Japan and using Japanese for daily life purposes. For L1-Japanese speakers, my only criterion was that they have some connection to an L2 participant. I did not impose any restrictions on the L1 participants in terms of, for example, their English language ability, present or past occupation or age.

For initial recruitment, I made use of professional and personal networks I had developed while living and working in Japan. Because I had lived in Ehime and worked first as a JET Program assistant language teacher (ALT) and later as an elementary school English teacher, many of my L1 and L2 participants lived in Ehime and were connected to the JET Program or English teaching. After I recruited the initial L2 participants, I used snowball sampling and asked them to introduce me to other possible participants, including other L2 speakers and L1 speakers. Not surprisingly, snowball sampling led to an increase in the number of participants living outside of Ehime, which made it possible to include participants in more urban areas, as well as participants in smaller cities and semi-rural areas.

L2 participants

All 27 of the L2 participants I recruited participated in at least one interview, and all interviews were conducted in English. I asked some L2 participants to speak with me in Japanese for a few minutes at the end of the interview (depending on the participant's availability and the time spent on the main interview). I also conducted participant observations and follow-up interviews with several L2 participants. All initial interviews were conducted in person. Audio-recordings were made of all interviews and follow-up interviews (except for follow-up interviews conducted by email). The location of the interviews depended on the L2 participant's availability and schedule. Locations included participants' homes, workplaces, restaurants, cafes, community centers and libraries. The follow-up interviews were dependent upon participants' availability and, consequently, some were conducted in person while others were conducted via online video conferencing or email. Participant observations occurred in a variety of settings, including participants' place of work, gyms or martial arts dojos where participants were members, and in public places such as grocery stores and restaurants. During participant observations, I did not make any audio- or video-recordings because there were usually people present who were not study participants. I took notes during and after the observations, focusing on the participant's role in the activity being observed, and the kind of language being used by all present. During observations in workplaces, I noted where the participant's desk was, how the participant and coworkers interacted and the kind of language being used. For leisure activities in which a participant was involved, e.g. sports groups, dance lessons, traditional Japanese arts, martial arts, I noted the participant's role in the group, the number of members, the age range of group members and the types of activities being undertaken. For all observations, I paid close attention to the language use involved, making note of the speech styles used and considering the degree of formality and any use of dialect, slang or gendered language. My observation notes helped inform my analysis, particularly with regard to the kinds of language a participant used and to which they were exposed. Table 2.1 presents a list of participants who are discussed in the following chapters.

I also interviewed a number of participants who are not introduced in the book. These participants nevertheless helped inform my analysis and I included their interview data and observation notes in my review and assessments of the experiences of L2 speakers in Japan. Table 2.2 shows the L2 participants who are not introduced by name in the book.

Information presented in Tables 2.1–2.5 represents the time of the study. For participants interviewed and/or observed more than once, the information is based on the last contact. Japanese level is based on a combination of the participant's self-assessment and their responses to Japanese questions in the background questionnaire, experience with any official Japanese tests (e.g. the Japanese Language Proficiency Test) and, where applicable, my assessment based on observations. Place names for rural areas are pseudonyms. Larger cities retain their real name.

L1 participants

I recruited 27 L1 participants who were friends, coworkers, significant others or spouses of one or more L2 participant. The fact that there are the same number of L1 and L2 participants is a coincidence. Not all L2 participants introduced me to an L1 participant, and some L2 participants introduced me to several L1 participants who ended up agreeing to participate. All of my interviews with L1 participants were conducted in Japanese. In principle, the L1 participant interviews were one on one; however, a few interviews happened in locations where the L2 participant was present (e.g. in a home in which both residents were participants). In those cases,

Table 2.1 L2 participants introduced in the book

Name	Age, gender	Nationality	Japanese ability	Years in Japan, place of residence	Appears in
Alyssa	30s, female	US	Intermediate	9 years, Matsuyama, Ehime	Chapter 4
Branden	20s, male	US	Advanced	2 years, Asahi (Tokyo)	Chapters 3, 5
Daniel	20s, male	New Zealand	Advanced	4 years, Miyaoka (Nagoya)	Chapters 3, 5
David	40s, male	US	Advanced	>20 years, Greater Tokyo Area	Chapters 3, 4, 6
Dean	50s, male	UK	Advanced	>25 years, Matsuyama (Kansai)	Chapters 3, 4
Grace	40s, female	UK	Advanced	10 years, Takata	Chapters 4, 5
James	30s, male	US	Advanced	10 years, Greater Tokyo Area	Chapters 3, 4, 6
Liam	20s, male	US	Advanced	3 years, Umikawa (Asahi)	Chapters 4–6
Louis	30s, male	US	Advanced	4 years, Miyaoka (Greater Tokyo Area)	Chapters 3, 4
Melissa	20s, female	New Zealand	Intermediate	3 years, Koyama	Chapters 3–6
Mike	30s, male	US	Advanced	7 years, Greater Tokyo Area (Hamada)	Chapter 4
Nicole	40s, female	Canadian	Advanced	16 years, Tokushima (Tokyo)	Chapters 3, 4
Nina	30s, female	US	Advanced	9 years, Kansai Area (Hamada)	Chapter 5
Peter	30s, male	UK	Advanced	11 years, Matsuyama (Koyama)	Chapters 3, 6
Sam	40s, male	US	Advanced	15 years, Takekawa	Chapters 3, 4
Scott	20s, male	US	Intermediate	1.5 years, Koyama	Chapters 4, 5
William	20s, male	US	Advanced	2 years, Sasaoka	Chapters 3–5

Note: All names are pseudonyms, presented in alphabetical order; place names in parentheses represent a participant's former place of residence in Japan.

Table 2.2 L2 participants not introduced in the book

Name	Age, gender	Nationality	Japanese ability	Years in Japan, place of residence
Alice	50s, female	US	Advanced/intermediate	>20 years, Tokushima
Austin	30s, male	US	Intermediate	4 years, Koyama
Elizabeth	20s, female	US	Intermediate	3 years, Matsuyama
Fionna	20s, female	UK	Beginning	1 year, Takekawa
George	20s, male	US	Intermediate	3 years, Matsuyama
Janet	20s, female	UK	Intermediate	2 years, Koyama
John	40s, male	Canadian	Beginning	5 years, Takekawa
Mary	40s, female	Canadian/UK	Intermediate	15 years, Greater Tokyo Area
Tyler	20s, male	UK	Beginning	2 years, Takekawa
Zac	40s, male	UK	Beginning	9 years, Matsuyama

Table 2.3 L1 participants introduced in the book

Name	Age, gender	Occupation	Area of residence	Connected to L2 participants	Appears in
Fujiwara	40s, male	JHS teacher	Koyama	Scott, all Koyama L2 participants	Chapter 4
Hamada	40s, female	JHS teacher	Koyama	Scott, William	Chapter 4
Kazuki	30s, male	Service industry	Matsuyama	Peter, Alyssa	Chapters 3, 6
Megumi	30s, female	Fitness instructor	Greater Tokyo Area	David, Mary	Chapters 3, 4, 6
Nakamura	50s, male	JHS teacher	Koyama	All Koyama L2 participants	Chapters 5, 6
Sakamoto	40s, male	JHS teacher	Koyama	All Koyama L2 participants	Chapter 5
Susumu	40s, male	Service industry	Koyama	Scott, Melissa, Austin	Chapter 4
Yoshio	50s, male	Civil servant	Sasaoka	William	Chapter 5

Note: All names are pseudonyms, place names for rural areas are pseudonyms but larger cities retain their real name.

Table 2.4 L1 participants not introduced in the book

Name	Age, gender	Occupation	Area of residence	Connected to L2 participants
Akemi	30s, female	Service industry	Koyama	Scott, Melissa, Austin
Chiyo	40s, female	Company employee	Koyama	Peter
Endo	50s, female	JHS teacher	Koyama	Austin
Fumihiro	30s, male	Self-employed	Koyama	Peter, Alyssa
Kawamura	40s, male	Elementary school teacher	Asahi	Liam
Kobayashi	40s, male	JHS teacher	Koyama	Scott
Kondo	50s, female	Civil servant	Matsuyama	George
Maeda	40s, male	Self-employed	Koyama	Janet
Naoki	20s, male	Self-employed	Koyama	Scott, Melissa, Austin
Saeko	30s, female	Company employee	Koyama	Peter, Alyssa
Sasaki	40s, female	Elementary school teacher	Koyama	Melissa
Shibata	50s, female	JHS teacher	Koyama	Melissa
Shinji	40s, male	Self-employed	Koyama	Scott, Melissa, Austin
Sugimoto	50s, male	JHS teacher	Koyama	Austin, Melissa, Scott, Sam
Takahashi	30s, male	Civil servant	Matsuyama	Liam
Tanaka	30s, male	Elementary school teacher	Asahi	Liam
Tomomi	30s, female	Elementary school teacher	Takekawa	John
Watanabe	30s, female	JHS teacher	Koyama	Austin
Yukiko	30s, female	Civil servant	Koyama	Koyama L2 participants

Note: All names are pseudonyms, place names for rural areas are pseudonyms but larger cities retain their real name.

sometimes the L2 participant spontaneously joined in during the L1 participant's interview. When this happened, I kept recording and allowed the discussion to evolve according to what both participants talked about. As with the L2 participant interviews, the L1 participant interviews were conducted in a variety of locations, depending on participants' availability, including workplaces, restaurants, cafes and community centers. I did not conduct follow-up interviews with L1 participants, and there was no English portion in the Japanese language interview. Table 2.3 shows a list of L1 participants who are introduced by name in the following chapters.

Table 2.4 shows the L1 participants who are not included by name in the book. As with the L2 participants, these L1 participants nevertheless informed my observations and assessments of the L1 participants as a group.

Where Participants Lived and Worked

Many of the participants lived in Ehime, one of the four prefectures located on the island of Shikoku. Ehime is fairly removed from Japan's more urban/metro areas and has a reputation, both in and outside Ehime, as more rural than areas closer to Tokyo or Osaka. It is difficult to travel to Ehime from Japan's major cities and, once there, the mountainous terrain makes travel within Ehime quite difficult. The population of Ehime is approximately 1.3 million people (Ehime Prefectural Website, 2021), and the foreign population is almost 13,500 (Japan Ministry of Justice, 2021). Ehime has a lively capital city, Matsuyama, with an airport and all the amenities of a regional, medium-sized city. Outside of Matsuyama, however, the availability and quality of many urban amenities decrease, including options for public transportation, entertainment, shopping, lifelong learning activities and medical facilities. Other limitations in smaller cities and towns include types and availability of services directed at L2-speaking residents, especially English language resources or municipal services, English-speaking health care providers and English-speaking town workers.[1] Proximity to other L2-Japanese speakers is limited, and travel to and from other parts of Japan or to an L2 speaker's home country is challenging. These factors serve to further limit options for social networks and community as well. Ehime's rurality is also evident in the limited

Table 2.5 Locations where interviews and on-site observations were conducted

City/town	Rurality	L2 participants	L1 participants
Asahi-shi	Slightly rural	Branden	Kawamura, Tanaka
Greater Tokyo Area*	Urban/metro	David, James, Mary, Mike	Megumi
Hamada-cho	Very rural	Mike, Nina	
Kansai Area*	Urban/metro	Nina	
Matsuyama-shi*	Ehime capital city	Alyssa, Dean, Elizabeth, George, Peter, Zac	Kazuki, Kondo, Takahashi
Miyaoka	Rural	Daniel, Louis	
Sasaoka-cho	Very rural	William	Yoshio
Takata-cho	Very rural	Grace	
Takekawa-cho	Very rural	Fiona, John, Sam, Tyler	Tomomi
Umikawa-cho (part of Asahi)	Very rural	Liam	

Note: Locations are in alphabetical order. All cities and towns are given a pseudonym except those followed by *.

employment options in terms of type and availability of local jobs. Although Ehime has a number of factories and Matsuyama's economy is relatively diversified, agricultural and marine industries make up a significant portion of the economy in other cities and towns in Ehime. Unlike metropolitan areas in other parts of Japan, there are few IT, financial or trading companies, with the result that the most readily available jobs for English-speaking foreign residents are principally in English teaching.

Study participants also lived elsewhere in Shikoku, as well as in the Kansai area and the Greater Tokyo Area. L2 participants' place of residence can be a significant influence on the Japanese language use they encountered; L2 participants in Ehime and Kansai and those in more rural locations tended to encounter more dialect use than participants in the Greater Tokyo Area. Furthermore, the rurality of a location also impacted the kinds of interactions and activities that L2 participants could engage in. Table 2.5 shows the names of the cities and towns where participants lived. All the place names are pseudonyms with the exception of capital cities and large urban areas.

The JET Program

Out of the 27 L2 participants in this study, all but 2 were current or former participants in the JET Program, a popular way to secure English teaching jobs in Japan. Teaching English is one of the most common ways for an English-speaking foreign national to find work in Japan and a number of placement agencies are involved in connecting overseas job seekers to teaching positions in Japan. The largest and perhaps most well known is the JET Program, which is coordinated by the Japanese government. The JET Program recruits recent college graduates to come and work in Japan; every year there are more than 4000 participants (JET Program, n.d., a). Of these, approximately 90% are hired as assistant English teachers (called ALTs) who are placed in elementary, junior high or high schools. The remaining positions are coordinators of international relations (CIRs), who make up just under 10% of positions, and sports exchange advisors (SEAs), who make up less than 1% of positions (JET Program, n.d., a). JET Program participants are placed in schools or city offices throughout Japan. Most JET placements are not in major cities but in regional cities and towns, with some placements in rural farming or fishing villages. Detailed statistics about rural placements are unavailable, but some estimates suggest that more than half of all JETs are in rural areas (Metzgar, 2012).

The Japanese language ability of JET Program participants varies widely. CIRs are required to 'have a strong, functional command of the Japanese language (ability equivalent to the Japanese Language

Proficiency Test Level N1 or N2 is desirable)' (JET Program, n.d., b). On the other hand, ALTs are not required to have Japanese proficiency as a condition of employment. Some ALTs go to Japan with little or no Japanese background, while others go after years of high school and college-level study. ALTs may end up in workplaces with other ALTs as well as Japanese coworkers who have excellent English skills, or they may be sent to workplaces where they are the only JET participant, and most or all of their Japanese coworkers are unable to speak English. In such cases, general Japanese language ability is an essential skill. When the JET placement is in a dialect-using region, the ability to acquire knowledge about dialect also becomes important. Thus, it is not surprising that, although JET Program participants are hired by virtue of their status as native speakers of English, when they arrive at their placements, they often find that it is their Japanese language ability and how they navigate the complex system of Japanese speech styles that shape their experiences in local communities.

JET Program employment contracts generally begin in August, are initially for one year and have the possibility of renewal for a total of up to five years of employment. This means that, although employment through the JET Program allows extended residence in Japan, it is not a means of permanent employment. Carlson (2018) criticizes the JET Program for failing to help participants transition into long-term employment and argues that the JET Program's policies are part of a larger pattern of excluding foreigners and viewing them as inherently short-term residents.

In the chapters that follow, I introduce findings from the interviews and on-site observations collected for this book. Although I can only include a fraction of the data collected, the large number of participants and the inclusion of both L1- and L2-speaking participants, along with the participant observations I conducted, made it possible to identify patterns in the experiences of L2 speakers living in Japan. As with any qualitative study, the findings and arguments shared throughout the book may not apply to other L2 speakers in Japan, or even in the same locations as the L2 participants. Nevertheless, I believe these participants, and my analysis of the data I collected with them, offer insight into how L2 speakers encounter and navigate language ideologies in Japan.

Note

(1) I focus on English in this discussion because the L2 participants in this study speak English as their L1. However, access to languages other than English is even more limited.

3 'Foreigners Don't Need *Keigo*': Excusing L2 Speakers from *Keigo*

Introduction

Keigo, the system of polite and honorific language, is famous or, possibly more accurately, infamous among Japanese language learners and teachers as challenging to teach and to learn. In this chapter, I examine first language (L1) and second language (L2) participants' beliefs and opinions about *keigo*, with particular attention to how native speaker bias and *keigo* ideologies intersect to reveal depictions of *keigo* as essential for 'native speakers', while for L2 speakers, it may be depicted as not necessary, or even at times detrimental or off-limits. My analysis of beliefs and ideologies about the relevance of *keigo* for L2 speakers underscores the impact of native speaker bias on the speaker legitimacy of L2-Japanese speakers.

The discussion begins with an overview of politeness registers in Japanese and ideologies about *keigo* and its importance for Japanese language speakers. Of particular interest are research studies that examine *keigo* in workplace and professional contexts and consider how ideological views depict *keigo* as an essential part of Japanese. One result of the ideological valuation of *keigo* is that *keigo* is invested with linguistic capital (Bourdieu, 1991), meaning that speakers who can deploy *keigo* in ways that conform to sociolinguistic norms will benefit in terms of access to contexts and interlocutors. I also discuss how language ideologies impact L2 speakers, and I review studies that explain how L2-Japanese learners approach or resist learning *keigo* and how they navigate decisions about incorporating it into their own Japanese language repertoire.

The rest of the chapter focuses on participants' beliefs and opinions about *keigo*. I present findings from interviews of a representative selection of L1 and L2 participants. This is followed by an in-depth discussion of two participants, a married couple, 'David' and 'Megumi'. Examination of David and Megumi demonstrates the disconnect between L1 and L2 speakers' beliefs about *keigo*. As we will see, David views *keigo* as an important linguistic resource and as the final, just out-of-reach skill that could push his Japanese to the next level. On the other hand, Megumi takes the position that L2 speakers, including David, do not need to adhere to the social and linguistic norms of *keigo* that are applied to L1 speakers. In fact, Megumi even suggests that David's speech is better without *keigo*. Her stance is an example of how expectations for L2 speakers can sometimes be fundamentally different from those for L1 speakers. The chapter concludes with a consideration of how ideologies that excuse or discourage L2 speakers from using *keigo* deny them the status of legitimate speakers of Japanese, however inadvertently. The case of David and Megumi is of particular interest because it shows that, even in the context of intimate interlocutors, legitimacy is often tenuous for L2 speakers. Participants' views also demonstrate the need for a more nuanced understanding of how *keigo* interacts with what it means for L2 speakers to be legitimate speakers of Japanese.

Previous Studies of *Keigo*

Keigo basics

All languages have a variety of registers that make it possible for speakers to be more or less formal or informal. Japanese is distinguished because these registers are highly codified. It is often said that Japanese does not have any truly neutral forms and, further, that Japanese does not exist without *keigo* (e.g. Carroll, 2005; Wetzel, 2004). In other words, no one can speak Japanese without taking account of politeness. Barešova (2015: 2) describes *keigo* as 'grammaticalized features of politeness', which highlights the systematicity and rule-bound nature of *keigo*.

A brief description of the different levels of polite and honorific speech in Japanese gives a sense of the elaborateness of *keigo*. The complete system of polite and honorific language is often referred to simply as '*keigo*', although there is a taxonomy of different levels of politeness and numerous ways to categorize different types of politeness. For example, forms that show politeness to one's interlocutor are called 'addressee honorifics', while forms that show politeness to the person being talked about are called 'referent honorifics' (e.g. Barešova, 2015; Barke, 2010, 2011; also see Barešova, 2015, for a discussion of the debate surrounding these labels). Indeed, categorizing and classifying the different kinds and levels of *keigo* has been one of the major objectives of Japanese linguists and government organizations tasked with making language-related recommendations.

Taxonomic debates aside, at a most basic level, Japanese could be said to have three levels of speech: plain, neutral polite and *keigo* which includes honorific and humble forms. Plain speech, sometimes called *da-tai* ('*da*' form), is generally used with interlocutors who are close, for example, close in age or socially close in status, or those who have a personal relationship, such as family members or close friends. The plain form can also be used by an interlocuter who is older or 'socially superior' to other participants in an interaction. As the term *da-tai* suggests, plain speech is characterized by the use of the short-form '*da*' copula, short-form verb endings, a lack of honorific prefixes and plain or neutral vocabulary in place of humble or honorific vocabulary.

A step above plain speech in terms of politeness is *teineigo*, or neutral polite language. *Teineigo* can be used among people who are more distant socially or in status and can also be used with strangers. *Teineigo* is often the first and sometimes the only speech style taught to learners of Japanese as a foreign language (JFL) and JFL teachers often tell students that this is a 'safe' speech style that can be used to avoid offending an unknown interlocutor (e.g. Niyekawa, 1991; Wetzel, 2004). *Teineigo* is also sometimes called *desu/masu-tai* or '*desu/masu*' form because it is characterized by the longer '*desu*' copula and '*masu*' verb endings.

The third speech level is *keigo*, which includes both *kenjōgo*, 'humble speech' to describe one's own actions, and *sonkeigo*, 'exalted honorific speech' to describe the actions of some higher-status other person. *Kenjōgo* is characterized by special humble vocabulary, including special verbs that 'lower' the speaker and special nouns that convey a sense of the speaker as humble. *Sonkeigo*, the counterpart to *kenjōgo*, is characterized by special honorific verbs and nouns that a speaker can use to honor either the interlocutor or the person being referred to. In addition, both *kenjōgo* and *sonkeigo* make use of grammatical patterns that can be used to conjugate otherwise neutral verbs into humble or honorific forms (see Barešova, 2015; Okamoto & Shibamoto-Smith, 2016; Shibatani, 1990; Wetzel, 2004).

Speakers of Japanese must take account of a complex array of factors in choosing which speech level to use with whom. In addition to the social distance between interlocutors, speakers need to consider the topic at hand, the degree of formality of the interaction and the location of the interaction. The following are examples based on language use I heard during my on-site observations; they give an idea of how these considerations result in real-world language use. I observed an office worker who used a mixture of *teineigo* and *keigo* in general when speaking to a supervisor. This same worker used more formal language overall, and more features of *keigo*, when the interaction with the supervisor was part of a formal discussion as compared to a casual chat while standing in the hallway waiting for the elevator. On the other hand, I observed that schoolteachers who were long-standing coworkers sometimes used *sonkeigo* (honorific) or *kenjōgo* (humble) verbs but with short-form endings while chatting with each other in the staff room. However, they switched to the same (honorific or humble) verbs with long-form (*desu/masu*) endings when speaking during a meeting in the staff room.

According to Wetzel (2004: 107), *keigo*'s complexity cannot be fully described without a complete account of the speakers and their relationships. This is one reason why *keigo* is challenging to teach in classroom contexts, because there is no single rule that encompasses all of the choices speakers make with regard to *keigo* and speech style. In addition, it is impossible to recreate all the contextual elements speakers take into account when making linguistic choices. These details may give the impression that each politeness level is neatly delineated and that any instance of speech is characterized by the use of a single speech level, but this is rarely the case. Instead, speakers often use a combination of politeness levels within the same interaction, as described above in the example of teachers, and sometimes even within the same utterance. Cook (2008) and others argue that speaking in a mixed style should be seen as the norm rather than the exception. The flexibility of *keigo* makes it possible to distinguish between politeness shown to an interlocutor present in the interaction and politeness shown to someone not necessarily present but being spoken about during an interaction. This distinction also makes it possible to use *sonkeigo* or honorific verbs to describe the action of one's supervisor, for example, but use that verb in its short-form ending because the interlocutor is a coworker.

Okamoto and Shibamoto-Smith (2016: 193) describe mixing politeness forms as 'a resource for achieving the right degree of deference and formality versus solidarity and casualness' and speakers use mixing to achieve a balance 'between the prescriptive and the socially constructed individual'. Okamoto and Shibamoto-Smith argue that, despite numerous rules about *keigo* usage, there are considerable differences in speakers' attitudes toward *keigo* rules and in actual language use practices. This underscores that *keigo*, like all linguistic choices, is always the result of negotiations of social relationships, and at the same time, 'speaker agency plays a vital role' (Okamoto & Shibamoto-Smith, 2016: 175). As Okamoto and Shibamoto-Smith (2016: 175) observe, 'this does not mean speakers can use any forms they please… speakers are clearly affected by the dominant norms of speech'. Thus, Okamoto and Shibamoto-Smith conclude that speakers actively make linguistic choices about honorifics and politeness forms, and their choices are also strategic. They note that, while speakers are influenced by sociolinguistic norms, the degree to which any individual speaker conforms to those norms depends on the speaker's attitude and stance toward aligning with specific norms.

Keigo ideologies

Given *keigo*'s central role in both social relationships and social identities, and the influence of norms on *keigo* usage, it is not surprising that numerous linguists have examined the ways that language ideologies are embedded in beliefs about *keigo*. Okamoto and Shibamoto-Smith (2016) describe the historical background of *keigo*, beginning with the Meiji era, and explain how *keigo* was constructed in conjunction with the ideological construction of Standard Japanese. Language standardization was promoted as part of Japan's nation-building efforts, and *keigo* was depicted as a way to distinguish Japanese from English and European languages, while still asserting that Japanese language was civilized. Okamoto and Shibamoto-Smith (2016: 131) observe that these efforts have been obscured in order to promote a 'romanticized version of *keigo* as an inherent and timeless trait of the Japanese language'.

In addition to emphasizing the uniqueness of the Japanese language, another way that language ideologies can be seen in *keigo* is in the strong push for appropriateness and correctness. Okamoto and Shibamoto-Smith (2016) point out that *keigo* norms are promoted and reinforced in scholarly work and government documents, and also by for-profit language trainers who teach correct *keigo* to L1 speakers. *Keigo* norms are reinforced in popular media, including self-help books designed to teach proper *keigo*, as well as television shows and internet blog articles devoted to the subject. In such materials, the importance of correct *keigo* is stressed, conveying the idea that being able to use *keigo* is a part of common sense and that *keigo* mistakes should be seen as a source of embarrassment. Such depictions create 'the illusion that *keigo* expertise is sadly lacking in the speaking population but necessary for successful adult life' (Okamoto & Shibamoto-Smith, 2016: 149). One result is what we might call the *keigo* industry, which commodifies *keigo* and is dependent on the book-buying and television-watching public, who are assumed to be insecure about their *keigo* skills while also believing that improving their *keigo* skills is both achievable and valuable. Okamoto and Shibamoto-Smith argue that the ultimate message of the *keigo* self-help genre is that *keigo* is a key source of the uniqueness, and crucially, the non-Western-ness, of the Japanese language.

Dunn (1999, 2011, 2013) examines business etiquette training for L1-Japanese speakers, which many Japanese companies require their new hires to complete. Such training is the result of implicit and explicit beliefs about *keigo* as an essential element for Japanese people to become *shakaijin*, adults who are full-fledged members of society. Dunn writes:

> mastery of honorific language is expected to develop as part of the process of becoming a mature, socially-responsible adult. The appropriate use of honorifics is ideologically linked to a variety of social values including social maturity and tact, grammatical correctness, good-breeding, and even Japanese national identity (Dunn, 1999: 89)

Dunn observes that although children and teens learn formulaic expressions that are part of *keigo*, L1-Japanese speakers rarely learn to use *keigo* fully before they enter the workforce. Thus, using *keigo* is one way to perform being and becoming an adult.

Other researchers, including Barke (2010) and Cook (2008), have described ways that Japanese speakers use *keigo* to express different aspects of their social identities, and, as a result, shifts in register (e.g. from casual to formal or from plain speech to *keigo*) often represent a shift in affective stance, which can function as a way for speakers to cultivate their social identities.

Keigo and L2 speakers

Japanese linguists examining *keigo* in use and *keigo* ideologies have tended to overlook 'the use of honorifics by ethnic others born in Japan or coming to Japan as immigrants' (Okamoto & Shibamoto-Smith, 2016: 143). However, researchers in second language acquisition (SLA) have considered the challenges *keigo* presents for L2 learners and JFL teachers (e.g. Carroll, 2005; Cook, 2008; Miyamoto Caltabiano, 2008; Takeuchi, 2021). Early work examining the experience of American exchange students in Japan described ways that L2 speakers resisted learning and using *keigo* (Siegal, 1996). However, Carroll (2005), Niyekawa (1991) and others argue that *keigo* is important for L2 speakers because of the role that *keigo* plays in ensuring 'smooth communication', an idea that is found in *keigo* guides geared to L1 speakers (Carroll, 2005). Writing 30 years ago, Niyekawa (1991) argued that L1 speakers react to *keigo* mistakes differently than other mistakes (e.g. grammar, tense). Specifically, she described *keigo* mistakes as being more likely to be interpreted as a personal insult rather than as a lack of language proficiency. Niyekawa did not explain the basis for this claim. Carroll (2005: 233–234) repeats this concern, arguing that 'although errors in *keigo* may not be corrected overtly, they may not be tolerated internally'. The idea that *keigo* mistakes are more than simple errors has become gospel among JFL teachers. In a survey I conducted in 2020, many respondents repeated similar claims and explained that they told their JFL students that a *keigo* mistake has the potential to be received as an insult, using this idea as a way to encourage their students to work hard to learn *keigo* (Takeuchi, 2021).

Carroll (2005) critiques the way *keigo* tends to be taught in JFL instruction and points out that instruction often explains *keigo* usage as determined by factors like social hierarchy and age, while omitting the various ways *keigo* serves expressive functions and contributes to the social identity of the speaker. In addition, such instruction reinforces the impression that *keigo* is only used when the speaker wants to convey respect, a depiction that research in Japanese linguistics shows to be a serious oversimplification. Ultimately, Carroll argues, L2 learners should be encouraged not only to learn the rules of *keigo* usage, but also to develop a more nuanced understanding of *keigo*'s functions within the Japanese repertoire. This will allow learners to make informed choices about when and how to use *keigo* in their own speech.

Ishihara and Tarone (2009) expand the idea of learners making their own choices and take a critical view of the tendency to judge an L2 speaker's usage of polite forms and honorifics as correct when it adheres to Japanese sociolinguistic norms and incorrect when it does not. Observing that even L1 speakers do not always adhere to sociolinguistic norms, Ishihara and Tarone (2009: 19) argue that the agency of L2 learners should be respected: 'Learners should be able to produce the L2 in any way they choose to, once they have the knowledge of L2 norms and the risks involved of being negatively perceived when diverging from those norms'. Although Ishihara and Tarone do not discuss L2 learners' *keigo* usage in terms of speaker legitimacy, their arguments support the recognition of L2 speaker legitimacy.

Ishihara and Tarone (2009) make an argument for allowing L2 speakers to choose for themselves whether or how much to adhere to so-called 'native speaker' norms. Other researchers suggest that L2 speakers need not, or perhaps should not, try to emulate L1 speakers in attempting to adhere to Japanese sociolinguistic norms. Iino (2006) examines L2 speakers in different circumstances in Japan, including exchange students doing homestays and L2 speakers who were no longer students and were working in Japanese companies. Iino (2006: 160) questions the degree to which L2 speakers were 'expected or allowed to assimilate to native Japanese' and he argues that '"speaking like a native" can sometimes be inappropriate'. Iino (2006: 160–161) bases his arguments on findings from participants who felt that if they spoke Japanese, they would 'lose control' of the interaction, leading Iino to conclude that 'by playing a *gaijin* [foreigner] role, a foreigner may be able to avoid responsibility for complying with the social norms which would otherwise be expected in native situations'. Unfortunately, Iino does not problematize these notions and he fails to consider the negative impacts on L2 speakers of such a dichotomous view of native and non-native, with corresponding language expectations.

Moody (2018) studied American interns in a Japanese company and describes their use of *desu/masu* or plain forms in interactions with L1 coworkers.[1] Moody finds that the interns made efforts to 'establish belonging' within the company and that they were aware of social norms for polite language and tried to adhere to those norms in their Japanese language use. Moody describes a variety of instances of polite forms used by the L2 speakers, including some uses that were unnatural and others that were natural or appropriate. One of Moody's participants is described as struggling with polite forms and using them in unnatural ways, while another used polite forms in ways that closely aligned with how L1 coworkers used them. Moody finds that both types of usage could be met by responses from L1 speakers that were 'othering', in that the responses highlighted the L2 speakers' status as outsiders. A third participant is described as using polite forms in ways that did not conform to sociolinguistic norms. While this participant was seen as successful in establishing positive relationships with his L1 coworkers, his linguistic choices were seen as ultimately strengthening his 'outsider identity' (Moody, 2018: 794). Ironically, Moody concludes that both the participant who used polite forms in 'native-like' and appropriate ways, and the participants who used them in inappropriate or non-conforming ways, ended up foregrounding their foreigner identities. Moody (2018: 795) argues that these findings call for a reconsideration of how belonging is defined, pointing out that there are different kinds of belonging, including belonging as feeling 'accepted for who they are' or as 'a matter of equal access to workplace resources'. Moody fails, however, to recognize that the L2 speakers are set up to be 'damned if they do, damned if they don't'. Missing in Moody's article is a critique of the root cause of the challenges his participants experienced – native speaker bias. For example, Moody (2018: 790) describes a comment made by a participant who complained that having his Japanese complimented was bothersome 'because it implicitly frames him as someone who should not be expected to understand Japanese language and culture'. However, Moody misses the opportunity to examine assumptions about L2 speakers and what contributes to the 'othering' observed in his study. Moody argues that 'native-like' speech is not necessary and might actually be counterproductive for establishing belonging. The idea that an L2 speaker should not need to adopt 'native-like' speech has intuitive appeal. However, when an L2 speaker uses appropriate speech that is 'native-like', but is nevertheless responded to with unwanted attention, it has the effect of treating the L2 speaker like an outsider. The problem here is not the L2 speaker's use of 'native-like' speech; rather, it is the absence of L2 speaker legitimacy that makes othering possible.

Study Participants: *Keigo's* Relevance for L2 Speakers

Research underscores the complexity of *keigo* in terms of its elaborateness as a system of linguistic politeness, the contested nature of ideological depictions of *keigo*'s role in Japanese society and the challenges that *keigo* poses for L2 speakers. My research findings demonstrate these complexities. Analysis of interviews shows how L1 and L2 participants viewed *keigo* and how L2 participants viewed *keigo*'s relevance for them as part of their Japanese linguistic repertoire. Findings from interviews with L1 participants emphasize the vital role of *keigo* within Japanese language and, at the same time, underscore the ways that L1 speakers can downplay or deny the relevance of *keigo* for L2 speakers.

The interview protocol did not include questions that specifically addressed *keigo*. However, participants often brought up the subject of *keigo* and honorific usage, showing how important the topic was to them. Participants' comments about *keigo* occurred most often in response to the following interview questions:

Questions for L2 participants:
- How would you describe your Japanese language ability?
- Is there anything you're careful about when you speak Japanese?
- What's difficult about Japanese?

Questions for L1 participants:
- 日本に住んでいる外国人はどんな日本語のスキルが必要だと思いますか。What kinds of Japanese language skills do you think foreigners living in Japan need?

Beliefs about *Keigo*

In the following sections, I introduce participants whose views about *keigo* bring into relief the many ways that *keigo* beliefs are impacted by ideologies of speaker legitimacy and language ownership. I first discuss findings from the L2 and L1 participant groups as a whole and conclude with a discussion of two participants in greater depth. All participants who discussed *keigo* acknowledged its importance and its challenges and both L1 and L2 participants expressed complex and divergent beliefs about *keigo*. In addition, when some participants discussed their ideas about what was appropriate or necessary *keigo* usage, they revealed ideological beliefs about who counts as a legitimate speaker of Japanese. Particularly notable is the finding that some participants, both L1 and L2 participants, described the belief that L2 speakers can or should be 'excused' from learning or using *keigo*. Such beliefs in effect position L2 speakers as not legitimate speakers of Japanese.

Struggling with *keigo*

Many L2 participants focused on *keigo* when asked what is difficult about Japanese. Viewing *keigo* as difficult was not limited to recent arrivals or to those who had not formally studied Japanese – even participants who had lived in Japan for many years or who had studied Japanese extensively reported struggling with *keigo*.

Louis, a Japanese major in college, had been living in Japan for over four years at the time of the study. He described his *keigo* knowledge as 'missing' and explained that he could understand it when he heard it but could not correctly use it himself. Louis said that he had been laughed at by his L1-Japanese significant other when he tried to use formal or honorific speech. Grace, on the other hand, only started learning Japanese after moving to Japan and had no formal instruction in Japanese language. At the time of the interview, she had been in Japan for 10 years and had developed advanced Japanese functionality, especially in spoken Japanese. However, Grace lacked confidence in her *keigo* ability. Grace said that she felt insecure in formal situations because of her limited knowledge about how and when to use *keigo*. As a parent of school-aged children, Grace was involved in the parent–teacher association (PTA) at her children's schools. She was also highly active in community events. As a parent and active community member, Grace's participation was expected, but she was keenly aware of her inability to use *keigo* in the same way as L1 parents. Grace discussed relying on her L1 spouse, but she felt that, as her children got older, she needed to be able to do PTA and community activities by herself. Grace spoke at length about her struggles in the PTA and her painful awareness that, as tasks rotated among the members, when her turn came, she was unable to use the expected polite language to carry out her duties the way L1 parents did. Grace also shared the concern that her children were not receiving the necessary exposure to *keigo* because of her own inability. Thus, Grace recognized *keigo*'s importance in her daily life, but she struggled because she was unable to use it fully.

William, who had been in Japan for two years at the time of the study, described observing the use of *keigo* both in his workplace and in social and casual interactions. William, a member of a traditional Japanese music group, described how *senpai/kōhai* (senior/junior) relationships among members were conveyed through *keigo*. William's experience of having studied Japanese as a university student in the United States was evident in his recognition of the richness that *keigo* brought to the language. For example, he described the presence or absence of *keigo* in literature as a way for an author to share information with the reader about the personalities of the characters. William said he found it fascinating to notice the changing speech levels, terms of address, honorifics and other linguistic features in literature. Yet, he also described *keigo* as the 'weakest part' of his Japanese. William shared a story about being corrected by his supervisor for using the plain form, *sō da yo* (that's right), when he should have used the *desu/masu* (polite) form, *sō desu yo*. However, he said, being corrected for such mistakes was unusual. William explained that rather than being corrected for mistakes, he received 'leeway for being foreign' and his coworkers rarely corrected his *keigo*-related mistakes.

The experience of being forgiven for mistaken or missing *keigo* was shared by other participants as well. Melissa, who had been in Japan for three years at the time of the study, explained her sense that *keigo*, while important in Japan, was optional for foreigners. Melissa described 'getting away with' not using *keigo* in situations where it was probably expected and, like William, she recognized the leeway she received as a foreigner:

> **Melissa:** I get a lot of leeway for not speaking *keigo* and stuff because I'm foreign and I'm not saying that's a good thing, but you know I can kind of get away with it a bit more cuz sometimes I don't know how to say something super politely, but I figure if I smile and I say it a nice way then they will just, hopefully understand that I'm not trying to be rude but at least we're communicating and most of the time that's fine

Melissa emphasized the importance of communicating in a nice and friendly way to make up for her lack of *keigo* ability. At the same time, Melissa recognized that this was not necessarily a 'good thing', and, in other portions of the interview, she described wanting to be able to use appropriate *keigo* when speaking with her supervisor or other superiors at work.

L1-Japanese participants concurred with L2 participants in describing *keigo* as difficult and, therefore, optional for L2 speakers. When asked about what was difficult for L2 learners of Japanese, Shibata stated that *keigo* was especially challenging because of the difficulty in knowing when and with whom to use which type of politeness. Examples she shared included that it would be difficult for L2 speakers to make decisions between *kenjōgo* (humble speech) and *sonkeigo* (honorific speech) or to choose between *teineigo* (neutral polite speech) and *keigo* (honorific polite speech). Some L1 participants commented about specific L2 participants' lack of ability at *keigo*. For example, Yoshio specifically commented on William's lack of *keigo* ability, and Endo reported that none of the L2 speakers she had worked with were good at *keigo*. On the other hand, both Saeko and Akemi explained that the use of *keigo* was a sign that an L2 speaker's Japanese had improved.

Rejecting *keigo*

While the L2 participants introduced above described their struggles to improve at *keigo*, other participants felt differently. Sam, who had been in Japan for over 15 years at the time of the study, reported his dislike of *keigo* and his preferences for avoiding *keigo* as much as possible. Sam recognized that *keigo* played a role in workplace contexts. He said that he lacked confidence in his ability to use *keigo* and, in particular, he was uncertain about which situations called for *keigo* and which did not. Nevertheless, Sam made it a point to try to use *keigo* at work, especially when answering the phone or greeting visitors to his workplace. At the same time, he shared his dislike of honorifics and even of the neutral polite (*desu/masu*) forms. Instead, Sam said he preferred to dispense with those linguistic formalities as much as possible. He explained that using honorifics and *desu/masu* too much distracted from communication goals. Sam wanted to be able to have a 'friendly conversation' with anyone and, perhaps by way of explanation, he pointed out that he also did not wear a suit to work.

Nicole had lived in Japan for 14 years at the time of the study. After working as a coordinator for international relations (CIR) in the JET Program, she stayed in Japan and worked as a translator and interpreter. Not surprisingly, given her work experiences, Nicole was comfortable using the different levels of *keigo* and adjusting her speech style as needed. Further, Nicole said that 'if someone should be using *keigo* with me and they don't, I feel like they're not being respectful'.

The experience of L2 speakers who are long-term residents of Japan is of special interest. Dean had lived in Japan for close to 30 years at the time of the study. Over the years, he worked in various jobs, including teaching English and as an in-house translator, and, at the time of the study, he was running his own business. Not surprisingly, Dean had a wealth of experience using *keigo* in diverse contexts. Dean, more than other participants, discussed the complexity of *keigo*. For example, one of the first things he said about *keigo* was that it can be 'quite offensive'. Dean told a story about an unpleasant exchange he had with a salesman whose use of humble polite phrases, such as *sō de gozaimasu ka* (is that so?), was insincere. Dean called it 'being polite to be offensive', adding that such *keigo* was a 'waste of time' and 'doesn't make the client feel any better'. He contrasted this kind of *keigo* with the example of an '*okamisan*', the proprietress of a traditional Japanese inn, who used *keigo* that was both polite and humorous, which Dean called 'charming'. When I asked Dean if he was comfortable using *keigo* himself, he laughed and said 'no, I feel as though I'm about to crash through the ice at any point'. Nevertheless, Dean emphasized that *keigo* was important to use and that it was important for L2 speakers to develop *keigo* skills:

> **Dean:** I've bumped into foreigners who have obviously taken the position that they're not going to do it. I think it's a cop out and I think they just seem graceless, and I think you get marks for trying even if you don't quite do it, so I think it's important.

Dean's comment about receiving marks for trying aligns with comments from other L2 participants that L1 speakers are lenient and do not expect L2 speakers to use *keigo*.

Few L1 participants shared negative comments about *keigo*. However, one who did was Kazuki. Kazuki was younger than many of the other L1 participants and, unlike many L1 participants who were teachers or civil servants, Kazuki did not work in either a school or city office. Instead, he worked in a customer service position. It is well known that employees involved in customer service in Japan are expected to use *keigo*, in particular *kenjōgo* (humble) and *sonkeigo* (honorific) forms as well as numerous honorific set phrases. During his interview, Kazuki complained about the heavy emphasis placed on the use of *keigo* in his workplace. He described various expectations for *keigo* usage and said the amount of *keigo* he was expected to use was 'too much' (he used the English expression although we were speaking in Japanese). Kazuki's stance was similar to Sam's in that Kazuki also described *keigo* as a barrier to interacting with others. At the same time, Kazuki lamented to me the fact that he did not study enough in school, saying that he wished he had studied more and that his *keigo* skills were better. He contrasted himself to his L2 spouse, Peter, and said that Peter's *keigo* skills were better than his own. However, in a later portion of the interview, Kazuki was critical of Peter's *keigo* skills, saying that Peter, who worked as a university-level English teacher, did not have much opportunity to use *keigo* at work and mainly used casual speech outside of work. Kazuki then added that, in general, there was little expectation that 'foreigners' would use *keigo*. Kazuki made it a point to qualify this as 'not discrimination', suggesting that he was aware that these disparate expectations constituted differential treatment. Kazuki's comments highlight the complexities that *keigo* present for any speaker of Japanese and serve as further evidence of the kind of 'leeway' described by some L2 participants. (See Chapter 6 for more in-depth discussion of Kazuki's depictions of Peter's Japanese skills.)

Embracing *keigo*

Most L2 participants who talked about the challenges of *keigo* also recognized expectations for *keigo* usage in the workplace. While the participants described above did not make significant efforts to meet those expectations, other participants actively cultivated *keigo* because of its benefits as a professional resource. Daniel is representative of this approach. Daniel had been in Japan for four years at the time of the study and he planned to stay in Japan indefinitely. His Japanese ability was quite advanced: he studied Japanese in high school and university and had previously lived in Japan on a working holiday visa. Daniel expressed a strong commitment to continually improving his Japanese skills. For example, he described making an active effort to pay attention to how Japanese speakers used different registers of speech, both in the workplace and in social interactions, as well as while watching Japanese television and movies. Daniel said that he would regularly make adjustments to his *keigo* usage based on what he heard.

Daniel also had a unique work history. Unlike many L2 participants, he had worked in the service industry both in New Zealand and in Japan, and Daniel's work experience clearly made an impression on him regarding what kind of Japanese was appropriate in the workplace. Daniel described his experience during his working holiday as particularly impactful, because of his participation in regular training sessions designed for L1 speakers that coached staff in the proper use of *keigo* and polite expressions. As a result, Daniel had clear ideas about how supervisors and subordinates should speak to each other, and also about how staff should speak to customers. Daniel described his Japanese ability in general as being much better than 'the average foreigner living in Japan' and his ability to use *keigo* and polite Japanese was clearly a source of pride. Daniel shared with me an experience early on in his working life in Japan when a supervisor scolded him for speaking too casually. This experience clearly left a lasting impression and Daniel said it had a positive impact on his Japanese language development. It was also clear that Daniel's assessment of his Japanese ability was based not only on functionality, but also on assessments from Japanese people with whom he spoke. Daniel recounted being praised by Japanese people for his ability to speak politely, and he expressed pride in his Japanese accent, which, he said, allowed him to 'pass' for Japanese on the telephone.

Further evidence of Daniel's commitment to *keigo* was seen when he contrasted his own experiences and linguistic abilities with those of another L2 speaker living in Japan. Daniel assessed his friend as unable to 'speak *keigo* properly', which Daniel believed would be a barrier to finding a job in Japan when the friend's limited-term teaching position ended. Overall, it was clear from Daniel's interview that he took pride in his *keigo* ability and also in his understanding of *keigo* as an important professional skill, both for obtaining employment and maintaining positive relationships within the workplace.

While Daniel focused on the use of *keigo* as a professional resource, other participants focused on *keigo*'s expressive possibilities, including *keigo*'s role in creating an identity or voice. Branden is an example of how L2 participants connected *keigo* usage to speaker identity. Branden had been in Japan for two years at the time of the study; both his university experiences of majoring in Japanese and doing an exchange program in Japan contributed to his advanced Japanese level. In his interview, Branden explained that he paid close attention to how he sounded to himself in Japanese, and he wanted to ensure that his way of speaking matched his conception of his identity as a speaker of Japanese. He explained that his commitment to using *keigo* was connected to his experience studying it and also his feelings of attachment to polite speech:

> **Branden:** [in university Japanese classes there] was that emphasis on, you know, using polite expressions, and that's sort of like the first Japanese that I was able to really, to really use and really like, call my own, is all those formal expressions

Branden's view of *keigo* as language he could call his own is an example of how *keigo* can be used for the purposes of identity and self-expression. Branden also expressed a sense of ownership over polite Japanese.

James shared Branden's affinity for *keigo*. At the time of the study, James had been in Japan for 10 years, first as a member of the JET Program, then as a graduate student in a Japanese graduate program and finally as a university professor. James had advanced Japanese ability, having studied Japanese in high school and university, and he had passed the highest level of the Japanese Language Proficiency Test (JLPT) many years earlier. In addition to his spoken Japanese ability, James was also an experienced writer and translator. In response to my question about whether he liked speaking Japanese, James had this to say:

James: that's tough, my answer to that has probably changed over the years. at one point the novelty of the different politeness registers and the emotiveness of Japanese I really enjoyed, I thought it was an interesting language, um, now, I don't know, one thing I like about it, you know, it's a polite language with lots of indirectness and lots of needlessness, I would say it's very *jōchō* ((verbose)), everything is too much and I kinda like that. So writing a business email in Japanese *o-sewa ni natte orimasu* ((I am in your debt)) *da da da* ((blah blah blah))... *nani nani no ken ni tsukimasite* ((in regards to the matter of something something)) ... like, all that stuff
Jae: yeah, it takes a long time to get where you're going
James: yeah, I like that, I enjoy that, there's a sort of luxuriousness to that that I enjoy

One comment that stands out is James's depiction of *keigo* as luxurious, as if the complexity of *keigo*, the very thing that makes it challenging for learners, is what attracted him to it. In addition, while other participants discussed *keigo*'s role in the workplace or its use for acknowledging status differentials, James did not mention these details. Although he described *keigo* as 'too much', in the same way as Kazuki, James did not find this frustrating but instead explained that he enjoyed *keigo*'s complexity.

The disconnect: 'Foreigners don't need *keigo*'

The participants introduced so far convey contrasting views about *keigo* and its relevance for L2 speakers. These views are brought into sharp relief in the case of David, an L2 speaker, and Megumi, an L1 speaker, a married couple whose *keigo* beliefs were starkly misaligned. At the time of the study, David had been in Japan for over 20 years and for most of those years, he had been self-employed as a performer and instructor of martial arts and fitness. David also worked as a translator. Although he had learned Japanese primarily through self-study, David's language skills were quite advanced. In addition to David's other activities, he and Megumi lived in and managed a guest house, primarily for international visitors to the martial arts dojo (training school) to which they belonged. Megumi had previously lived abroad and at the time of the study, she was working as a fitness instructor in addition to running the guest house. Thus, David and Megumi differed from other participants in that they were both self-employed, and David, unlike many L2 participants, had never worked as an assistant language teacher (ALT) or English teacher.

David and Megumi were both active participants in the dojo, and many topics discussed in their interviews related to activities and interactions with their *sensei*, the head instructor at the dojo. The importance of hierarchy in Japanese martial arts is well known, and with hierarchy comes the expectation of polite speech for one's *sensei* or *senpai* (one's seniors or more advanced martial arts practitioners). The dojo to which David and Megumi belonged was run by a charismatic teacher who was well known for attracting a large number of international disciples. David's long-standing connection to the dojo and to this *sensei* gave him insider status at the dojo. During the interview, I asked David how he would describe his Japanese ability. Having heard David's spoken Japanese prior to the interview, I was surprised when he responded with 'fair', so I asked:

Jae:	what would it take for it to be better than fair?
David:	to fill in those gaps, particularly *keigo*, and uh, yeah, mostly *keigo*, and of course going back and reviewing vocabulary
Jae:	are there things you'd like to do in Japanese, and you can't?
David:	well, speak to *sensei* [martial arts teacher] in *keigo* ((laughs))

David's choice to focus on *keigo* in his answer indicates the salience of his assessment that his *keigo* ability was insufficient. It also shares the personal reason he had for wanting to improve, speaking with his *sensei*. David was the only participant I interviewed who mentioned a specific person with whom they wanted to be able to use *keigo*. In fact, David's wish to be able to use *keigo* better when speaking with his *sensei* came up numerous times during the interview. His feelings were readily apparent when I visited the dojo and saw the reverence and affection that David had for his *sensei*.

Megumi ran the guest house with David and worked as a fitness instructor. She interacted with international visitors from numerous countries who visited the guest house and the dojo. Megumi spoke Japanese with international guests who spoke Japanese and she spoke English with guests who had limited or no Japanese ability. My interview with Megumi was conducted in Japanese, and David was present for part of the time and participated in some of the discussion. Megumi commented about L2 speakers in general and also about David as an L2 speaker. For example, when I asked what kinds of skills L2 speakers need, Megumi discussed language skills as well as cultural knowledge. Her experiences at the guest house meant she had regular opportunities to encounter cultural differences. Megumi shared her observations about aspects of Japanese etiquette or customs with which international guests struggled. She described etiquette mistakes that guests made in the guest house, such as wearing shoes in rooms with tatami straw mat floor covering. This discussion evolved into one of etiquette at the martial arts dojo. It was in this context that I asked Megumi about *keigo* skills and whether she thought *keigo* was necessary. I had intended my question to be about the *keigo* skills of L2 speakers; however, Megumi interpreted my question to be about 'Japanese people'. The exchange that followed is presented below (all translations by this author).

Jae: さきDavidさんが少し話した、あのう、敬語は大切なスキルだと思いますか。それともいらないと思いますか。
Megumi: めっちゃいると思います。そんないらんって言う日本人いないと思う… え、たまにいたら、いや、いr-、いるよ、これは大事です、敬語は。本当に

Jae: earlier, David talked about it a little bit, but do you think *keigo* is an important skill? Or do you think it's not needed?
Megumi: I think it's super needed. I don't think there are any Japanese people who would say it's not needed, if there were people like that, well, no, it's needed, *keigo* is really important

In her remarks, Megumi made a point of stressing that there were no *Japanese* people who would say that *keigo* is not needed. I next asked her about David, but I did not notice that he had joined us and was sitting nearby:

Jae: Davidさんはあまり、あのう、得意じゃないというふうに話したんですけど、もっと学んでほしい？
Megumi: 学んでほしいか？いや、学ばなくていいでしょ、いや、Davidは使わなくていいです
Jae: それはどうしてですか
David: どうしてですかね ((slight laughter))

Jae: David said he wasn't that good [at *keigo*], do you want him to learn [it] more?
Megumi: do I want him to learn? No, it's ok if he doesn't learn, no, it's ok if David doesn't use [*keigo*]
Jae: why is that?
David: yeah, why is that? ((slight laughter))

Megumi's response to my question suggested that she had never thought about David needing *keigo* before. She repeated twice that David did not need to learn more *keigo* and that it was okay if he did not use it. When I asked Megumi why, David, who had been listening but not participating in the discussion, joined in. David repeated my question, laughing slightly, making his question sound both joking but also slightly offended.

David continued talking and shared that he wished he could use *keigo* better. Because he was off to the side, the audio-recording is unclear, and it was not possible to discern exactly what he was saying. The next portion was audible, and the following excerpt shows that part of the discussion.

Jae:	先生と話すと？
David:	そうそう。うまかったら、ね、もうちょっとね、いつも思うんだよね
Megumi:	そう？
David:	うーん
Megumi:	え？だって、面白いじゃん、今のしゃべり方
David:	((laughs/snorts))　いや、面白いけどね。先生と((hard to hear))
Jae:	when you speak with your *sensei* ((teacher))?
David:	yeah, yeah, I always think, if I was better, it would be a little more
Megumi:	really?
David:	yeah
Megumi:	huh? But, it's [more] interesting right, the way [you] speak now
David:	((laughs/snorts)) well yeah, it's interesting but, when talking to *sensei* ((hard to hear))

David sounded wistful, as if he were imagining himself speaking with his teacher using *keigo*. Megumi, however, questioned David's comments, asking 'really' with rising intonation. David answered 'yeah' and reiterated his desire to be better at *keigo*. Megumi then commented that David's current way of speaking was more interesting. It should be noted that Megumi's use of the word *omoshiroi* can be translated as either interesting or amusing. Further, Megumi prefaced her comment with *datte*, which can be translated as 'but' or 'because', and has the effect of emphasizing the sense of correctness of her view on the matter. Her use of *datte* as well as *jan* ('isn't it', translated above as 'right') made her statement sound as though agreement from David was a given. David then responded with a sort of half laugh, suggesting a sense of self-derision at the idea of his way of speaking being 'interesting' or 'amusing'. The implication was that being amusing was not his goal, especially when speaking to his *sensei*.

In the next excerpt, I again directed my question at Megumi and asked about the Japanese members of the dojo. Here again, Megumi initially misinterpreted my question:

Jae:	日本人の道場のメンバーたちは [name] 先生と敬語をよく使いますか。
Megumi:	敬語使っているし、ヘンな敬語を使っている人も、((she imitates)) お師匠さま、そうでございますか。みたいな
David:	それは外国人ね
Megumi:	うん外国人ね
Jae:	ああ
Megumi:	そ- あ、日本人ね？日本人はもちろん敬語ですよ。どのジャンルのお稽古ごとも、先生と生徒というのは、日本は、ほら、ね、マスターとディサイプルみたいな
Jae:	そうですね
Megumi:	関係性があるから
Jae:	弟子が
Megumi:	そんな、先生に敬語なしでしゃべる人はちょっとばかやろう
Jae:	do the Japanese members of the dojo often use *keigo* with Sensei?
Megumi:	they use *keigo*, and there are people who use weird *keigo* like ((she imitates using a funny, high-pitched voice)) 'Is that so, oh Honorable Master'
David:	that's foreigners right ((who do that))
Megumi:	yeah, that's foreigners
Jae:	oh
Megumi:	ye- ah, Japanese people? Of course, the Japanese people [use] *keigo*. With any genre of [traditional] practice/training, there's *sensei* ((teacher)) and *deshi* ((pupil)), right, so Japan has the thing like master and disciple
Jae:	yes
Megumi:	there's that relationship
Jae:	the disciple
Megumi:	so, someone who talks to Sensei without using *keigo* is just an idiot

Again, Megumi misinterpreted my question, and she began to talk about people who used incorrect (weird, *henna*) *keigo*. She used a high-pitched voice and excessive *keigo* that could be called obsequious. David, however, corrected her, pointing out that she was talking about foreigners. Megumi agreed and realized her mistake. She then stated that 'of course' Japanese people use *keigo*. After connecting this to the Japanese cultural tradition of master and disciple relationships found in traditional arts (which include martial arts), Megumi concluded by saying that anyone who did not use *keigo* when talking to the teacher was an idiot. The discussion then moved on to the kinds of mistakes people make when speaking *keigo*.

Following discussion of different kinds of *keigo* mistakes, I returned to the question of Megumi's opinion about David's *keigo* abilities. My field notes from this visit show that I was surprised by Megumi's comments about David, and I was worried that she had unintentionally hurt his feelings. To ease the conversation, I first returned to the question of Megumi's opinion about David and then focused on her own language use habits.

Jae:	えーと、敬語に関するほかの、じゃあ、さき、だから、Davidさんは、そんなに別に敬語をマスターしなくていい
Megumi:	うん、別に、ね、あのう、うん。。。そうだ、いや、いいんじゃないかなと思う
Jae:	Megumiさんも [dojo] に行かれるわけ
Megumi:	行きます、はい
Jae:	で、その、[martial arts]先生とかと話す時は敬語は
Megumi:	うん敬語でしゃべります
Jae:	尊敬語、謙譲語を使ったりはしますか。
Megumi:	うん、しますします。やっぱ日本人だしね ((laughing))

Jae:	well, other things related to keigo, so, earlier, David, [you said] it's ok if he doesn't master *keigo*
Megumi:	yeah, not especially, um, yeah, so, that's right, I think it's fine [if he doesn't]
Jae:	so you also go to the dojo
Megumi:	I do go, yes..
Jae:	then, do you [use] *keigo* when you talk to Sensei?
Megumi:	yeah, I speak in *keigo*
Jae:	so you use honorific ((*sonkeigo*)) and humble ((*kenjōgo*)) language
Megumi:	yeah, I do, I do. I'm Japanese after all ((laughing))

Megumi again repeated her view that David did not need to master *keigo*. In response to my next questions, she explained that she did indeed use *keigo* when talking to their teacher. Megumi concluded her response by saying that she is, after all '*yappa*' Japanese. I then confirmed her opinion that 'foreigners' did not need to use *keigo*, and she agreed but qualified her remarks, saying that a certain amount of respectful language was needed. The remainder of this portion of the interview discussed the importance of L2 speakers using *desu/masu* long form rather than short form, which confirmed Megumi's belief that L2 speakers did not need to learn or use *keigo*.

Discussion

The interview excerpts introduced above show that participants held diverse views with regard to *keigo* and its use by L2 speakers, but all participants recognized the important role that *keigo* plays in the Japanese language. Some L2 participants, including Louis, William and David, saw *keigo* as the weakest part of their Japanese skill set. However, this was tempered by the perception that L1 speakers would not have high expectations for L2 speakers to use *keigo*, a perception largely supported by L1 participants. Despite the shared belief that L2 speakers' *keigo* inability would be forgiven, some L1 and L2 participants described *keigo* ability as a marker of language proficiency for L2 speakers. Indeed, some L2 participants, most notably Daniel, took pride in their ability to correctly use *keigo*. While less common, some L2 participants, like Branden and James, connected with *keigo* as an expressive tool. Only one L2 participant, Sam, and one L1 participant, Kazuki, expressed outright dislike of *keigo* and a desire to avoid using it if possible.

In many ways, David and Megumi epitomize the dilemma that *keigo* represents for L2 speakers living in Japan. David, who had a high level of Japanese, was painfully aware that his *keigo* abilities did not measure up to the rest of his language skills. He also had a personal reason, his relationship with a beloved teacher, for wanting to improve his *keigo* skills. If we see Daniel as someone who has accomplished the goal of *keigo* mastery, then we might think of David's *keigo* as still aspirational. However, David's *keigo* aspirations were not supported by his spouse, Megumi, who downplayed the importance of *keigo* for David, even as she made strong statements about the importance of Japanese people being able to use *keigo* appropriately. From Megumi's point of view, L2 speakers did not need *keigo* in terms of the humble and honorific forms, instead basic politeness skills (*desu/masu*) were sufficient. In addition, Megumi made it clear that she felt David did not need to learn any more *keigo*, his Japanese was fine, perhaps even better without it, since his current way of speaking was more amusing. For Megumi herself, on the other hand, her own use of *keigo* was a given. Further, for Megumi, her *keigo* use was explained by the fact that she is Japanese; put another way, the fact that she is Japanese was sufficient explanation for her use of *keigo*. Thus, we see the disconnect between David and Megumi with regard to *keigo*'s relevance for L2 speakers in general and for David in particular.

Conclusion

This chapter began with a description of *keigo* and its role within Japanese. There is no question that *keigo* is an important part of the language, but the interview excerpts shared in this chapter raise a fundamental question: important for whom?

Previous studies confirm *keigo*'s role in showing respect and deference, as well as its importance in professional contexts. In addition, *keigo* is a multifaceted register that allows Japanese speakers to express elements of their identities and their subjective agency as speakers and interlocutors. The interview and representative excerpts shared in this chapter affirm that these features of *keigo* also apply to L2 speakers. *Keigo* is also a marker of linguistic proficiency for L2 speakers and a tool that makes it possible to use Japanese in strategic ways. *Keigo* offers L2 speakers a set of linguistic tools to display a respectful relationship, and at the same time, a way to express one's voice and identity as a speaker. Thus, *keigo* is a resource for both identity construction and for social and interactional goals for all Japanese speakers, both L1 and L2.

However, comments and observations by both L1 and L2 participants indicate that L2 speakers may not only be 'excused' from *keigo*, but may also be actively discouraged from pursuing *keigo* proficiency. A surface-level examination suggests that those who espouse the idea that L2 speakers are excused from *keigo* are doing so from a desire to be kind. However, when L2 speakers do not have access to *keigo*, they may also be denied access to resources, in terms of resources both for professional goals and for self-expression.

In Megumi's comments most especially, there is an unexamined, taken-for-granted understanding of *keigo* as a tool only for 'Japanese' people, which emphasizes and reinforces the speaker legitimacy of native speakers. For L2 speakers, speaker legitimacy is tenuous at best. The problem here is that excusing L2 speakers from *keigo* risks confining them to an infantilized and exoticized position as speakers of Japanese, as seen in Megumi's statement that how David speaks is amusing.

These divergent views of *keigo*'s role for L2 speakers can also be considered in terms of what it means to be a legitimate speaker of Japanese. Some researchers (e.g. Iino, 2006) suggest that L2 speakers should not try to emulate L1 speakers, while others (e.g. Moody, 2018) view attempts to use polite forms as 'trying to act like a native'. These depictions ignore an alternative interpretation: namely, that incorporating *keigo* may simply be acting like a competent Japanese speaker. Also missing from previous studies of *keigo* is an account of the impact that native speaker bias and language ownership have on L2 speakers. To be a legitimate speaker, at minimum, means the right to use Japanese in all of its iterations and registers, without being told 'you don't need to use *keigo*'. Beliefs that L2 speakers do not need to 'worry' about *keigo* also suggest the possibility that *keigo* may be more vulnerable than other speech styles to being the target of language ownership. We have to wonder if there is a sense that, while it may be fine for L2 speakers to speak Japanese, mastering *keigo* is taking it 'too far'. Regardless, as this chapter has shown, there are persistent differences in expectations for how L2 speakers use *keigo*.

Note

(1) Moody (2018) did not examine other types of *keigo*, including *sonkeigo* or *kenjōgo* forms; nevertheless, his study is relevant to this discussion because it presents an example of how L2 speakers negotiate speech styles and use of polite language.

4 Trying (Not) to Sound Like a 'Girly-Girl' or a 'Manly-Man'

Introduction

Second language (L2)-Japanese speakers are aware of the expectations for Japanese speakers to pay attention to distinctions between women's language and men's language, i.e. Japanese gendered language. Ideologies and social norms about Japanese gendered language are often in tension with how L2 speakers conceive of who they are and how they want to sound as speakers of Japanese. For the purposes of this book, Japanese gendered language refers to *joseigo*, Japanese women's language, and *danseigo*, Japanese 'men's language', which are words and linguistic forms that are normatively viewed as being for use only by women or only by men, respectively. L2 speakers, including those who study Japanese in formal classroom contexts and those who access Japanese literature and media products, get the message that there are some words and forms that are only appropriate for women, and others that are only appropriate for men. This chapter highlights L2 participants' concerns and fears about possibly inappropriate use of Japanese gendered language and considers how ideologies inform their word choices and at the same time complicate their attempts to be legitimate speakers of Japanese.

Research in Japanese linguistics finds that use of gendered language in spoken Japanese is decreasing (e.g. Matsumoto, 2002; Okamoto, 1995; Okamoto & Shibamoto-Smith, 2004). However, despite these observable changes in usage, ideologies about gendered language persist and are evident in stereotypical depictions of masculine or feminine speech in media and literature (Inoue, 2006; Nakamura, 2008; Suzuki, 2020, 2015). Moreover, L2 speakers encounter ideologies of Japanese gendered language, not only in media such as anime, but also in pedagogical materials used in formal classroom environments. A review of textbooks shows many examples of men and women characters using stereotypically gendered speech patterns, including in the popular *Genki* textbook series by Banno *et al.* (2011, 2020). Some textbooks include explanations describing Japanese language as 'gendered' and learners are explicitly cautioned against using forms for the opposite gender, as in the textbook *Tobira* (Oka *et al.*, 2009). Research findings attest to the impacts of such messages and describe how L2-Japanese learners attend to and often worry about whether and/or how to incorporate or avoid Japanese gendered language forms in their own speech (e.g. Brown & Cheek, 2017; Ohara, 2001; Siegal, 1996).

Findings discussed in this chapter demonstrate that concerns about Japanese gendered language were magnified for the L2 participants and awareness of gendered norms of Japanese language complicated their efforts to 'sound like themselves'. Many L2 participants struggled with how they wanted to sound as Japanese speakers, and they experienced conflicts when they felt that their Japanese speech was more or less masculine or feminine than they felt was appropriate for their sense of themselves as Japanese speakers. In addition, comments from first language (L1) participants show how L1 speakers reinforce ideologies about correct or appropriate ways to use Japanese gendered language. This chapter underscores the impact that ideologies of gendered language have on L2-Japanese speakers and demonstrates how native speaker bias emerges when L2 speakers lack ownership over their own Japanese.

Previous Studies of Japanese Gendered Language

There is extensive research on Japanese gendered language, although until recently, most studies focused on Japanese women's language while overlooking men's language. Below, I introduce some of the features of gendered language, consider the ideologies that underlie them and introduce previous studies that have considered L2-Japanese speakers and gendered language.

Describing Japanese gendered language

Japanese gendered language refers not to grammatical gender such as that found in Romance languages but instead to sets of words, linguistic features and stylistic patterns that are believed to be, or prescribed to be, used by only one gender. For ease of discussion, I use the term 'gendered language' to describe both *joseigo* or women's language and *danseigo* or men's language. According to Nakamura (2011), most Japanese speakers are able to list linguistic features that fit into *joseigo* or *danseigo*, regardless of whether their own speech conforms to ideological depictions of how men and women should speak. The most frequently listed examples include first-person pronouns, sentence-final particles and honorifics, while stylistic features tend to focus on degree of politeness and amount of *keigo* used (Okamoto & Shibamoto-Smith, 2008). Some commonly noted feminine examples include the first-person pronoun *atashi* and the sentence-final particles *wa* and *kashira*. Some masculine examples include the first-person pronouns *boku* and *ore* and the sentence-final particles *ze* and *zo*. There are also some vocabulary words that are seen as more masculine in that they are believed to be rougher or more vulgar, or more feminine in that they are believed to be refined or more beautiful. Thus, stylistically, men are said to use more rough or vulgar language, while women are said to use language that is more refined, beautiful and makes significant use of politeness language.

The situation with masculine first-person pronouns *boku* and *ore* is somewhat complex, in that two options are available and although the meaning is the same, the degree of masculinity conveyed is believed to be different. First, *boku* is regarded as moderately masculine, and appropriate for use by younger male speakers, while *ore* is regarded as strongly masculine. *Boku* is seen as gentler while *ore* is rougher and sometimes seen as vulgar. At the same time, there are regional distinctions as well, and which pronoun is used by younger male speakers can differ by region (Ohara, 2019; SturtzSreetharan, 2009). An additional distinction is that, where *ore* is used more commonly, as in Western Japan, it tends not to carry a negative or vulgar connotation, whereas in areas where *ore* is less common, as in Eastern Japan, it may be seen as more negative or more roughly masculine. Lastly, *ore* may be used by female speakers in some dialects (Sunaoshi, 2004) and there are studies showing use of both *boku* and *ore* by high school-aged girls, which is generally attributed to linguistic rebelliousness. (For an in-depth discussion of these distinctions, see Kroo, 2014, 2018; Miyazaki, 2004; SturtzSreetharan, 2009, 2015, 2017.)

Despite the prevalence of beliefs about men's and women's language, research on naturally occurring Japanese language has found significant diversity in linguistic practices. It is common for researchers to find that male and female Japanese speakers' speech patterns differ from stereotypical depictions of *danseigo* and *joseigo* (Okamoto, 2021). Matsumoto (2002), Nakamura (2011), Okamoto (2021) and others find ample evidence of speakers mixing masculine and feminine linguistic forms in the same interaction or even utterance, suggesting that mixing registers or speech styles appears to be the rule rather than the exception in spoken Japanese (cf. Okamoto & Shibamoto-Smith, 2016).

Nevertheless, the idea that Japanese has gendered versions is taken as commonsensical, and it is widely believed that 'those women who do not talk in a feminine manner and men who speak like women are socially sanctioned' (Nakamura, 2011: 6). Concerns about speaking 'correctly' seem to be particularly strong with regard to women's language and explains the popularity of self-help books intended to help women cultivate more feminine speech habits (Nakamura, 2011; Okamoto & Shibamoto-Smith, 2016). Nakamura (2011) also pointed out that it is common for Japanese as a foreign language (JFL) textbooks and other pedagogical materials to present guidance on how men's and women's speech differ and, crucially, *should* differ.

Japanese gendered language as an ideological construction

Research demonstrates that naturally occurring spoken Japanese rarely adheres to canonical depictions of men's and women's language, underscoring the view that Japanese gendered language is more ideology than reality. Okamoto and Shibamoto-Smith (2008: 88) argue that the speech styles thought of as *joseigo* or *danseigo* 'represent a prescriptive societal norm rather than an accurate description of actual speech practice'. An additional point, and one with particular relevance to my study, is the belief that gendered language, along with honorifics, is part of what makes Japanese unique and different from other languages and this uniqueness is seen as a source of pride (Ohara, 2019). For a discussion of the construction of Japanese gendered language, readers are directed to Okamoto (2018, 2021), Okamoto and Shibamoto-Smith (2004, 2016) and Ohara (2019) for discussions of how Japanese women's language was actively created as part of Japan's nation-building efforts in the late 1800s and early 1900s and the movement to create and promote Standard Japanese.

Okamoto (2018), Okamoto and Shibamoto Smith (2008, 2016) and Suzuki (2018) describe how gendered linguistic norms are maintained, promoted and reinforced in self-help books and by internet blog posts that encourage women to speak in particular ways. They also report on representations of women's speech that can be found in literature, television dramas, anime and other media products that present female characters as speaking in Standard Japanese-based *joseigo*. That men's language is less often the target of self-help books is perhaps explained by the fact that men's language is presumed to be the norm, with women's language then defined based on how it differs from men's language (Ohara, 2019; SturtzSreetharan, 2009). Ohara (2019) also describes how literature, media and etiquette guides all work to reinforce gendered linguistic norms, in particular because Japanese gendered language that is presented in scripted dialogues tends to be both 'exaggerated versions of gendered speech' (Ohara, 2019: 288) and highly conformist in its adherence to normative depictions of gendered language.

Japanese gendered language used in media and literature is part of what Kinsui calls *yakuwarigo* or role language (e.g. Kinsui, 2003, Teshigawara & Kinsui, 2011). Role language refers to the ways that scripted speech, such as in literature, anime and television dramas, draws on linguistic stereotypes which associate certain kinds of speech with characteristics ascribed to age, gender, nationality, occupation or social status. The most common linguistic features used to create a fictional character include first-person pronouns and sentence-final particles, and the use of feminine sentence-final particles or masculine first-person pronouns helps the audience to understand whether the character is a man or a woman. The use of role language results in persistent stereotypes about what counts as masculine or feminine speech. Further, it seems likely that the frequency with which Japanese gendered language is used in scripted speech may contribute to the salience of gendered language norms for both L1 and L2 speakers who consume Japanese media.

Japanese gendered language and representations of non-Japanese speakers

Researchers have also studied how the speech of non-Japanese speakers is represented in Japanese, including both the speech of actual people translated into Japanese, as well as fictional accounts of non-Japanese characters and non-native-speaking characters who are given Japanese language dialogue. Takatori (2015) examines how interviews with non-Japanese-speaking athletes were translated into Japanese. She finds that their Japanese translations contained numerous gendered forms, including sentence-final particles like *ze* or *zo* used in translations for male athletes, and *wa* or *yo* used in translations for female athletes. This is surprising not only because the original languages used by the athletes did not include gendered forms, but also because there were more gendered forms in the Japanese translations for non-Japanese athletes than were observed in similar interviews with L1-Japanese athletes.

Suzuki (2018) examines the scripted speech of non-Japanese characters in contemporary Japanese novels and finds that the Japanese speech of female non-Japanese characters included more occurrences of gendered sentence-final particles in their speech than did the Japanese speech of male non-Japanese characters. According to Suzuki, there is ample evidence of the sociolinguistic norms of femininity being imposed more on female speakers than on male speakers. Suzuki also describes female non-Japanese characters who were depicted using feminine sentence-final particles regardless of whether or not they were depicted as speaking fluent Japanese. Male non-Japanese characters, however, were only scripted with masculine sentence-final particles if they were also depicted as being fluent in Japanese. Suzuki concludes that this distinction is because masculine forms were associated with language competence, but feminine forms were not.

Suzuki (2018) also shows that the association of masculine linguistic forms with casual speech means that masculine forms are used to display insider status and authenticity. Conversely, the association of feminine linguistic forms with refined or polite speech does not lend itself to such displays. Suzuki (2018: 295) argues that the result of these distinctions is that 'masculine forms are treated as the linguistic resources exclusively available to the Japanese more so than feminine forms'. Further, Suzuki concludes that her findings from contemporary novels show that ownership of Japanese gendered language is more relevant for masculine forms than for feminine forms. Suzuki's findings are suggestive of how scripted speech reinforces the view that only Japanese people, in other words, those native speakers who are ethnically Japanese, can claim ownership of the Japanese language, and further, that they are the only speakers who can be expected to be truly fluent speakers of the language. In these ways, Suzuki's work supports a connection between gendered language and language ownership.

Similar to her earlier work, Suzuki (2020) examines fictional non-Japanese characters and compares non-Japanese East Asian male characters with white male characters. Even when both types of characters are depicted as fluent in Japanese, Suzuki finds that East Asian characters tend to be scripted with more strongly masculine forms (e.g. *ore, omae*) compared to white characters (e.g. *boku*). Suzuki argues that this pattern matches research studies of real language use that find that white L2 speakers may be discouraged from using masculine forms (e.g. Iwasaki, 2011, cited in Suzuki, 2020), while East Asian L2 speakers do not receive such feedback and as a result are able to use masculine forms in beneficial ways when interacting with L1 speakers (e.g. Itakura, 2008, cited in Suzuki, 2020). These findings add further evidence for viewing masculine forms as more likely to be subject to language ownership, since the dialogues Suzuki (2020: 238) analyzes show that masculine forms were part of the 'insider code perceived to be only available to ethnic Japanese or those who are considered racially close to the Japanese'.

Suzuki (2018, 2020) explains that although her research is based on scripted speech, her findings nevertheless have important implications for understanding the language use of actual people, and especially of L2 speakers. Researchers have described resistance to L2 speakers using Japanese skillfully (e.g. Burgess, 2012), and Suzuki's findings confirm that, although Standard Japanese is available for use by L2 speakers, problems may arise when 'foreigners' attempt to incorporate the full repertoire of Japanese speech styles and registers, including gendered forms, honorific language and regional dialects. These speech styles play an important role in using Japanese for expressive purposes, and it may be that it is just this kind of language use by L2 speakers that triggers a claim of language ownership, asserting that such expressive Japanese is only for L1-Japanese speakers. Suzuki argues that language ownership manifests as a view that only Japanese people are allowed to use authentic language, while Japanese gendered language, dialects and slang are off-limits to non-Japanese. The problem here is that such ideologies are likely not confined to fictional accounts, and restricting access to authentic language may make it difficult for L2 speakers to express friendliness, vulgarity, anger, etc. If we understand authenticity as using Japanese to its full expressiveness, it is this kind of language use that is in danger of being treated as off-limits for L2 speakers. Although Suzuki does not use the term 'native speaker bias', native speaker bias emerges from the kind of language ownership she describes, in which L2 speakers lack access to the full range of Japanese speech styles, including gendered language, *keigo*, dialects and slang.

Japanese gendered language and L2 speakers

While it is unclear to what degree L2 speakers read Japanese language literature, many L2 speakers are consumers of Japanese media, such as manga and anime, and often access these media in Japanese, as opposed to translated or dubbed versions. Increasingly, these authentic media products are also used for language study (e.g. Armour, 2011; Carlson, 2018). There can be no doubt that L2 speakers encounter ideological messages about Japanese gendered language contained in such media.

One recent example is the popular Japanese anime, *Your Name* (Shinkai, 2016). The story involves a Japanese teenage girl, Mitsuha, and boy, Taki, who swap bodies. The first time this happens, Mitsuha, in the body of Taki, goes to his school and has lunch with his friends, who assume they are talking to Taki. A key moment occurs when Mitsuha uses the first-person pronoun '*watashi*' (the neutral or feminine pronoun), to which the friends react with surprise. Mitsuha gets the message that she has used the wrong pronoun and cycles through the other options, trying the highly polite first-person pronoun '*watakushi*', then the slightly masculine '*boku*'. The friends continue to show their disapproval, until she finally uses the strongly masculine '*ore*'. The friends nod to affirm that *ore* is correct. In the translated version of the film, the friends' surprised reaction is subtitled as 'feminine pronouns?' because there is no other way to translate or convey this exchange in English. Both the original and the subtitled version send a two-fold message to viewers (1) that these first-person pronouns are gendered and (2) that using the 'correct' first-person pronoun is of great importance.

Japanese gendered language in textbooks

One intermediate-level textbook popular in US universities is *Tobira* (Oka *et al.*, 2009), which includes a chapter devoted to speech styles with a short section about male and female speech styles. The section begins by explaining that in Japanese novels, it is easy to tell whether a speaker is male or female based on the character's use of Japanese gendered language, which tends to occur most often in casual speech. The textbook includes a sample conversation to show how Japanese gendered language might be used but does not say which speaker is male and which is female. Instead, students are directed to try to figure it out for themselves. The section concludes with this explanation:

友達や恋人や家族と話す時、男性は自分のことを「僕」とか、「俺」と言い、女性はたいてい「私」を使います。

最近は男女の差が小さくなって、[例文]のように、文末に「わ」「わよ」を使う女性や「ぜ」「ぞ」を使う男性は少なくなっていますが、でも、女性が「俺も腹へった」と言ったり、男性が「いやよ！」と言ったら、びっくりされてしまいます。話し方の差が小さくなっても、使わない方がいい表現もあるということを知っておいて下さい。

　When speaking to friends, lovers, or family, men refer to themselves as '*boku*' or '*ore*', and women usually use '*watashi*' [first-person pronouns]. Recently, differences between male and female [speech] have gotten smaller, and there are fewer people who use '*wa*', '*wa yo*', or '*ze*', '*zo*' as in [the example conversation], but if a woman said '*ore mo hara hetta*' ((I'm also hungry, rough)) or a man said '*iya yo!*' ((no, I don't like it, feminine)) people would be surprised. So even though the differences in speech have decreased, please keep in mind that there are some expressions that [you] shouldn't use. (Oka *et al.*, 2009: 29, translation by this author)

Although the explanation points out that the use of gendered forms is decreasing, the failure to mention any diversity of language use and the lack of details about gendered language is a missed opportunity for a more nuanced discussion. We may well wonder about the impact of this type of instruction on how JFL students understand Japanese gendered language and, in particular, on how they understand their own linguistic choices in Japanese. Because the use of gendered first-person pronouns is presented as a taken-for-granted practice, it gives the impression that this is how *all* Japanese speakers use these pronouns. In addition, the statement that use of incorrect gendered forms will receive a negative reaction reads as an admonishment, suggesting possible social sanctions for using forms assigned to the opposite gender. Further, the textbook not only advocates for gender-normative language use, but it also suggests that L2 learners should self-censor to ensure their language use is not mis-gendered.

L2 speakers' concerns about Japanese gendered language

　Although research on L2-Japanese speakers and Japanese gendered language is less extensive, studies of L2 acquisition and sociolinguistics offer some insights. Early work by Siegal (1994, 1995, 1996) examines the experience of Western women in Japan and finds that some of them resisted using polite forms and feminine expressions because they viewed such forms as being subservient and overly humble. A particular concern for Siegal's participants was to ensure they used Japanese that fit their identity conceptions, and they struggled to adhere to Japanese linguistic norms without adopting linguistic femininity. Ohara (2001) examines pitch level and voice quality in female L2 speakers with various proficiency levels. She finds that the L2 participants took a critical stance toward gender expression in Japanese and made choices that sought to strike a balance between Japanese sociolinguistic norms and their own identity expression.

More recent works demonstrate that Japanese gendered language remains a significant issue for JFL students and L2 speakers. For example, Bohn (2015) surveyed JFL students to explore their perspectives on gendered language. JFL students reported a variety of views about gendered language and described their linguistic choices as being influenced by their understandings of the meanings of different Japanese speech styles. Bohn explains that students encountered gendered language when they consumed Japanese media, including television programs, magazines and anime, but they learned about the differences in gendered forms during in-class discussions. Roughly half of Bohn's respondents felt that gendered differences should be taught as an aspect of Japanese culture, while other respondents felt that students should decide for themselves what Japanese speech styles to use. Students in the latter group also tended to have a negative view of gendered language as dated and discriminatory.

While the vast majority of research on L2 speakers and Japanese gendered language has focused on women, a few scholars focus on male L2 speakers and how they deal with issues related to masculine linguistic forms. Itakura (2008, 2009) examines L2 speakers in Hong Kong and how they navigated Japanese speech styles in their multilingual workplaces. Itakura finds that L2 speakers' perceptions about gendered language styles influenced their linguistic choices. Some L2 participants used masculine forms to display advanced Japanese proficiency and insider status. Itakura also describes how L2 participants made strategic choices about when to use or avoid gendered language, such as using it for solidarity and to encourage friendly relations but avoiding it in formal business situations. An additional benefit of gendered language for Itakura's (2008: 475) participants was being able to use gendered language as an additional way to demonstrate Japanese proficiency, which had positive impacts on their 'in-group membership'. Some L2 speakers also used gendered language as a way to 'gain native-speaker status in the language' (Itakura, 2009: 29).

On the other hand, Itakura describes participants who were aware of the difficulty that gendered language choices presented. One participant described *danseigo* as 'secret forms' (Itakura, 2008: 474) that were only available for use by native Japanese speakers. Similarly, Itakura (2009: 276) finds that L2 speakers tended to associate Japanese gendered language more closely with 'the broader category of Japanese cultural identity'. It is not surprising that the view of gendered language as an insider's code meant some participants felt that having a command of gendered forms was a way to demonstrate their language competence and attain native speaker status. For other participants, the forms' association with

'Japanese-ness' resulted in an 'unwillingness to use masculine Japanese', because gendered forms were believed to be reserved for Japanese people. One participant in Itakura's (2008: 476) study is described as having a 'feeling of resignation that, try as he might, he would never "become like a Japanese person"'. This participant also explained that 'I used to believe that I would be able to become like a Japanese person, but now I feel that *unless I think like a Japanese person, I won't be able to speak like a Japanese person*' (Itakura, 2008: 477, emphasis added). Itakura (2008: 477) explains that this participant also had 'a strong sense of himself as a Hong Kong person. At the same time, he appeared to feel that, as a foreign language learner of Japanese, he did not need to adopt a Japanese cultural identity'. Another participant 'also appeared to feel that, as a foreign language learner of Japanese, he should not be expected to adopt a Japanese cultural identity through facility with masculine Japanese' (Itakura, 2008: 477). Itakura suggests that because these L2 speakers were located in Hong Kong, it was easier for them to consider not aligning with Japanese sociolinguistic norms than if they had been in Japan.

Similarly, Brown and Cheek (2017) examine how male JFL students studying at a US university used gendered first-person pronouns (*watashi, boku, ore*), and explore how L1 speakers reacted to L2 speakers' pronoun choices. Brown and Cheek note that L2 speakers made conscious choices about which pronouns to use for themselves, based on such concerns as a desire to display language competence and to align their language choices with their own identity self-conceptions. Brown and Cheek find that some L1 speakers were not accepting of the pronoun choice made by an L2 speaker. Brown and Cheek also find that, when an L2 speaker's linguistic choices were seen as appropriate, the L2 speaker was seen as creating a 'legitimate L2 identity' and this resulted in benefits such as increased chances to interact with an L1 speaker. However, when an L2 speaker's pronoun choice was not successful, the loss of opportunity could be detrimental for that L2 speaker's learning experiences.

Study Participants and Japanese Gendered Language

Research confirms that L2 speakers negotiate Japanese gendered language as they strive to convey content or information, while also trying to speak in ways that reflect the social and cultural norms of spoken Japanese. Many of the L2 participants in my study struggled with Japanese gendered language and expressed concerns about appropriate use of gendered forms. For these participants, awareness of gendered norms of Japanese language complicated their efforts to sound like themselves.

Here, I present findings that explore L2 participants' perceptions of their Japanese use with regard to Japanese gendered language, including their beliefs and concerns about sounding 'too' masculine or 'too' feminine. It is important to note that the L2 participant interview protocol did not ask about participants' gender identity. Also, no specific questions asked participants to discuss aspects of Japanese with regard to social norms about gendered language. Nevertheless, it was quickly apparent in my discussions with L2 participants that they were attentive to how they understood themselves in terms of gender identity with regard to Japanese gendered language. Specifically, L2 participants' observations and comments about themselves as Japanese speakers conveyed that ideologies about gendered language created tensions for them between how they saw themselves and how they perceived restrictions on their speech connected to Japanese gendered language. As such, my analysis focused on the comments and observations participants shared about themselves as Japanese speakers and about their experiences as L2 speakers in Japan.

In my analysis of the interview data, I found that female L2 participants frequently shared concerns about sounding either too masculine or too feminine. Similarly, male L2 participants shared concerns about sounding too feminine, not masculine enough, or too rough or vulgar. These L2 participants wanted to sound like themselves in terms of how they understood themselves and how they wanted to sound to others when speaking Japanese. Thus, when participants talked about their concerns about themselves as Japanese speakers, they revealed ideologies and beliefs about gendered language. Participants' comments related to gendered language most often occurred in response to the following interview questions:

- Have you ever given any thought to how you want to sound in Japanese?
- Do you like how you sound when you speak Japanese?
- How would you describe your Japanese language ability?

It is important to note that L2 participants often brought up Japanese gendered language despite the fact that none of the questions in the interview protocol specifically asked about gendered language or issues related to gender. Gendered language was a salient topic for them and, for some participants, it was a sticking point in terms of how they assessed both their Japanese ability and their ability to improve their language skills.

The interview protocol for L1 participants asked about the gender of the L2 speakers they knew and asked their impressions of the way those L2 speakers used Japanese. This resulted in some L1 participants sharing comments about whether or how L2 speakers should use Japanese gendered language. However, none of the L1 participants discussed their own use of gendered language. The excerpts included from my interviews with L1 participants affirm the importance of choices about Japanese gendered language for L2 speakers and suggest the complexity faced by L2 speakers living and working in Japan.

L2 participants' beliefs about Japanese gendered language

A girly girl?

Many female L2 participants discussed the degree to which their Japanese use included gendered features. When I asked Alyssa if she had thought about how she wanted to sound in Japanese, she proudly emphasized that her Japanese was not 'girly' and she gave examples of gender-neutral forms she used, specifically mentioning *yarō*, the dialectal form of *deshō* 'probably, right'. She also shared feminine forms she actively avoided, citing *wa*, the feminine sentence-final particle, as one of the forms she avoided because she felt it was overly feminine. Alternatively, Nicole noted that she had sounded more masculine in the past when she had interacted with more male L1 speakers at work. But at the time of the interview, Nicole felt her speech had become less masculine, since she was now a parent and interacted primarily with L1-Japanese-speaking mothers through her daughter's activities.

While Alyssa and Nicole both seemed confident in how they navigated questions of Japanese gendered language, Melissa, on the other hand, was less sure of her Japanese skills in general and was concerned about how to project a friendly persona without sounding what she thought of as 'cutesy' or 'weak':

Jae: have you ever given any thought to how you want to sound in Japanese?

Melissa: oh yeah, that's interesting, because there's the really girly talk over here, like all that *atashi* [feminine first-person pronoun] and all the *wa* [feminine sentence-final particle] on the end of things and, that's probably one thing where I thought I don't want to sound like that, you now, cuz, I don't want to sound aggressive or something, but I don't want to sound like I'm being all, kind of cutesy all the time, I don't know why that sounds like a slightly weaker position, but you want to be taken seriously, and for some reason that doesn't sound serious to me

Melissa's comments shed light on several issues L2 speakers must negotiate with regard to gendered language. First, Melissa had a clear image of what counted as 'feminine speech' in Japanese, and she shared some of those features (*atashi*, *wa*). Second, she had a negative opinion of these linguistic features, labeling them 'girly', 'cutesy' and 'weaker'. Third, Melissa was clear that she herself did not want to incorporate these features into her own speech, in part because she felt they would contribute to sounding weak and she might not be taken seriously. In the next excerpt, Melissa gives the impression that she envisions a continuum of speech styles from weak to aggressive, and she wants to be somewhere in the middle.

Jae: who do you hear using that kind of cutesy language, like other female teachers or coworkers here [at the board of education] or friends?

Melissa: it's more, a lot of the time it's students, um, but they're at that [junior high school] age, I suppose and sometimes people who are a similar age, but not here [at the board of education], or just like sometimes on TV and stuff. You see all that, and I've heard that that's more like a TV kind of thing, but that's the one thing I've heard and thought, uh, I don't want to sound like that, and I think I would feel weird saying it. So, you know, like, whereas I wouldn't feel so weird speaking Koyama-*ben* [Koyama Dialect], but I would feel really weird speaking the girly girl talk. And, I mean, I want to sound approachable, um, and like I'm being respectful, but still relatable, and so I feel like the middle ground there is, not polite Japanese, but just, you know, uh, I don't know, just the usual Japanese, do you know what I mean?

Although Melissa did not hear overly feminine linguistic features in the speech of coworkers or friends, she may have heard them from her junior high school-aged students and from characters in television programs. Melissa did not convey that she recognized these features as stereotypical, but instead she stressed her desire to not incorporate those features into her own Japanese speech. It is also notable that she made a point of saying that, while she would not feel weird speaking the local dialect, she would feel weird speaking what she considered 'girly girl talk'. Instead, Melissa was clear that she wanted to sound approachable and respectful, and speak 'just the usual Japanese'.

Melissa also discussed her concerns about how she wanted her speech to be perceived by others:

Melissa: everyday Japanese, not like that really manly one or really girly girl, just something relatable and easy, easy to communicate, and that way more of the focus is on the words rather than how I'm saying it, and I feel like, if you're a Japanese person and you've got a kind of a, you've got like, I don't know, your speech has a certain type of character, because you're Japanese, the emphasis is still on the words. But when you're foreign, people are quite interested in how you speak Japanese, and so as soon as you kind of deviate from what's considered standard or normal Japanese, all of a sudden, the focus isn't on your words anymore but on how you're speaking it. And that's fun with kids or people sometimes, but if you're just in everyday communication, if I just want to communicate a point, it's easier to stick with the standard

Melissa, in effect, sees 'manly' Japanese and 'girly girl' Japanese at opposite ends of a continuum of Japanese language, and places 'everyday Japanese' in the middle, depicting it as the most effective way for her to communicate. Of particular relevance is Melissa's implication that L1-Japanese speakers can use a wider variety of speech styles than she can, and they can do so without having interlocutors lose sight of the topic at hand. At the same time, Melissa was concerned that 'foreigners' who 'deviate from what's considered standard or normal Japanese' will find that their interlocutors pay less attention to the content and focus more on the form of their speech. Thus, in order to keep the focus of conversation on the content, Melissa was careful to avoid any speech styles other than standard, and gender-neutral, Japanese.

Another participant who was worried about the degree to which their speech matched or deviated from gendered norms was Grace, who was concerned about sounding too masculine. Specifically, she worried about the negative influence of speaking primarily with her L1 husband. Grace also shared that she made it a point to apologize to people for sounding like a man:

Grace: but my husband, I mean he's not, he speaks very much in dialect, and he was my main exposure to Japanese, um, it's kind of frustrating that when I speak, I might sound like a man, because I haven't spent that much time with women

Jae: so you were worried about sounding too masculine. Has your husband ever said, you know, that's too masculine or have other people said that? Or is that a concern you just have yourself

Grace: um, usually, when I met people and start talking with them, I usually make that apology early on, as a way of explanation, for the way, um you, an excuse for the way I speak, I just say, at first they say 'your Japanese is really good' and then I say, well, it's not that great, and I'll tell them that, cuz they'll say 'how did you get so good', and I just say, well I just picked it up and I explain about how I've just learned it and that's why I speak like this, that's why I sound, perhaps, or I might say things that are inappropriate or that a man would say, not a woman, you know, sometimes it's not a very feminine way to speak. They're so fixed on being feminine and pretty and dainty and ladylike here so, I do make that apology quite early on when I meet people

It is unclear whether L1 speakers had ever commented on Grace's language use; however, her comments indicate that she has an understanding of what women are 'supposed' to sound like in Japanese, and she is quite aware that her own Japanese speech does not fit that image. Grace's comment about a tendency for L1 speakers to be 'fixed on being feminine and pretty and dainty and ladylike' suggests her frustration with these gendered norms and conveys that she did not want to adhere to them. Nevertheless, Grace was also self-conscious about sounding 'like a man' to the degree that she preemptively apologized to L1 interlocutors.

A man's man?

Concerns about the use of Japanese gendered language was not unique to female L2 participants. Male L2 participants also had concerns about their use of Japanese gendered language, and they discussed their struggles to settle on which masculine first-person pronoun to use and how to avoid sounding stylistically feminine. Louis, who had lived in Japan for more than four years at the time of the interview, explained that his girlfriend did not speak English and they spoke only in Japanese. As a result, he said, 'I tend to talk like a female'. As we discussed further, Louis shared that not only was he aware of this himself, but he had also been told by both L1 and L2 speakers that he sounded feminine. He described participating in hobby activities with male L1 speakers and having some difficulty understanding their speech because it included a lot of slang and male speech features. When I asked Louis if anyone had influenced how he thinks about Japanese, he told me about a friend who was a fellow assistant language teacher (ALT) from a Western country:

Louis: [my friend] speaks [Japanese] more like a male, yeah, he speaks more like a Japanese male because he's had a lot of Japanese male friends. Sometimes he'll point that out and say no, you shouldn't, say it like this...

Louis did not elaborate on what he meant by 'speaking like a Japanese male', but he seemed certain that there was a more masculine way to speak in Japanese, which was different from how he himself spoke. But Louis seemed resigned to the fact that his own speech was overly feminine and there was little he could do about it.

Mike had been in Japan for more than seven years when I met him, and his approach to gendered language was more proactive. During the interview, I asked Mike about whether he had ever given any thought to how he wanted to sound in Japanese, and he responded by discussing male versus female speech patterns:

Mike: I guess things that I've been conscious of in terms of my own casual speech would be things like male versus female speech patterns. Like, I'm conscious of the difference that I, what I see often is people will be influenced, for instance, English-speaking males will be influenced by their wives or their girlfriends and end up using female speech patterns and I'm aware of that, I've spent more time with my Japanese girlfriend over the last year than with any other single person but I try to maintain male speech patterns, but, and you know, I'm conscious of what constitutes like gruff or rude or, turning it into a class thing is kind of strange, but like low class speech and I don't tend to use that

Mike paid attention to the speech of other male speakers in order to make note of how male L1 speakers sounded. Mike was clear that he did not want to pick up the speech patterns of his girlfriend, saying he preferred to 'maintain male speech patterns'. Mike, like Louis and other participants, did not give specific examples of what he considered male speech patterns, but compared to some other participants, Mike seemed more confident with his current abilities and his choices about Japanese gendered language. And although he wanted to sound masculine, Mike was also clear that he did not want to sound 'gruff', 'rude' or 'low class', suggesting that he viewed at least some elements of masculine speech in more negative ways. I asked him where he heard low-class speech, and he explained that he watched a lot of Japanese television, particularly comedy shows.

Some male L2 participants described having role models for how they spoke in Japanese. Sam, who had been in Japan for 15 years, described modeling his speech after his L1-Japanese father-in-law. He also said that he used 'guys [his] age' as examples of language use in general and particularly with regard to dialect and casual speech styles. Similarly, Branden described how he disliked hearing his own voice in recordings and said he wanted to 'mimic' the deep voices of men he heard on Japanese radio programs and podcasts. Neither Sam nor Branden provided specific examples of linguistic forms they want to use or avoid, but rather focused on stylistic features, such as the casual authority of Sam's father-in-law or the voice quality of radio personalities Branden admired.

Scott, who had only been in Japan for about a year when I met him, was more explicit in his attention to finding a role model for his Japanese. When I asked him if he had given any thought to how he wanted to sound in Japanese, he told me about a male L1-Japanese friend whose speech he particularly admired. Scott then compared his friend to his supervisor, whose speech he did not want to emulate.

Scott: I actually tell my friend [name of male L1-Japanese speaker], I said I like the way you speak Japanese, I want to speak like you
Jae: so how does [he] speak?
Scott: um, he speaks politely without sounding like... ((laughs)) without sounding like a whipped office employee, you know what I mean? A little bit, um, cuz there's a different language with... I mean, he's a young cool guy who also ah, he, is respectable, you know, and I like the way his Japanese sounds, and it seems like it's received well by anyone. Um, I'm a bit of a mimic, and I just, I kinda like to talk to people who, they're talking to me, like I'll find myself kinda playing along with the same intonation and stuff and my supervisor right now at the office has um a really distinctive, kinda older man Japanese ah, I mean, it's very funny, at *enkais* ((drinking parties with coworkers)) I've been asked to do impersonations of him because, I mean, he is kinda like intimidating, ((Scott imitates his supervisor, using a deep voice and imitating 'difficult to understand' speech)) *o, Scott-kun, o,* that's kinda like, ((imitating)) *o, shiranakatta sore a sugoi na* ((oh, Scott, really? I didn't know that, wow))

Scott juxtaposed a 'whipped office employee' with the description of his friend, who was not only cool but also respectable and well-received.

In contrast to female L2 participants, several male L2 participants focused on the challenge of choosing which Japanese first-person pronoun to use and they specifically discussed their process for, and sometimes struggles with, choosing from among *watashi* (neutral), *boku* (masculine) and *ore* (strongly masculine). For example, when I asked William what he found easy or difficult about Japanese, he mentioned 'methods of self-identification' which, he said, 'tells you a lot about a person':

William: well I mean, for instance, I use *boku*, rather than like *ore* for instance and the main reason I ended up doing that was because I asked [another L2 speaker] which one was actually more common, you know cuz I know in some places *ore* is the more common term for boys to address themselves with and *boku* is not quite so much. So that was more of a decision that I made, less about like self-identification and more about like, how do they do it

	where I live, as opposed to how do I feel like I should address myself and to be honest I don't really think I fit the *ore*-stereotype anyways
Jae:	what do you think the *ore* stereotype is?
William:	it's like very self-confident, self-assured. Not necessarily arrogant, but like they know what they're about and that's not really me, ((laughs)). I mean like, I've never actually seen it, but I know that there are girls in Japan that will use *boku* as self-identification which makes them stand out, cuz that's traditionally a masculine, you know, and like, you may have like, older people who use like *ware* ((formal, literary 'I')) um, you know, or like when you're talking in more formal scenarios sometimes, you'll hear people use *ware-ware* ((formal 'we')) or something like that. It's really interesting and it definitely tells you a lot about, it's easy information about the kind of person that they are, and like, the setting, I guess, if it's gonna be more, like, informal place, they'll probably use *boku* or *ore*, but if it's more formal, then they start using *watashi* and that kind of thing

One thing that stands out in William's comments is his account of the masculine first-person pronouns. Earlier in the interview, William talked about how much he had learned in his university Japanese classes, and his attention to pronouns reflects that education. He was also aware of the influences of regional differences in terms of how the use of *ore* was perceived. William weighed his options and considered both local practices as well as his own preferences. Ultimately, he decided that he did not fit the *ore* 'stereotype', despite not having a negative view of *ore*.

Unlike William, other male L2 participants did view *ore* negatively, including James, who had been living in Japan for over 10 years. During his interview, James talked about aspects of Japanese speech styles and explained how he had refined his approach over the years. With regard to whether there was someone he wanted to sound like, James mentioned a male L1-Japanese *senpai*, a mentor, who had a 'cool' way of speaking. James also said that although he was not able to succeed in sounding exactly like his *senpai*, paying attention to how his *senpai* spoke was a big influence. James also shared that he was conscious of influences from the past, including past Japanese language teachers and former girlfriends. When I asked him to describe this more, he discussed choosing which first-person pronoun to use:

James:	so, for example, I don't use *ore* at all, even privately
Jae:	any reason why?

James: yeah, I think, I found it distasteful when I first started speaking Japanese, because, I mean, [my college Japanese teacher] didn't teach it. So, when I first came to [Japan], I remember not knowing what it meant. And hearing other people use it and thought, who is this guy *ore* ((laughs)) ... but, um, I guess, you know, I always think the differences in *ichininsho* ((first-person pronouns)) are kind of like clothing, right? *Ore* is like a wife-beater, you know, just like, no sleeves, the fact that I'm, I don't know ... I always think it's funny when a person is really good at Japanese, like a male from another country who's good at Japanese uses *ore* because it seems almost antithetical to the kind of personality of the person who would become good at Japanese, you know what I mean

Jae: that's super interesting. Do you use *boku*?

James: yeah, I use *boku*

Jae: and then do you use *watashi* very much?

James: ah yeah, I use, I mean, for work I use *watashi* and when I'm speaking with my coworkers, in spoken language, I use *boku* but when I'm writing emails and things like that, or if I'm speaking, say I'm making a statement at a conference or even in a meeting with the same people that I use *boku* with all day, I'll use *watashi*

Several details stand out in James's comments. First, James reported not learning *ore* in his university Japanese classes, which is surprising, given its common usage. Second, James had a strongly negative opinion of *ore*, calling it distasteful, and he was equally critical of the kind of person who uses *ore*. He compared using *ore* to a man wearing only a sleeveless undershirt when he should be more well-dressed – for James, this image did not match his image of 'the kind of person who would become good at Japanese', presumably someone who studied diligently and was highly educated. Third, James's use of clothing as a way to describe the choice of first-person pronouns speaks to the role pronouns play in presenting oneself to others and in cultivating one's Japanese language identity.

James had lived in both the Kansai and Tokyo regions, and during his interview, he also discussed regional comparisons. For example, he explained that in the past, he had used *uchi* (inside) and *jibun* (self), both words that can be used as first-person pronouns in some dialects of Western Japan:

James: because I'm self-conscious about language, I remember I picked *jibun* ((self)) up from a friend who did it, who was female, and then I was wondering about the male/femaleness of it, so I think I looked up some information online and, you know, you just go google everything, right, and yeah I think, based on some regions it was sort of male, or it was female rather, also *uchi* ((I, house, inside)) is the same way. So, I used to use *uchi* a lot just because I had a friend who used it, um and then I realized it was sort of female, so I kind of, well I don't use it anymore but there was a period where I used it a lot

As his ability and experience with the Japanese language increased, James attended to the gendered nature of the various first-person pronoun options and, over time, he made an effort to choose the pronouns that he felt fit him best. James described making active efforts to control his language and he was particularly aware of being influenced by female L1 speakers whose linguistic habits he did not want to adopt. At the same time, it does not seem that James agonized over these questions, rather, he presented them as examples of how an L2 speaker gradually adjusts, modifies and refines language use over time and as awareness about language use increases. It may also be that his advanced proficiency, coupled with his length of experience in Japan, allowed James to control his linguistic choices more easily in comparison with some other participants in this study.

When I asked James if he liked how he sounded when speaking Japanese, he explained that one thing he wanted to work on was his ability to control his language use, especially the highly polite registers, so that he could be 'ultra-polite' without sounding feminine:

Jae: do you like how you sound when you speak Japanese?
James: yeah I think I'm happy with it, I do think that I, one thing that I want to work on, I was just thinking about this the other day because I was in a meeting with, like I said, I went to talk to the head of the dept. and he's also the vice president, right, so I went to his office and it was in the administrative complex and I put on a suit and everything, I was very nervous, I was sweating, and when I get in a situation like that and I'm speaking ultra-polite Japanese I tend to become a little bit too redundant you know what I mean, and I also think, I become sort of, I don't, not feminine in words, I don't mean in the words I'm using, but tone of voice? Tends to go way up and, which I mean I guess that happens with everybody, but I'd like to control that a little more

Again, we can see the challenge of using Japanese language in a way that is appropriate for the context and interaction while also being true to how the speaker wants to present himself or herself. Just as David saw *keigo* as the last missing piece of his Japanese competency in Chapter 3, for James, being able to be 'ultra-polite' without sounding feminine, was perhaps the last skill he needed to acquire.

The male L2 participants introduced thus far were explicit about their desire to avoid sounding feminine when speaking Japanese. They also rejected using the first-person pronoun *ore*, which suggests a rejection of sounding overly masculine as well. Some male L2 participants described avoidance of adopting the linguistic habits of a female partner as a key concern. Others discussed how having a same-gender linguistic role model was helpful for them.

It is important to note that few male L2 participants described making conscious efforts to sound strongly masculine when speaking Japanese, including general speech styles as well as choice of first-person pronouns. One exception to this was Liam, who had been in Japan for three years at the time of the study. Liam shared that one of his main goals for his Japanese ability was to be able to use as many registers in Japanese as he could use in English. While some participants sought to develop their *keigo* abilities, Liam was particularly focused on developing his ability to use rough and even profane Japanese. Liam actively cultivated the ability to use what he called 'rough-sounding Japanese', something of which he was quite proud. For example, he explained that his skills with this kind of language were due to his habit of watching television dramas with characters that included yakuza gangsters and *furyō* or delinquent high school students. Liam also paid close attention to the slang and rough language used by the high school boys he taught. Here is his response when I asked if he had given any thought to how he wanted to sound in Japanese:

Liam: my goal for how I sound in Japanese would be how I sound in English, and when I speak English with friends I curse a lot, I curse a lot and I speak very frankly and am often very loud and bombastic, so my goal for Japanese, where I would like to be and consider myself to have … where I would consider myself to have, say, perfected or feel like a fluent point when I feel like I can speak in Japanese the same way I can speak in English and can be myself in Japanese the same way I can be myself in English … which means being able to speak politely when I feel the need to and want to but also when I'm with friends, being able to comfortably curse

Liam explained further that his linguistic goals were due to the kind of language he heard being used around him, where he lived and in the schools where he taught:

Liam: so I want to make sure, for one, this is a place where I feel, I like using *hōgen* and dialects in that, at school, if I walk into a school with country hick kids, or the fisherman village kids, and say *desu kara* ((because, long-form)) or *achira ni* ((over there, formal)), they make fun of me, cuz it sounds really silly to them, in a village of people who speak exclusively in hard dialect, to then walk in and be speaking what I guess would be the equivalent of in America and suddenly an English kid would walk in and speak very enunciated English, so that is one time where if I'm with the kids I particularly want to, I'm very careful about it, I can get very worried about how I sound, because they'll make fun of me, the children will make fun of you

It is hard to know how accurate Liam's description is of how his neighbors and students spoke Japanese – but more important than the question of the accuracy of his perceptions is the fact that Liam's goal was to match his Japanese use to the Japanese he heard spoken around him, including what he called 'hard dialect', as well as slang and rough or vulgar expressions. In describing the importance of sounding natural, Liam added:

Liam: I've been told things like, slow down, you're speaking too fast. It's cooler for a man to speak slow, so I've been told things like that

This was Liam's only explicit comment about gendered language, but coupled with his statements that he was 'very worried' about how he sounded and wanted to avoid being laughed at, it suggests that a tough and masculine image was not only something he felt aligned with his self-conception, but also something he felt was necessary because of where he lived and worked. By using rough language and dialect and by being careful to sound 'cool for a man', Liam made conscious attempts to ensure that his Japanese would not be perceived as silly but would sound natural and appropriately masculine.

While Liam wanted to avoid being laughed at, another L2 speaker, Dean, sought to avoid being taken advantage of in business deals. Similar to Liam's approach to using language defensively, Dean described a kind of protective language use, something he described as sounding like a 'yakuza'. Dean, who was self-employed and had lived in Japan for more than 25 years, shared with me some of his experiences living in the Kansai region and hearing Kansai dialect. I asked Dean if he used Kansai dialect himself:

Dean:	I did yes, I still do, when I get cross, I do my yakuza thing which I do occasionally to persuade people who are being unreasonable, the Osaka-*ben* [Osaka Dialect] comes out a bit ((he changes his voice)) *omae, aho chau ka* ((are you stupid?)) I'll say while slapping the counter
Jae:	how do people respond when you do that?
Dean:	oh, surprise, horror
Jae:	yeah? Are they scared?
Dean:	yes, where did that come from, that kind of thing, yes.
Jae:	do you ever get pushback from that, like you're this Caucasian person why are you
Dean:	uh, no. And if they did ((laughing and sitting up to show his height)) I would have a response to that

Dean described a kind of weaponization of language, especially when he described using Osaka dialect to 'persuade people who are being unreasonable'. This impression was strengthened when Dean, who was much taller than me, sat up in his chair to demonstrate how easily he could tower over other people. Like Liam, Dean was proud of his ability to use rough Japanese and unsurprisingly, Dean, who had been in Japan much longer than Liam, also seemed to rely on this skill strategically in disagreements. Dean felt that his ability to employ a highly masculine speech style allowed him to accomplish things he otherwise might not be able to do.

Another L2 participant who described wanting to sound tough and manly was David, who, like Liam and Dean, used yakuza as a way to describe tough speech. When I asked how he wanted to sound in Japanese, David explained that he wanted to sound like a 'man's man'. David also shared that he had a role model for this kind of speech, and he made it a point to use *ore*.

Jae:	have you ever thought about how you want to sound in Japanese?
David:	well, I went through stages, right, you know, first I wanted to sound real proper, then as a street performer I wanted to sound real funny and of course I wanted to sound manly and I wanted to sound, you know, tough, so I went through stages. You know, now, I would just like to be, you know, able to speak at any level, proper, at the right time, right moment

Jae:	is there anything or anyone who has influenced how you think about Japanese?
David:	I'd have to say my friend A-san (Mr A), he was at the dojo, we train together a lot, he's kinda tough looking, kinda looks like a yakuza guy, he kinda was on the borderline of those two worlds, right ... and yakuza, so he always spoke really, like you know
Jae:	rough?
David:	rough like gangster, so I would mimic that a lot to become more manly, *ore sa*, *omae sa*, right and these kinds of things ((laughs))

David's desire to be able to speak at any level was similar to what Liam expressed, and this stance was especially common among participants who had been living in Japan for more than a few years. Like Scott, David had a language role model, A-san, and earlier in his tenure in Japan, David described making conscious efforts to imitate A-san. David described A-san as looking and sounding tough, 'like a yakuza guy' and explained that he imitated A-san because of his desire to avoid sounding like a woman:

Jae:	so, you wanted to sound like him
David:	well, I mimicked him because I didn't want to sound like a woman, I wanted sound a little tough, you know, I wanted to sound like a man's man, right, but he's pretty much gangster, so ((laughs)) so I had to realize that too, wait a minute, that's a bit, that's a bit, overkill

Later, David talked about being able to make people laugh, which was especially important when he worked as a street performer. David described his ability to use strongly masculine language as surprising and, thus, it was a good tool for making people laugh. Similar to Liam, David had a strong desire to be able to control his speech register, to speak in ways that were appropriately masculine and to be able to make people laugh. In interviews with both Liam and David, their goals of sounding like a 'man's man' and not sounding 'like a woman' are indicative of the influence of gendered norms on their linguistic choices.

Most of the L2 participants in my study were keenly aware of the gendered nature of their speech, especially when they felt that there was a mismatch between how they wanted to sound and how they actually sounded. This awareness was magnified when L1 speakers reacted to such mismatches or otherwise depicted an L2 participant's speech as not aligned with an expected male or female speech style. There was a tendency for female L2 participants to want to avoid sounding overly feminine, and some of them also wanted to avoid sounding masculine.

For the male L2 participants, most mentioned wanting to avoid sounding feminine, and many were concerned with avoiding picking up the speech habits of a female Japanese significant other. However, when it came to sounding masculine, there was more variety of viewpoints among the male L2 participants. Some wanted to avoid sounding overly rough or too masculine, and these participants tended to specifically mention avoidance of the first-person pronoun *ore*. For all participants, concern with getting the details right and being able to sound appropriate and correct was forefront in their minds. And for participants like Liam, Dean and David, a key desire was being able to use language defensively and also to use profane and vulgar language and strongly masculine speech styles.

L1 participants' opinions about L2 speakers and gendered language

L2 participants discussed their concerns regarding Japanese gendered language without being asked specific questions to prompt such comments. However, the interview protocol for L1 participants included questions that asked about the gender of the L2 speakers with whom they interacted. Interview questions also asked L1 participants to think about the L2 speakers they interacted with and any differences they noticed between male and female L2 speakers. Although many L1 participants reported that they did not notice many differences, some L1 participants responded to these questions by sharing their ideas about L2 speakers and Japanese gendered language.

My interview with Megumi, an L1-Japanese and L2-English speaker, were especially informative about perceptions and beliefs concerning Japanese gendered language. She shared her expectations for L2-Japanese speakers with regard to Japanese gendered language as well as her concerns about her own speech when speaking English. Megumi explained that she worried about picking up masculine expressions in English from David, her husband. Megumi's concerns about her English suggest that she may expect to hear differences in how women and men speak, regardless of the language, but especially when they speak Japanese.

Megumi had many opportunities to hear L2 Japanese spoken because she and David owned a guest house that catered to L2-Japanese speakers, primarily men, who came to visit a local dojo where they practiced martial arts. Megumi explained that many of the male L2 speakers she met had learned Japanese from L1-Japanese girlfriends and often picked up feminine speech habits in the process. When she heard male L2 speakers using Japanese that was too feminine, Megumi said she would pull them aside and tell them they sounded feminine in order to help them change those speech habits. When I asked whether Megumi thought it was relevant for L2 speakers to pay attention to *danseigo* or *joseigo*, she replied that it was very relevant, and she demonstrated by mimicking a male L2 speaker who sounded overly feminine. Megumi used both prosodic features, such as pitch or elongating the end of a word, and various words and expressions to demonstrate what she meant by too feminine:

Megumi: 例えば、((imitating, raising pitch slightly)) あ、これ、めっちゃおいしいって私やったら言うけど、男の人やったら、((imitating, lowering pitch slightly)) あっ！うま！とか言うよね。

Megumi: for example, ((imitating, raising pitch slightly)) '*a! kore, mecha oishii!*' ((oh, this is super delicious)) so I would say that, but if it was a man, it would be ((imitating, lowering pitch slightly)) '*a! uma!*' ((oh, good!))

Megumi then discussed the correct ways for male and female speakers to use the terms *oishii* and *umai* (which is sometimes shortened to *uma* for emphasis), explaining that both words mean 'delicious', but that it sounds 'better' for women to use *oishii* and for men to use *umai*. Megumi concluded by commenting that it would be helpful for L2 speakers to watch Japanese television shows, especially anime, to become more aware of these differences.

In the context of discussing L2 speakers and dialect use, another speaker, Yoshio, shared his views about differences between male and female L2 speakers. Yoshio's job included supervising JET Program ALTs and he had supervised several L2 speakers in the past, both men and women. At the time of the study, he was William's supervisor. During the interview, I asked Yoshio about any differences he noticed regarding the speech of male and female L2 speakers. Yoshio focused on dialect in his response to my question. Yoshio began by explaining that he hoped William would use the local dialect. He next explained that, although it might seem 'old-fashioned', he had different expectations for male and female speakers. For example, Yoshio explained that he often encouraged male L2 speakers to use the local dialect as a way to convey friendliness, but he did not encourage female L2 speakers to use the dialect. As we continued our discussion, it became clear that Yoshio wanted male L2 speakers to learn and use the local dialect as a way to connect to the region. He also encouraged female L2 speakers to connect to the region, but in different ways, for example, by learning about local traditions and local foods. In terms of speaking Japanese, however, Yoshio's hope was that the language spoken by female L2 speakers would be '*kirei*', pretty, and '*josei rashii*', feminine. In suggesting men add dialect to their Japanese repertoire, Yoshio implied that men would benefit from using dialect, but he gave no indication that women would experience similar benefits.

Other L1 participants also discussed gendered language. Although Fujiwara's comments were brief, they were similar to Yoshio's. Fujiwara explained that he preferred male L2 speakers to sound friendly and female L2 speakers to sound polite. Similarly, Susumu explained that he thought it sounded overly feminine when male L2 speakers used too much honorific speech or *desu/masu* style. Sugimoto and Hamada also described their preference for how male and female L2 speakers should speak. Sugimoto said that he did not like it when a male speaker sounded feminine or a female speaker sounded masculine. Hamada described hearing the L2-Japanese-speaking mother of one of her students, a woman who Hamada described as picking up the speech habits of her L1-Japanese husband. Hamada felt the mother's way of speaking was '*kitsui*', 'too strong' and she said that the person's way of speaking gave her a sense of '*iwakan*', that it sounded 'off' to her. In these ways, L1 participants showed that they had expectations about how male and female L2 speakers should sound, and they noticed, sometimes with some displeasure, when those expectations were not met.

Discussion

The participants introduced above show how L1 and L2 speakers attend to gendered language and also demonstrate how L2 speakers often struggle with linguistic choices of gendered forms. A common concern for female L2 participants was to avoid sounding overly feminine and several listed specific examples of feminine linguistic features that they did not want to use, including the sentence-final particle *wa* and the first-person pronoun *atashi*. Concerns about *wa* were particularly notable in light of research showing that *wa* is more of a stereotype than a form regularly used in actual speech. It seems likely that L2 participants were exposed to these normative gendered forms in media and pedagogical materials. Grace's concern with overly feminine language came from her dislike of feminine speech. Melissa expressed a different concern, specifically she worried that sounding overly feminine might prevent her from being taken seriously. Separate from concerns about sounding overly feminine, both Grace and Melissa wanted to avoid sounding overly masculine. Grace also mentioned being aware of the influence of her L1-Japanese spouse, and she worried that she had picked up his speech habits, making her sound masculine.

Interestingly, many male L2 participants also worried about sounding too feminine, and several mentioned the importance of avoiding taking on the speech habits of their female significant others. Whether to use masculine first-person pronouns *boku* and *ore* was a common concern among the men in the study and many shared stereotypical views of *ore* as reasons for wanting not to use it. Male L2 participants differed from female L2 participants in the frequency with which they discussed having a role model for how they wanted to sound. While some male L2 participants reported that they did not want to sound overly masculine and wanted to avoid rough or vulgar ways of speaking, others actively sought to cultivate a roughly masculine way of speaking, and some made strategic use of masculine linguistic features, for example in contentious interactions.

In general, L2 participants expressed preferences that their Japanese speech would align with normatively gendered speech styles, although there was some variation in the degree to which participants wanted to sound more gendered, for example, Liam, or less gendered, for example, Melissa. L1 participants showed similar preferences for L2 speakers' speech to align with normative usage. Although we saw in Chapter 3 a belief that L2 speakers would be forgiven for linguistic (*keigo*) mistakes, it seems that L1 speakers were more likely to offer correction, or at least guidance, to an L2 speaker whose speech did not match normative gendered usage. That was particularly the case with male L2 speakers, as we saw with Megumi, who described making it a point to coach male L2 speakers if they sounded feminine. Other L1 participants, like Yoshio, noted their preference for female L2 speakers to align, at least stylistically, with the stereotype that women sound pretty and polite.

The interview data introduced above confirms that L2 participants have clear ideas about what counts as feminine or masculine Japanese, and many have internalized stereotypes about the connotations of different gendered features (e.g. sentence-final particle *wa*, first-person pronoun *ore*). Both male and female L2 participants wanted the gendered aspects of their Japanese speech to be aligned with their identity self-conceptions, which may be at least a partial cause for the frequency with which L2 participants worried about being influenced by (opposite sex) significant others. Similarly, L1 participants took a critical view of L2 speakers who used speech forms or stylistic features of opposite sex speakers, and L2 Japanese use that did not align with the sociolinguistic norms of gendered language was seen as something to correct. At the same time, there were no reports of L1 speakers advising L2 speakers to incorporate specific gendered linguistic features.

There was agreement about some gendered features, especially with regard to feminine features like *wa* that were recognized as strongly feminine or 'girly'. At the same time, there was disagreement about others features. Some participants felt strongly that masculine features such as *ore* were 'low class' or 'distasteful', while others felt that those same features were desirable. Male L2 participants focused much more on first-person pronouns than did female L2 participants, and male L2 participants were more concerned than female L2 participants about choosing the right first-person pronoun. The interviews also showed that some male L2 participants actively cultivated an ability to use strongly masculine speech. However, no female L2 participants in this study actively sought to acquire a strongly feminine way of speaking.

Conclusion

The findings introduced in this chapter demonstrate the impact of ideologies of Japanese gendered language, not only on how L2 participants view their own speech, but also on how L1 participants view L2 speakers' Japanese language use. The findings demonstrate that, for the L2 participants, concerns about gendered language were magnified, and awareness of the gendered sociolinguistic norms of Japanese language complicated their efforts to sound like themselves. Many L2 participants struggled with how they wanted to sound, perceiving gaps between their desired speech and their actual speech, in particular when they felt that their Japanese was more or less masculine or feminine than they felt was appropriate in terms of their sense of self and how they wanted to sound to other speakers. The concerns expressed by L2 participants underscore how fears about inappropriate use of gendered language impacted their sense of language ownership.

Perhaps most notable is the disconnect between how participants wanted to sound and how they believed they actually sounded. Both male and female L2 participants worried about sounding inappropriately gendered: some female participants did not want to sound too masculine or like 'girly girls', while male participants wanted to sound 'manly', like a 'man's man'. Further, while concerns about Japanese gendered language impacted both male and female L2 participants, these concerns emerged differently for men and women. For example, male participants did not report pressure to sound manly, although some actively sought out those skills. On the other hand, female participants did not want to sound stereotypically feminine in Japanese and tended to reject stereotypical feminine features. There were, however, expectations that female L2 speakers should adhere to linguistically feminine speech styles, especially in terms of avoiding slang and dialect and using polite speech.

Also notable were comments that suggest ways that L2 speakers are 'corrected' by other speakers for using gendered language that is believed to be mismatched. While very few participants reported receiving feedback about incorrect *keigo* use, it was more common for L2 participants to report receiving advice about how to speak that guided them to conform to stereotypes of gendered language. It was also more common for L1 participants to report giving advice or otherwise seeking to correct L2 speakers' Japanese use so that it better aligned with gendered language norms. It may be that there is less forgiveness for transgressions related to the use of gendered language. Or it may be that L1 speakers' ownership of Japanese gendered language facilitated such advice – an interpretation that is supported by research findings such as those introduced by Suzuki (2018, 2020).

Missing from this discussion is a consideration of how gendered language norms impact L2 speakers who identify as lesbian, gay, bisexual, transgender, queer and others (LGBTQ+) and it is difficult to say how the concerns of L2 speakers who identify as transgender might differ from those of the participants introduced here. However, given that participants in this study were often painfully aware of the challenges presented by navigating gendered language, it is important to consider the concerns of L2 speakers who may wish to use language in ways that do not align with the heteronormative sociolinguistic norms of gendered Japanese language use.

In short, Japanese gendered language presented challenges to L2 participants. Their interviews revealed tensions between how they wanted to sound and the messages they got about how they should sound. L2 speakers' lack of ownership of Japanese resulted in an acute awareness of the consequences for not aligning with sociolinguistic norms about how men and women 'should' speak.

5 'You're Speaking Dialect, That's Funny Cuz You're a Foreigner'

Introduction

A discussion of Japanese speech styles would be incomplete without considering regional dialects. Despite efforts to standardize Japanese, dialects remain prevalent (Carroll, 2001b; Jinnouchi, 2007; Sanada, 2019) and some dialects are different enough to pose comprehension challenges for Japanese speakers from other regions (Okamoto & Shibamoto-Smith, 2016; Shibatani, 1990). Japanese dialects have been the focus of a significant body of work within Japanese linguistics (e.g. Inoue, 2011; Kobayashi, 2004; Sanada, 2019). Japanese regional dialects can be considered contested linguistic forms because, both historically and in particular on a national scale, dialects have been stigmatized. Nevertheless, dialects can sometimes be a source of linguistic capital (Bourdieu, 1991). Despite the relevance of dialect, there has been little research on Japanese dialects from the perspective of second language (L2-)Japanese speakers. In this chapter, I examine Japanese dialects and consider whether L2 participants can be seen as legitimate speakers of Japanese Dialect and whether L2 speakers' dialect use, or non-use, impacts their community membership. Examination of participants' interviews shows that L2 participants experienced constraints that differ from first language (L1) speakers in terms of linguistic choices related to dialect. In addition, as in previous chapters, L2 participants were vulnerable to linguistic censure by L1 speakers, in particular when L1 speakers commented on or gave directives about the speech and dialect use of L2 speakers. As a result, L2 participants lack language ownership, which impacts their ability to incorporate dialect into their Japanese linguistic repertoire.

I begin the discussion with an introduction to Japanese dialects and focus on studies that shed light on the role of language ideologies in Japan's push for language standardization. This review demonstrates the complex and dynamic position Japanese dialects occupy within the larger repertoire of Japanese speech styles, in particular with regard to notions of prestige and stigma. I conclude with examples from the dialects of Ehime to show how dialects and Standard Japanese differ.

Against this background, I present my analysis and study findings. I draw on theories of linguistic capital (Bourdieu, 1991) to consider the important role that dialect plays in local communities and introduce research on L2 identity and investment (Norton, 2006, 2013). As seen in previous chapters, analysis presented in this chapter demonstrates the diversity and complexity of participants' stances toward dialect use. My analysis sheds light on the question of whether dialect functions as linguistic capital for L2 speakers and how dialect as linguistic capital differs for L2 speakers, as compared to L1 speakers. Dialect presented both possibilities and pitfalls for L2 participants: L2 participants saw dialect use as a way to fit in to local communities and align with local linguistic norms, while at the same time, they recognized the potential for unwanted attention as a result of using dialect.

Previous Studies of Japanese Dialect

Contemporary spoken Japanese includes Standard Japanese (*hyōjungo*), common language (*kyōtsūgo*) and numerous regional dialects. Standard Japanese is Japanese that conforms to normative depictions of so-called correct Japanese (e.g. Sanada, 2019) and it is sometimes described as the Japanese speech used by newscasters on NHK, Japan's government-owned public broadcaster. Common language refers to Japanese that may not completely conform to Standard Japanese but is nevertheless mutually intelligible by speakers from different regions (e.g. Okamoto & Shibamoto-Smith, 2016; Sanada, 2019). Common language may include the phonological patterns of a regional dialect but tends not to include lexical or morphological features that might be harder to understand for speakers from other regions. Regional dialects are associated with specific regions and may be more or less intelligible to L1-Japanese speakers from other regions.

Dialects differ from Standard Japanese in a number of ways, including pitch accent, phonology, grammar, morphology and lexical items (e.g. Sanada, 2019). Dialectal differences can be slight, as when the pitch accent of a word differs in dialect and standard. Differences in accent or phonology generally do not have an impact on communication. However, other differences, particularly morphological or lexical differences, can be significant enough to impede comprehension and this is why Japanese dialects have sometimes been described as 'mutually unintelligible' (Shibatani, 1990: 185).

Creating Standard Japanese, vilifying dialects

Japanese linguists regard Standard Japanese as an ideological creation and describe how it was intentionally promoted as part of Japan's nation-building efforts in the Meiji era (1868–1912) (e.g. Gottlieb, 2005;

Heinrich, 2005, 2012; Kubota, 2014). Sanada (2019) explains that having a standard language was essential to the goal of presenting Japan as a unified nation to the rest of the world. The model for Standard Japanese was based on a dialect used by middle-class speakers in Tokyo (e.g. Carroll, 2001a; Gottlieb, 2005). Standard Japanese was promoted in education, print media and eventually radio and television (e.g. Carroll, 2001a; Gottlieb, 2005; Ramsey, 2004). Along with the promotion of Standard Japanese came a concerted effort to vilify dialects. Official documents described Standard Japanese with words like 'beautiful', 'refined' and 'polished', while dialects were called 'bad', 'coarse' or 'awkward' (Sanada, 2019: 67). Efforts to eliminate dialects resulted in the *hōgen bokumetsu undō* (movement to eradicate or beat down the dialects) in which dialect use was vilified and, in some cases, actively punished (e.g. Okamoto, 2008b; Sunaoshi, 2004). For example, numerous scholars have reported on the punishment of children who used local dialects at school (Gottlieb, 2005; Ramsey, 2004). Consequently, dialect stereotypes emerged, and dialects came to be associated with 'backwardness' (Heinrich, 2012: 6). The standardization of Japanese continued in the decades following World War II and various governmental bodies and non-government institutions were established to create and promote language-related recommendations to the nation. These developments led to a growing sense that the push for standardization was oppressive, and the term 'common language' (*kyōtsūgo*) came to be used to describe speech that was not dialectal, but which allowed people from different regions to communicate in a common language (Sanada, 2019).

Despite efforts to eradicate dialects, dialect use persisted and official policy toward dialects gradually softened (Carroll, 2005; Ramsey, 2004). Carroll (2001a) reports that by 1989, the Ministry of Education's curricular guidelines had been revised to include provisions for elementary school students to understand differences between their local dialect and Standard Japanese. Changes in curricular guidelines represented official recognition of the value of dialects, primarily because they acknowledged dialect as an important part of cultural heritage. Carroll (2001a) notes that one result of the revised curricular guidelines is that there is now official sanction of code-switching between Standard Japanese and dialect. At the same time, however, scholars point out that dialect continues to be impacted by years of vilification and notions of stigma and dialect-as-inappropriate persist (e.g. Carroll, 2001b; Kubota, 2014; Okamoto & Shibamoto-Smith, 2016). Standard Japanese retains its status as the 'legitimate language', especially because it is the medium of instruction in educational contexts, as well as the language of print and broadcast media. Nevertheless, as changes in educational policy took effect, popular attitudes toward dialect also shifted. Over the last few decades, surveys of popular opinion often report positive feelings associated with dialect. Recently, surveys have shown that dialects are evaluated positively in terms of nostalgia and positive emotions, while Standard Japanese continues to be associated with intelligence and sophistication (e.g. Heinrich, 2022; Inoue, 2006; Okamoto, 2008b; Okamoto & Shibamoto-Smith, 2016; Ramsey, 2004; Watanabe & Karasawa, 2013).

Code-switching between Standard and Dialect

In light of the ways that Standard Japanese and dialect are valued differently in different contexts, it is no surprise that *tsukaiwake*, a kind of code-switching that distinguishes between standard and dialect, is common in contemporary spoken Japanese.[1] Researchers find that speakers switch between dialect and standard depending on the situation, topic or interlocuters (e.g. Carroll, 2001a). Jinnouchi (2007) describes the ability to use both standard and dialect as a form of bilingualism and argues that the practice of code-switching should be regarded as one among many varieties of Japanese. These findings are supported by a public opinion poll by the Japan Agency for Cultural Affairs (2010), which found that almost 80% of respondents felt it was appropriate to choose between Standard Japanese and Japanese Dialect depending on factors such as context and other speakers.

Although dialect use is seen more favorably than in past decades, speakers sometimes experience code-switching between dialect and standard as a site of struggle. Occhi (2008) describes how Japanese university students from Miyazaki Prefecture, on the island of Kyushu, viewed dialect use and dialect users. She finds that participants 'expressed feelings of affection towards dialect' (Occhi, 2008: 108) but adopted a practical stance toward choosing speech styles to align with local norms. When moving from a smaller area to a larger regional city, participants used the dialect of the regional city even when it differed from their original dialect. Their code-switching was not without adverse effects. One participant reported feeling homesick upon hearing his local dialect. Another participant described her use of either dialect or 'standard-like' speech as being dependent on contexts and reported that 'her dialect and standard switching behavior [was] consciously performed, necessary and stressful' (Occhi, 2008: 101). Occhi also describes how dialect speakers adopt Standard Japanese when they move to urban areas, as seen when students at universities in Tokyo hide their regional origin by concealing their dialects and adopting Standard Japanese as a protective measure. Occhi (2008: 102) describes their use of Standard Japanese as 'passing', and she notes its similarity to a dialect speaker described in Inoue (2006) who also adopted Standard Japanese after relocating to Tokyo because it was perceived to offer access to upward social mobility.

Researchers have drawn on Bourdieu's (1991) notion of linguistic capital to understand the complex roles of standard and dialect. Standard Japanese is said to have more linguistic capital in contexts where intelligence is valued, such as in workplace interactions, while Japanese Dialect is said to be valued in contexts where emotions are valued, for example in interactions with family and friends (e.g. Watanabe & Karasawa, 2013). The research introduced thus far sheds light on what counts as linguistic capital for L1 speakers. Code-switching affords linguistic capital but is highly context and interlocutor dependent, dynamic and changing, rather than static or fixed.

From code-switching to de-standardization: Shifts in dialect and standard usage

With dialect stigma dissipating and speakers increasingly code-switching between standard and dialect, some Japanese linguists argue that Japanese is undergoing de-standardization. Inoue (2011) traces the evolution of attitudes toward Japanese Dialect and explains that attitudes toward dialect went through three stages: first, in the Meiji era, the goal was dialect eradication. Next, after World War II, use of Standard Japanese became widespread, and coexistence became the norm as speakers actively code-switched between dialect and standard depending on contexts and interlocutors. As dialect use decreased, scarcity contributed to a 'renewed appreciation' (Inoue, 2011: 114) of dialects. From the 1990s on, dialect's stigma lessened, and Inoue argues that dialects in Japan now function as a form of amusement and are used to fulfill speakers' goals for freedom of self-expression.

Inoue also explains that the evolution in the language used in media has played a significant role in de-standardization. First, widespread use of Standard Japanese in radio and television programs resulted in exposure to Standard Japanese across all regions of Japan. This included news reports as well as television dramas that used everyday language. At the same time, 'street interviews and on-the-spot reporting', along with dramas set in regional locales, created numerous opportunities for the broadcasting of local dialects to other regions across Japan. Thus, Inoue argues that the influence of television and radio broadcasting on language is not the unidirectional path to standardization as often described.

Inoue (2011) identifies additional factors involved in the current de-standardization of Japanese. Large-scale urbanization has resulted in a tendency for people to evaluate their hometowns more highly, which has been reinforced by the favorable treatment of dialects on television as features of local color. In addition, colloquial spoken Japanese, especially that used by young people, has contributed to dialect's treatment as merely another speech style, much like slang and youth language. These shifts in usage have brought about what Inoue (2011: 115) calls 'new dialects', in which speakers seek out dialect forms from regions other than their own to make up for a sense that Standard Japanese is merely 'colorless language'. Inoue argues that these changes suggest a growing tendency to see language variation as an asset and a resource for self-expression. All of these developments contribute to language diversification after decades of a reduction in language diversity and have led to dialect revitalization.

The idea of dialect as a resource for self-expression and playful language is found in research that examines the increasing use of dialect by young people. Kobayashi (2004) and Tanaka (2007) describe the various ways young people, especially in Tokyo, incorporate dialectal features into their speech. Kobayashi calls this the 'accessorization' of dialect, while Tanaka calls it *hōgen-kosupure* or dialect cosplay (costume play). Tanaka explains that a defining feature of dialect cosplay is that it draws on linguistic stereotypes and, as a result, dialect cosplay does not need to make use of a 'real' or 'authentic' dialect as long as it matches speakers' perceptions of what dialect sounds like. Like Kobayashi, Tanaka finds that dialect cosplay is mostly used by young people in urban areas, although its use in internet blogs and social media means that dialect cosplay should not be dismissed as a phenomenon relevant only to Tokyo. Further, Tanaka and Kobayashi describe the use of isolated dialect features such as sentence-final particles or emotive expressions, demonstrating how dialect can perform a symbolic function by being inserted into speech that would otherwise be characterized as standard.

Similar uses have been found in research that examines scripted language, such as dialogue written for movies and novels. For example, Shibamoto-Smith and Occhi (2009) examine how gendered linguistic norms are recreated through differential use of dialect in the scripted speech of characters in a Japanese romantic television drama. The authors find that when dialects are used by a romantic heroine in a television drama, urban and/or prestige dialects, such as the Kobe Dialect, can be used but more rural dialects are not used by romantic heroines. Echoing other authors (e.g. Okamoto, 2008a; Sunaoshi, 2004), Shibamoto-Smith and Occhi point to such use of urban, prestige dialects as evidence that not all dialects are equal. In fact, prestige dialects can be said to have greater linguistic capital than more rural dialects. While Jinnouchi (2007) argues that Japan is experiencing a dialect boom, Shibamoto-Smith and Occhi (2009: 538) suggest that dialect is treated only as a 'cute accessory', and may be seen as attractive by Standard Japanese speakers who view dialects as 'exotic, like foreign languages'. Shibamoto-Smith and Occhi (2009: 531) also argue that television viewers ultimately seem to prefer 'dialect lite', or dialect that has been reduced to a few key, and often stereotyped, features. The authors conclude that although the use of dialects in a television drama appears to recognize dialects as valuable, because dialects are mainly used by supporting characters and for 'language play', it 'marks dialectal speech as "other" and peripheral' (Shibamoto-Smith & Occhi, 2009: 538–539).

Heinrich (2017, 2018, 2022) expands on Tanaka's (2007) work examining dialect cosplay, and agrees that the phenomenon is most common in urban locations. He also argues that the impact of de-standardization on Japanese language has resulted in blurring the boundaries between Standard Japanese and Japanese Dialect. Nevertheless, ideologies of Standard Japanese and stereotypes about dialects and dialect speakers persist and, although actual speech often mixes standard and dialect, speakers tend to see a clear boundary between the two (Okamoto & Shibamoto-Smith, 2016). Heinrich (2017) argues that because of these persistent ideological depictions of dialect as wrong or inappropriate, modern uses of dialect cosplay are what Heinrich calls examples of 'linguistic transgressions'. Linguistic transgressions allow speakers to display stances such as affiliation toward an interlocutor or identity stances such as masculinity. Heinrich argues that dialect as linguistic transgression allows speakers to resist expectations and display coolness. Heinrich (2018) draws on Bourdieu's notion of legitimacy to show how use of dialect cosplay takes advantage of the ideological association of dialect as not-legitimate language. Dialect cosplay could thus be described as subverting ideologies of legitimacy. These new ways of using dialect allow speakers to add 'a new layer of social meaning' to their language, and cultivate a linguistic repertoire that is 'illustrative, vivid, innovative and cool' (Heinrich, 2022: 293).

Expressing coolness is not the only function of present-day dialect use. While speakers in Tokyo may use dialect primarily for language play, dialect continues to perform membership functions in regional locales. Kobayashi (2007) argues that in addition to its communicative function, dialect allows speakers to convey a sense of belonging. Similarly, Ohuchi (2014) examines the use of dialect in emergency radio programs (*rinji kasai hōsōkyoku*) after the Great East Japan Earthquake of 2011 and finds that dialect use in emergency radio programs had three functions: (1) to display a sense of belonging and feelings of hometown even when listeners were in evacuation shelters far from home; (2) to provide relief from the stress of the disaster and instill courage in the listeners; and (3) to aid in the preservation of the dialect even when dialect users were separated from each other (Ohuchi, 2014: 15–16, translation by this author).

Ball (2004) also examines discourse data and finds that the function of dialect is not only as an index of regionality, but that dialect also performs a socioindexical function, allowing a speaker to index solidarity with an addressee and index the speaker and addressee as members of the same in-group. Similarly, Ball argues that Standard Japanese can index out-group membership and highlight the differences between speaker and addressee. Barke's (2018) work further demonstrates the functionality of dialect. He examines workplace language at a company in the Kansai region and finds that shifts between Standard Japanese and Japanese Dialect occurred in a range of contexts and for a range of expressive functions. While the association of dialect with humor is widely acknowledged, Barke (2018: 144) finds that dialect was also used for anger and other 'expressions of affect', as well as informality, spontaneity and in-group depictions. Barke's analysis also shows that shifting between Standard Japanese and Japanese Dialect allows speakers to display changes in stance and allows them to manipulate language for their own interactional goals. All the studies above offer diverse evidence for the valuable role that regional dialects serve as a linguistic resource for social meaning making.

Japanese Dialect and L2 speakers

Research that considers how L2 speakers experience Japanese Dialect is less common, but it is clear that L2 speakers in Japan encounter dialect and when they do, they have to negotiate issues surrounding its understanding and use. Iino (2006: 152) finds that American exchange students participating in homestays in Kyoto were exposed to various non-standard forms, including regional dialect and 'foreigner talk'. Iino (2006: 168) explains that host families believed that Standard Japanese was the most appropriate speech to use with the American students, but they actually spoke a 'hyper-normalized' Japanese that was neither standard nor dialect, leading Iino to call it 'foreigner talk'. Iino suggests that the host families may have believed that using Kyoto Dialect was not appropriate or that the American students would not be able to understand dialect. However, although foreigner talk may have been easier to understand, Iino notes that foreigner talk also emphasized the students' foreign-ness and highlighted the distance between the homestay students and the host families.

Iino (2006) also describes American students' struggles to define their identities and roles within Japanese society. One issue they faced was the extent to which 'non-Japanese in Japan are expected or allowed to assimilate with native Japanese' (Iino, 2006: 160). According to Iino (2006: 160), 'speaking fluent Japanese may not always be sufficient or even appropriate in some situations. In fact, "speaking like a native" can at times be inappropriate', although Iino does not specify what these situations might be. Iino (2006: 171) also considers various expectations for how L2 speakers speak or should speak, arguing that L1 speakers do not necessarily expect L2 speakers to 'speak and behave like a native, and at the same time non-native speakers themselves may not wish to speak and behave like a native'. Iino (2006: 171) concludes that 'if the American students behave like a native Japanese, then the Japanese hosts may feel that the student is *henna* (strange) *gaijin* [foreigner]'. Unfortunately, Iino neither problematizes notions such as *henna gaijin* nor discusses how these notions affected American students.

While Iino examines the experiences of short-term American exchange students, Mori's (2012) study includes L2 speakers who were long-term residents of Japan. Mori considers what factors influenced whether L2 learners became members of a new community. Similar to Iino's findings, Mori notes that it was likely that foreign exchange students heard dialect used and, like Iino, Mori (2012: 155) argues that while a host family's speech adjustments may help the homestay student's comprehension, language adjustments may also serve to 'reconfirm the students' status as outsiders'. Mori concludes that L2 learners in Japan will encounter a variety of speech styles, including Standard Japanese and Japanese Dialect. Drawing on Bourdieu's (1991) notion of linguistic capital, Mori (2012) points out that although Standard Japanese offers L2 learners a certain amount of linguistic capital, not all Japanese speakers will use an easy-to-understand version of Standard Japanese. Thus, Mori argues, L2 learners need to be able to comprehend the different types of speech styles (including dialect) that they encounter. Further, she makes the important point that learners need sufficient knowledge of Japanese to understand how their own choices about speech styles will influence the impressions they make on others.

One L2 participant in Mori's research has particular relevance for my study, 'Ms Wang'. Mori details Ms Wang's ambivalence toward Japanese Dialect and describes her attempts to avoid using dialect forms, even though her L1 coworkers used them so frequently that Ms Wang found the forms slipping into her own speech. Ms Wang discussed her previous work as a translator and explained that her Japanese speech needed to be accessible to all Japanese speakers. At the same time, Ms Wang acknowledged that if she used some dialect forms, it might decrease the distance between her and her coworkers. Mori's descriptions of this type of ambivalence demonstrate the conflicting concerns that L2 speakers may struggle with as they navigate choices between standard and dialect.

Japanese Dialect and teaching Japanese as a foreign language

Given that L2 speakers will be exposed to Japanese Dialect when they go to Japan, it is important to address how dialect is handled in Japanese as a second or foreign language (JSL/JFL) instruction. Long (1996) argues that, because L1 speakers are sometimes unaware of mixing standard and dialect forms, some instruction about non-standard forms is needed. Long is one of few researchers, along with Iino (2006) and Jones (2003), to acknowledge that the frequency with which dialects are used all but guarantees L2 speakers in Japan will encounter dialect use, and some dialect instruction would be beneficial. However, Long (1996) assumes that L2 learners would not need or want to use dialect themselves, although he did not explain why this might be. As such, Long, along with Iino (2006), is (perhaps unwittingly) participating in othering in which L2-Japanese speakers are treated as if they do not need to learn or use Japanese to its fullest extent and in all of its varieties (cf. Burgess, 2012).

Jones (2003), on the other hand, argues that JSL/JFL curricula should include instruction in non-standard forms of Japanese. He criticizes traditional JSL/JFL instruction that seeks to prepare JSL students primarily for business settings, saying that this approach makes less sense for obvious reasons: Japanese language learners are likely to be involved in a variety of occupations, they may have a Japanese spouse and family members and, ultimately, they may intend to stay in Japan indefinitely. Jones points out that such students have various Japanese language needs that are not met when JSL/JFL curricula is limited to Standard Japanese, and he argues that the ability to adapt to local dialects will help L2 speakers integrate into the Japanese communities in which they find themselves.

Mukai (2000) looks specifically at L2 speakers' awareness of dialect and explores their attitudes toward dialect use and instruction. Mukai surveyed 34 foreign exchange students attending university or graduate school in Matsuyama, Ehime. Mukai reports that almost all respondents believed it was necessary to understand the local dialect to some extent and most also said it was necessary to be able to speak the dialect to some extent. In addition, more than half said they wanted to be taught dialect. Regarding their experiences, most respondents said they had experienced difficulties due to being unable to understand the local dialect. Mukai finds that students experienced difficulty in the following kinds of situations: talking to friends, working part-time jobs, while shopping and during class. Mukai also finds that some dialect forms were misunderstood, and students frequently misunderstood the pragmatic intent or level of politeness encoded in the dialect forms. Finally, when asked about their language use habits, almost half of the students responded that they spoke Standard Japanese, only some used both standard and dialect and others appeared to be confused about what they were speaking. Similar to Jones's argument that dialect knowledge helps L2 speakers fit into Japanese communities, Mukai concludes that students recognized the importance of dialect as a way to have better relations with people in the area where they lived. Departing from Long (1996) and Iino (2006), Mukai (2000) also argues that instruction in JSL should be designed not only to facilitate students' understanding of dialect forms and their ability to distinguish between standard and dialect but also to help students learn how to use the dialect forms they encounter.

Case Study: Ehime Dialect

Common questions regarding dialect use in Ehime include how common it is for speakers in Ehime to use dialect, which speakers use dialect and in which situations, especially given increasing standardization. Dialectology research relating to Ehime's dialects focuses primarily on grammatical aspects (e.g. Kubo, 2018; Nakagawa, 2019), phonetic description (e.g. Arimoto, 2006) or accent (e.g. Kodama, 2019; Shimizu & Akiyama, 1999). Fewer studies examine or seek to quantify how many people use dialect or how often dialect is heard in daily interactions. My fieldwork in Ehime suggests, however, that dialect is regularly heard in daily interactions, including in workplaces and businesses. Dialectologists who study Ehime's dialects confirm that dialect is commonly used by speakers across a wide range of age groups and in a variety of situations. For example, with regard to Matsuyama's dialect, Kubo explains that although some dialectal features are becoming standardized (particularly pitch accent), dialect use remains common across age groups, especially with regard to word endings, sentence-final expressions and grammatical structures. Lexical items also remain common in school settings, although adults in other settings may be less likely to use dialect lexical items (H. Kubo, personal communication, 9 September 2022). Similarly, Nakagawa reports that while standardization and grammaticalization are impacting the use of some dialect features, dialect forms specific to particular regions within Ehime are commonly used across age groups (H. Nakagawa, personal communication, 13 September 2022). These observations do not allow us to quantify dialect use; however, they underscore the relevance of dialect as part of the linguistic repertoire of present-day Ehime.

A brief introduction to Ehime Dialect shows how it differs from Standard Japanese and gives readers an idea of how L2 speakers encounter dialect while in Ehime. Ehime, formerly called Iyo, has three regions: Chūyo (central-Iyo) is the central region and includes the prefectural capital of Matsuyama, Tōyo (Eastern-Iyo) and Nanyo (Southern-Iyo). Although there are some commonalities, each region has a distinct dialect. For example, accent patterns differ across Ehime, with some areas having accents that are similar to the Kansai region, the Kyushu region or even the Tokyo region (Doinaka, 2005; NHK, 2005).

I will use the Nanyo dialect as an example because I lived in the Nanyo region for 12 years and it is the dialect with which I am most familiar. The differences between the Nanyo dialect and Standard Japanese can be categorized in terms of lexical, morphological and phonological differences. Examples of lexical differences include the use of *oru* (to be) instead of the standard verb *iru*; the use of *ken* (so, because) in place of the standard *kara*; and the use of *hiyai* (cold) instead of the standard *samui*. One representative morphological difference is found in the verb conjugations of the present progressive and the resultant state, which in Standard Japanese are both expressed with the *te*-form of the verb plus *iru*. For example, to express 'is doing' in Standard Japanese, the conjugation is '*yatte-iru*'. The difference between the present progressive, 'is doing', and the resultant state, 'has done', can only be expressed either by adding an adverb (like *mō*, already) or by relying on context. In the dialect form, however, either *yoru* or *toru* is attached to the verb stem, and these two endings allow for a distinction not made in Standard Japanese: verb stem + *yoru* is used for the present progressive, while verb *te*-form + *toru* is used for the resultant state. To express 'is doing' (i.e. the present progressive) in the dialect, '*yari-yoru*' is used. To express the resultant state 'has done' (i.e. was doing and is now finished), the form becomes '*yat-toru*'. A similar example can be seen with the present progressive 'is coming' and the resultant state 'has come' (i.e. has arrived): in Standard Japanese, both are expressed as '*kite-iru*', and context or an added adverb is needed to make the distinction. In the dialect, '*ki-yoru*' is the present progressive 'is coming', while '*ki-toru*' is the resultant state 'has come'. For Japanese speakers not familiar with these dialect conjugations, the *te*-form + *toru* conjugation appears to be similar to the standard *te*-form + *iru*, but the dialect *te*-form + *toru* has a more restricted meaning than the standard *te*-form + *iru*.

Other examples of differences between dialect and standard involve phonological differences such as the use of vowel lengthening and shifting to change adjectives into adverbs, as in *yō* (well/often) compared to the standard *yoku*. There is also a different conjugation pattern for negative verbs, as in *dekin* (cannot do) instead of the standard *dekinai*, and *taben* (not eat) instead of the standard *tabenai*. These words appear to be similar to Standard Japanese, but they are often used in ways that do not have the same meaning or nuance. One example is the Nanyo dialect phrase *yō taben*. Due to the sound similarity, it might be assumed that the equivalent to this phrase in Standard Japanese would be *yoku tabenai*, 'don't eat very much' in terms of either frequency or amount. However, *yō taben* actually means 'can't eat'. These forms are additional examples of how dialect features can pose comprehension challenges. Table 5.1 presents another example which shows how different dialect tokens can be used together. As the example in Table 5.1 shows, some of these dialect tokens can differ enough to have the potential to impede comprehension for speakers from other regions.

Note that the dialect example in Table 5.1 shares only one word in common with its standard equivalent (*ame-ga*, rain), while the rest of the example is composed of dialect tokens. However, it is common for speakers to use what can be described as a mixed form in which dialect tokens are used along with standard features. It is especially common, even in speech that is largely standard, for the following forms to be used in dialect: verb endings, sentence-final particles and iconic lexical items such as *ken* in place of *kara*. These observations are based on my fieldwork as well as on descriptions that participants shared with me during their interviews. Findings from research in Japanese dialectology provide additional evidence with descriptions about how dialect and standard variants are mixed in complex ways that serve interactional and stylistic needs (e.g. Okamoto, 2008a, 2008b; Tanaka, 2007, 2014). Another pattern I observed was the use of dialect tokens mid-sentence, with sentence endings made up of standard features; this pattern was especially common in workplace settings, as shown in Table 5.2.

Table 5.1 Dialect in a sentence – Example 1: 'It's really raining, so come home soon'

Standard Japanese	sugoi	ame ga	futte-iru	kara	hayaku	kaette-kite	ne
Ehime dialect	gaina	ame ga	furi-yoru	ken	hayō	monte-kisai	ya
English	really	rain	falling	so	soon	come home	SFP
Type	L	N	M	L	M, P	L, M	L

Note: L: lexical; N: no change; M: morphological; P: phonological; SFP: sentence-final particle.

Table 5.2 Dialect in a sentence – Example 2: 'I have to go to Matsuyama, so I can't attend the meeting'

ED	ashita wa	Matsuyama ni	ikan to	iken	ken	kaigi ni	derenai	n desu
SJ	ashita wa	Matsuyama ni	ikanakereba	ikenai	kara	kaigi ni	derenai	n desu
Eng	Tomorrow	to Matsuyama	not go	won't do	so	meeting	can't attend	E C
Type	N	N	M	M	L	N	N	N N

Note: N: no change; M: morphological; L: lexical; E: explanation marker; C: copula.

L1 Study Participants' Views about Dialect and L2 Speakers

Having introduced Ehime Dialect, I begin the discussion of participant findings with the L1 participants. One key way that this chapter differs from the other chapters is that the interview protocol for both L1 and L2 speakers included questions that asked specifically about dialect. This is because I was interested in issues related to dialect before starting the study. The interview protocol for L1 participants included three questions about dialect in general as well as two questions about dialect and L2 speakers:

- 方言についてどう思いますか 'what do you think about dialect?'
- 方言が好きですか 'do you like dialect?'
- 方言を使いますか 'do you use dialect?'
- (この町) に住む外国人は方言を理解することは必要・大切だと思いますか 'do you think it's necessary/important for foreigners living in this town to be able to understand dialect?'
- 外国人は方言を使うことは必要・大切だと思いますか 'do you think it's necessary/important for foreigners to use dialect?'

I concluded each L1 participant interview by asking if they had any advice for L2 speakers who live in their area. Examining the answers to these questions revealed patterns and similarities in L1 participants' views about dialect and its role in local communities, as well as how L1 participants regarded use of dialect by L2 speakers.

Most L1 participants shared favorable views about dialect and many of them expressed their ideas about dialect using the same words:

'*atatakai*' warm, '*shitashii*' friendly, '*omoshiroi*' interesting/funny and '*inaka*' rural or rustic. Some comments suggested a romanticized view of dialect, as when participants said dialect made them feel '*natsukasii*' nostalgia or talked about dialect's role in local culture. Nakamura, for example, described dialect as '*kuni no takara*' (the country's treasure) and said that people should cherish their local dialect. Other participants shared examples of specific dialect tokens, such as the sentence-final particles *ken* or *ya-ken*, 'so' or 'because', which loosely correspond to the Standard Japanese *kara* or *da kara*.

Almost all of the L1 participants who lived in regional locations, as well as some in larger urban areas, reported that they used dialect regularly. Participants most often described speaking dialect with family members, friends and neighbors. L1 participants who worked in public schools described using dialect, sometimes intentionally, with schoolchildren and parents of schoolchildren. Yoshio even described using his local dialect when visiting Tokyo for work events, explaining that he used dialect as a way to promote his region.

When explaining why they liked dialect, many L1 participants described dialect as a way to connect to others and strengthen interpersonal connections. Some participants discussed dialect's connection to local communities and talked about using dialect to express affection for their '*furusato*' (hometown) and also as a way to demonstrate identity. At the same time, participants stressed the importance of *tsukaiwake* or making distinctions in terms of when and with whom to use dialect. Participants were especially attentive to notions of appropriateness and described paying attention to 'TPO', a loanword from English used to refer to the importance of taking account of time, place and occasion when making linguistic choices. In discussing TPO, there was wide agreement among L1 participants that dialect was less appropriate in workplaces, particularly in formal discussions or with people from outside of one's workplace. However, their views about using dialect with people they did not know or did not know well were more complex. Some participants said that they would not use dialect if they did not know the other person, while others said that they would intentionally use dialect as '*chikamichi*', a short cut to becoming more friendly.

L1 participants who reported that they did not use dialect themselves explained that this was because dialect was not personally relevant, rather than due to any negative feelings about dialect. Only a few L1 participants expressed negative views about dialect, and only one participant, Sakamoto, shared negative comments in a more personal way. Sakamoto explained that, in his youth, he had moved from a small island to a larger town, 'Koyama', to attend junior high school. He feared that his Koyama classmates would make fun of his '*namari*' (accent) or dialect words he regularly used from his hometown. As a result, Sakamoto was self-conscious throughout his school years and always tried to avoid dialect. As an adult, however, Sakamoto explained that he used dialect often, and he used it numerous times during our interview.

When I asked L1 participants about whether they thought dialect was important for L2 speakers, most agreed that it was important for L2 speakers to be able to understand dialect. Not surprisingly, this view was particularly common for L1 participants in more regional or rural locations. However, many L1 participants expressed concern that learning Japanese language was already a difficult task and thus it would be unfair to expect L2 speakers to also learn dialect. Often, the sentiment that L2 speakers would not use dialect was implied in their comments, and they indicated that other L1 speakers would not expect L2 speakers to use dialect. In fact, many L1 participants said that an L2 speaker using dialect would be surprising. At the same time, however, many L1 participants said that if an L2 speaker tried to learn their local dialect, L1 speakers would react positively. Some L1 participants also shared that they would feel closeness toward an L2 speaker who used the local dialect, and others said an L2 speaker's dialect use would be seen positively, as proof the L2 speaker was trying to fit in. A few L1 participants observed that, if L2 speakers used dialect, it would help them to stand out from other L2 speakers.

Although most L1 participants' comments about L2 dialect use were favorable, there were also some concerns. Some L1 participants explained that it would be a problem if an L2 speaker used dialect exclusively. There was a general belief that L2 speakers might have a difficult time making distinctions between when to use dialect and when to use Standard Japanese. A few L1 participants also mentioned that, while they would be happy to hear a male L2 speaker using dialect, they would prefer female L2 speakers not to use dialect and instead focus on acquiring polite, Standard Japanese skills, as discussed in Chapter 4. Lastly, a few L1 participants expressed the belief that it would be better for L2 speakers not to use dialect and to focus only on speaking Standard Japanese.

In short, dialect use was common among L1 participants and most of them shared positive views about dialect. At the same time, their messages about L2 speakers were mixed. Often, they suggested that L2 speakers were unlikely to use or need dialect, despite the benefits that dialect use would afford, especially in smaller communities.

L2 Study Participants: Encountering and Negotiating Dialect

My first round of data collection with L2 participants took place in Ehime and other prefectures in Shikoku. Based on my own experience as a resident of Ehime, I expected that L2 participants would encounter dialect, which was confirmed by the many L2 participants who brought up dialect before being asked. L2 participants often discussed dialect in response to the following questions:

- What's easy/difficult about Japanese?
- Have you ever had any problems understanding (or being understood by) your Japanese coworkers/neighbors/friends?
- Have you ever given any thought to how you want to sound when you speak Japanese?

When an L2 participant did not discuss dialect, or follow-up was needed, I asked one or more of the following questions from the interview protocol:

- Did you know that Japanese language has dialects before you came to Japan?
- Do you understand (the dialect of your town)?
- Do you use (the dialect of your town)? Why or why not?
- Do you think dialect is important here? Why or why not?
- Do you think it's important for you to understand dialect? Why or why not?
- Do you think it's important for you to use dialect? Why or why not?
- (If this has not come out yet, ask) What do you think about this dialect? (or: Do you like the dialect? Why or why not?)

Thus, in each interview, these questions led participants to discuss whether they wanted to use dialect or consciously avoided using it or whether they were unsure and possibly conflicted about dialect.

Using dialect

Some L2 participants intentionally and even enthusiastically used dialect. For such participants, it was typical for them to have spent time thinking about dialect and deciding explicitly to use it. Grace, who had lived in Ehime and elsewhere in Shikoku for over 10 years, brought up dialect before I asked. Grace explained that dialect was one of the things that made Japanese difficult for her, especially in the beginning, because she had to learn to distinguish dialect and standard. However, she heard dialect so often that she naturally began to use it. I asked Grace if there were any benefits to living in a dialect-using region:

Grace: the people you meet, especially people you meet for the first time, they are more relaxed. If you speak, first of all, when they see my face they don't expect me to be able to speak Japanese at all, so they're uneasy when they see me initially and there's always that relief when they realize you can speak Japanese, but if you speak Japanese, their Japanese, they're like ooh, and you're instantly friends, you can instantly, you relate to them and they're like ah and

> instead of talking to you as a foreigner, they'll comment on something else, unrelated to me being a foreigner and I like that. I don't like being the foreigner all the time, so it's nice just to have an instant connection with people

Grace referred to dialect as 'their Japanese', the Japanese that belonged to the people with whom she was speaking. At the same time, this view of dialect did not prevent Grace from using it herself. Grace emphasized that using dialect allowed her to make an 'instant connection' and to avoid 'being the foreigner all the time', suggesting that dialect had an immediate benefit in making connections to the community.

William also felt that how he used Japanese impacted his membership and identity in the local community. William consciously worked to improve his Japanese language skills, not only to improve his ability to communicate, but also because he recognized that dialect helped him create and maintain connections with L1 speakers in his workplace and community, something that was clearly important to him.

Jae: do you think it's important for you to be able to understand dialect?

William: uh, I think for like day to day living, yeah. Um, and especially you are trying to fit in, like, being able to understand it means that, you know, you're not having to constantly ask for clarification. And especially being able to use it in conversation shows the people that, you know, you're not just there to, you know, like dick around for a couple years and teach English and go back home, you're actually interested in the language and the people that you're around.

For William, dialect was an important way to convey a deeper commitment to the local community. In addition, he placed a high value on being able to understand dialect. William also valued the role of dialect in facilitating membership and participation, as evidenced by his characterization of dialect for 'trying to fit in'. In addition, William emphasized the importance of understanding dialect to avoid interrupting conversational flow and calling attention to his status as a non-native speaker.

I asked William if he heard a lot of dialect and he shared examples of dialect phrases used throughout Ehime, as well as phrases used only in the immediate area where he lived. He enthusiastically explained which phrases were more common and which ones he used most, depicting dialect as an established part of his Japanese linguistic repertoire. William made a point of learning more about dialect because he saw dialect as a way to cultivate memberships in his workplace and hobby communities.

Liam, another L2 participant, was also enthusiastic about using dialect. Unlike William, Liam had not studied Japanese extensively before coming to Japan. But since arriving in Ehime, Liam enjoyed studying Japanese and learning the local dialect. He explained that dialect use was common where he lived, and he used it because that was how people around him spoke. Liam also felt that dialect fit his personality and allowed him to express himself. Issues of identity and voice were prominent in his comments, and he reported that dialect fit his personality in spite of, or perhaps *because* of, his foreigner status. He used dialect frequently, explaining 'it's what I've learned naturally'. Liam mentioned his belief that dialect use was natural for him several times during the interview and, like William, Liam gave examples of specific dialect words that he used exclusively, saying that he did not use the standard equivalents for those words. Liam's comments conveyed that he was comfortable with his dialect use. When I asked Liam why he used dialect, he replied:

Liam: because it's what I learned firsthand… because I learned firsthand from speaking, I learned Japanese from being here, I made sure I progressed by using textbooks, but then, as much as I did stuff in textbooks, I then just learned stuff from drinking parties with old men. So I've been learning Japanese through a combination of textbook studying and then using it practically, so I know words that have come from both … and all of my speaking practice has only ever come from using it locally, so I use [dialect] because that's how I speak Japanese, cuz that's how the people around me speak Japanese

Liam made an implicit claim about the legitimacy of his dialect use: using dialect was 'natural' for him because it was what he learned 'firsthand', which was also evident in how he displayed his identity as a Japanese speaker. Specifically, Liam explained that he was a particular kind of Japanese speaker: one who used dialect, because 'that's how I speak Japanese'. Thus, dialect was a key part of Liam's understanding of who he was as a Japanese speaker, specifically, someone who used dialect as a matter of course. His claim was further legitimized by depicting his dialect use as being aligned with local linguistic practice, as seen in his comment that he used dialect because 'that's how people around me speak Japanese'. It was clear that Liam viewed his dialect use as in keeping with local norms, and his justification for his use of dialect was that he had learned it 'naturally'.

Although Liam described his use of dialect in a matter-of-fact way, he also described experiences which suggest his dialect use sometimes became a contested code choice. There was tension between Liam's depiction of dialect as the local linguistic norm in general and his experiences which called into question whether or to what degree dialect use by an L2 speaker was treated as normal or acceptable by L1 speakers. Liam told me about his girlfriend, an L1-Japanese speaker, who used dialect with her Japanese friends and family. However, Liam said that she did not use dialect when speaking with him, 'she always said she couldn't use it [dialect] with me, it just didn't come naturally'. Nevertheless, her reluctance did not seem to influence Liam's own dialect use.

Liam also described how some L1 speakers reacted when he used dialect. The following comment came after I asked Liam when he first learned that Japanese has dialects:

Liam: I learned that almost right away because it's just a big topic of conversation among a lot of Japanese people, and it's almost like *jiman* ((boasting)) in that many Japanese people just have conversations about what's that *hōgen* ((dialect))... so it came up a lot in conversation, also because it was what I was learning naturally from kids and things, people would be like, ah you're speaking *hōgen*, that's funny, cuz you're a foreigner

Liam described learning dialect not only by hearing it, but also by participating in conversations about dialect. Despite his comfort with and regular use of dialect, however, Liam was also told that it was 'funny' for him to use dialect because he was a 'foreigner'. Although Liam was exposed to beliefs that dialect use by an L2 speaker was unusual or unexpected, he did not regard this as problematic, and it did not appear to cause him to reconsider his own use of dialect. Since he had mentioned being teased or made fun of for using dialect, I returned to the question of how L1 speakers responded to his dialect use:

Jae: so if you use dialect, do they make fun of you for using dialect?

Liam: um... yes, or that would be more like laughing, and adults do that a lot, because, and really much more now than earlier, because now that I'm speaking so much and I'm using dialect so much, now it's getting to be very amusing of, look at the foreigner, he's speaking Asahi-*ben* [Asahi Dialect], foreigners aren't supposed to speak Japanese like that, so that's happening a lot, and it might also be that I'm speaking with a particularly heavy accent, I'm probably not sounding like a 25 year old Japanese man sounds like, I maybe sound like what a 25 year old fisherman shipbuilder sounds like, I maybe sound like what a 60-year-old old man sounds like, but my Japanese doesn't really match people's expectations, and then coupled with that, that I have an accent, I have an American accent when speaking Japanese which causes me to stress vowels and consonants in Japanese words more than a Japanese person would, so therefore my accent might sound even a bit more kind of silly, cuz it's not only a heavy accent but it's also a heavy accent thrown in with an American accent

Liam seemed to want to present L1 speakers' reactions in a less negative light than being 'made fun of'. Further, he explained that, over time, he came to use dialect more frequently and again referred to reactions of L1 speakers that showed their belief that foreigners are not expected to use dialect. By continuing to use dialect despite such comments, Liam seemed to enjoy the fact that his Japanese did not 'match people's expectations' of how a foreigner should sound. He also speculated about reasons for L1 speakers' reactions to his Japanese use other than his status as a foreigner. For example, he described his 'heavy accent' as being both an American accent and an accent that sounded like someone much older, and he acknowledged that these things may have made his speaking seem incongruent to L1 interlocutors. In addition, although he was in his early twenties, Liam recognized that his speech style may have been more appropriate for someone much older, or someone who worked as a fisherman rather than an English teacher. Regardless of L1 speakers' reactions to his Japanese, Liam continued to use dialect, clearly enjoyed doing so and seemed comfortable with how he spoke.

Liam's perceptions of local linguistic norms of dialect and his experiences of dialect use are complex. We may well wonder why Liam's enthusiasm for dialect did not dampen in response to comments he received from L1 speakers. Perhaps it was because, beyond viewing dialect as a local linguistic norm, Liam viewed it as a resource for self-expression, a way to get closer to achieving his ideal self and his ideal voice. Liam clearly enjoyed what he viewed to be the rough parts of dialect, as well as rough speech in general, and he was proud of his ability to use rough dialect and slang. Liam said that he was 'very good at the very bad, rough sounding Japanese'. In the next excerpt, Liam discussed his feelings about Asahi dialect and how he wanted to sound when speaking Japanese:

Jae: have you ever given thought to how you want to sound in Japanese

Liam: my goal for how I sound in Japanese would be how I sound in English, and when I speak English with friends I curse a lot, and I speak very frankly and am often very loud and bombastic, so my goal for Japanese where I would like to be and consider myself to have, say, perfected

> or feel like a fluent point, when I feel like I can speak in Japanese the same way I can speak in English and can be myself in Japanese the same way I can be myself in English ... which means being able to speak politely when I feel the need to and want to but also when I'm with friends, being able to comfortably curse.

This excerpt shows how Liam viewed both his desired voice in Japanese and also the local dialect. In addition to seeing dialect as a tool for self-expression, he also described his goal of being able to sound the same in Japanese as he did in English, which he described as 'loud and bombastic', and being able both to 'speak politely' and to 'comfortably curse'. These comments demonstrate how Liam used dialect to construct his ideal voice and identity in Japanese. Thus, Liam's decision to incorporate dialect into his linguistic repertoire was connected to his belief that dialect allowed him to express himself, and his feeling that dialect fit his desired voice and allowed him to create a Japanese language identity that was more like his English language identity. This may also explain why experiences that might otherwise have been discouraging did not dissuade him from continuing to use dialect.

Rejecting dialect

Some L2 participants took a negative stance toward Japanese Dialect. Daniel rejected dialect use and indicated that dialect had neither personal relevance nor benefit. Instead, Daniel prioritized Standard Japanese and especially polite language ability, which he saw as important for professional and personal interactions. He made frequent mention of the correctness and appropriateness of Standard Japanese during his interview and his desire to use correct and appropriate language played a significant role in his linguistic choices. Daniel's view of the importance of Standard Japanese also informed how he created his identity and voice in Japanese, and he saw no benefit to using dialect.

Daniel had studied Japanese throughout high school and he had lived in Japan for several months as part of a study abroad program. After high school, he took advantage of Japan's working holiday visa to live and work in different regions of Japan, including Kanto, Chubu and Kansai. He then returned to New Zealand for university and resumed formal Japanese language study. At the time of the study, Daniel was nearing the end of a three-year tenure as a JET Program assistant language teacher in Ehime; he had already secured post-JET employment and was planning to stay in Ehime after finishing his JET contract.

Daniel's experience working in a service industry position while on a working holiday was particularly influential. In this position, Daniel learned workplace Japanese, including differences in the language used with supervisors, coworkers and customers. Along with his L1-speaking coworkers, Daniel participated in weekly training sessions focused on proper greetings and proper pronunciation because he was required to master the polite greetings and honorific language used in service interactions. Daniel discussed these details as a way of accounting for his overall Japanese development as well as his ability and comfort level with honorific language and he conveyed pride in his language skills and in his 'unaccented' Japanese.

Daniel's experiences also meant that, unlike many L2 participants, he arrived in Ehime having already established an understanding of what kind of Japanese speaker he wanted to be. His comments below suggest that he focused on making appropriate speech style choices early in his language learning trajectory:

Daniel: when I first started working there [in the service industry job], there was a lot of dialects being thrown around and um, at first you know it was hard to tell which was the dialect, and which was, you know, normal Japanese, and yeah I was, at first I had to just check with people towards it, especially you know, after I got told off [by my boss for speaking too casually] I sort of thought, maybe I'm not supposed to be using dialects and that to my bosses

Similar to participants who referred to 'proper Japanese', Daniel described Standard Japanese as 'normal Japanese', and, after being scolded by his supervisor for speaking too casually, he concluded that he was 'not supposed' to use dialect in situations where casual speech should be avoided. Daniel had a long-term girlfriend, an L1-Japanese speaker, and he described being very close to her family. He explained that he spoke mostly Japanese with his girlfriend and Japanese only with her family. Although her family used dialect, Daniel said that he always used Standard Japanese with them, and he was careful to use only *desu/masu* or polite style with her parents. Daniel said that his girlfriend used dialect with him, but Daniel used only Standard Japanese with her, explaining that he preferred not to allow dialect to be 'mixed in' his speech.

Daniel planned to stay in Japan indefinitely and his goal was to become part of a professional community in Japan. Daniel was confident that his ability with Standard Japanese had played an important role in his success in securing a new position, and he believed that Standard Japanese and appropriate honorific language would continue to be important in his professional endeavors. Daniel contrasted his approach with an L2-speaking friend who used a lot of dialect. Daniel worried that using dialect would become a bad habit, saying 'if you start to use it and it sort of sticks, and then you can't stop using it'. Daniel believed that his friend's habit of using a lot of dialect, along with his inability to use *keigo*, would limit his friend's future employment opportunities in Japan.

Being able to control his speech style was important for Daniel and he paid close attention to how he spoke and with whom. Ability to use Standard Japanese and appropriate honorific language allowed him to cultivate an identity, a voice for himself that fit the image he wanted to project. His past experiences of living and working in other parts of Japan also influenced his valuation of Standard Japanese. Further, Daniel saw Standard Japanese as the best fit for his future goals of living and working in Japan.

Daniel's concern that dialect would become a bad habit was shared with many other L2 participants. Nina had been in Japan for nine years at the time of the interview, initially as a JET Program participant for three years in a small town in Ehime. After finishing the JET Program, Nina moved to the Kansai region and completed a graduate degree at a local university. Nina remained in the Kansai region and was pursuing a career in global business. Nina's career path set her apart from many participants who continued to teach English even after finishing their JET contracts. During the interview, Nina described some of her experiences in Ehime. She first learned about Japanese dialects while living in Ehime. Initially, Nina did not know which words or expressions were dialect and which were Standard Japanese. However, as her Japanese abilities progressed, she was gradually able to distinguish between standard and dialect. At the time of the interview, Nina had also become comfortable with the Kansai dialect, and she mentioned how famous and popular it is. However, when I asked Nina if she wanted to use Kansai dialect, she explained her goal, what she called her 'agenda', which was to achieve business-level Japanese proficiency and establish a successful professional career in Japan. She also shared that she had been encouraged to use dialect but chose not to do so.

Nina: last year, my friend and I were having a conversation and he was like, you should use more dialect, you should say this way, and I tend not to, consciously because, I think that, first of all, I'm not from here, so it's not what I learned, it's also not, it's not that it's not professional, but it definitely, Kansai people tend to use different words in different situations, and I'm sensitive to that and I find myself largely in the situations right now where it would be too casual or, it's so affected, so it's sort of like, it becomes the thing that I'm using it instead of what I'm saying. And I try to avoid all of those things, cuz right now, I have a different agenda. When I'm with my friends, it doesn't matter what I say, but I'm not spending much time with friends right now, so [it's] business level Japanese and get a job here

It is instructive to compare Nina's comments with Liam's, who focused on his interpersonal connections and friendships and fostering a self-identity that was not connected to any professional goals. Nina, on the other hand, was not worried about her friendships, in the sense that her friendships were established and were not going to be impacted by her linguistic choices. Instead, her focus was on her professional goals, which she felt would be impacted by her linguistic choices. Nina's comments show her desire to keep interactions focused on the topic and on what she said, rather than on *how* she said it.

When I asked Nina if dialect was important for L2 speakers, her answer suggested that dialect's relevance depended on one's trajectory in Japan, and where one was in terms of a timeline for 'living in Japan'.

Jae: do you think it's important for non-native speakers of Japanese to be able to understand dialect?

Nina: yes. I mean, if you want to understand what's being said around you, then it depends on their goal, it's spoken, and it can be quite different, but I don't know, there's an evolution of your life in Japan, where, at some point you want to get beyond the differences and you want to just live your life, and so, what happens is, I mean, I don't have these conversations where people try to teach me, in Kyoto we say this way and in Osaka, we say... I'm over that. I don't pretend to know everything, by any means, it's just not where I'm at, so I don't think about it as much anymore, except for when my friend had said that, and I realized that, no I probably won't talk that way because, if it's not sort of the way the NHK speaker is speaking on the news, then I probably shouldn't, you know

Jae: yeah, so is that a sort of a marker for you, NHK

Nina: yeah, I think if I have to model myself after something, right now, then yes

Nina saw Japanese Dialect as being important to understand what people were saying. However, she made it clear that in her own trajectory of living in Japan, she had moved past the stage where she needed linguistic differences explained to her; indeed, she was 'over that'. Nina concluded her comments by referring again to her goals and invoked the 'NHK speaker' as an ideal model of Standard Japanese, and the kind of Japanese that would be appropriate in professional settings.[2]

Like Nina, Scott also decided that he did not want to use the dialect he heard around him. Scott recognized dialect's role as a resource for L1 speakers, but he felt that dialect was inaccessible to him because of his status as a 'white foreigner'. At the time of the interview, Scott had been in Ehime for one year and was preparing to begin his second JET contract year. He participated in many community and public activities, including festivals and performances as well as numerous hobby and sports groups that met regularly. In some of these groups, Scott participated as a student or general member, in some other groups, he acted as an instructor and played a leadership role. Scott's many group activities may explain why he had a large circle of L1 friends who were close to his age.

Despite Scott's many local connections and activities, he did not use the local dialect at all. Nevertheless, he easily gave examples of well-known dialect words along with their Standard Japanese equivalents, demonstrating that his Japanese knowledge was sufficient to distinguish between standard and dialect and to recognize dialect in the speech of others.

Scott: I think I don't really want to learn it [dialect] very, I don't want to input that kind of accented Japanese and then later on, if I am trying to work in a job that uses Japanese to have that kind of very heavily accented country Japanese that I can't fix, and so I don't really try very hard to learn it, just so that I can understand what people are saying, but to use it myself, I'm not really too interested in it

Scott's reasons for rejecting dialect were clear: he saw Standard Japanese as the more appropriate speech style for workplace language use, and he regarded dialect as inappropriate and less correct. Scott shared the concern voiced by other L2 participants that dialect use would become a bad habit. He also described dialect as 'very heavily accented country Japanese', and implied that such language would require 'fixing', which would be difficult. In addition, by describing dialect as 'heavily accented country Japanese', Scott expressed a common stereotype of dialect as an undesirable accent that lacked sophistication.

In addition to disliking dialect and regarding Standard Japanese as more proper, Scott's ideas about his desired voice and how he wanted to sound also pointed him away from dialect use. At several points during the interview, Scott made comments that suggested the kinds of people who used dialect, namely, fishermen and older people. Interestingly, Scott's characterization was almost identical to Liam's; although Liam liked this way of speaking, Scott was clear that he did not.

When asked, Scott agreed that he had made a conscious decision to avoid dialect. I next asked if he thought dialect was important in Koyama:

Scott: it [is], with some people, but only a few people, and so, overall, not really ... yeah, I think the [sports] guys, that use it, I think, if I were to use it, it would kinda be like, ah! He's one of us! Type of feel, so for those relationships, yes, I think [dialect] is important, but the majority of the relationships in the workplace, and other places in Japan, and other places just around Koyama, I don't really think it's too important

Jae: so do you think it's important for you to be able to understand dialect? because you wanted to be able to understand your [sports] friends

Scott: yeah, I think it's important to understand, and it's interesting, you know? It's culture, so, yeah, I think it's important to understand it at least, maybe not speak it but to understand it

For Scott, dialect might be important with some people in limited contexts, such as members of the sports club he participated in. While he described dialect as having the potential to facilitate his relationships with club members, he also explained that in other communities, e.g. workplace communities or communities outside of Ehime, he did not think dialect was very important. Instead, he felt that for him and other L2 speakers in general, dialect comprehension was the most important skill. Scott also made reference to the cultural value and uniqueness of dialect, but he was careful to point out that *speaking* dialect was not important. I followed up by asking why he thought dialect use was unimportant. His reply demonstrated how his membership and identity concerns overlapped:

Scott: um, good question, well... I think, it's funny, being a white foreigner who lives in Japan, I will always be different, and I will always look different, and at some point, no matter what I do, or how good my Japanese is, I'm not going to be Japanese, and probably until I die, people will say *nihongo ga jōzu desu ne* ((your Japanese is very good))... which I'm sure you get, and ah... I don't know, I guess if I were able to assimilate into the culture fully and do things like speak the local dialect, and, feel like I'm one of the Japanese, it would be more important ... but because I don't see that happening in Japanese society, a foreigner fully being viewed as not a foreigner, I guess I don't really think it's too important

Scott referred to himself as a 'white foreigner' and explained his belief that, regardless of how advanced his Japanese was, his foreigner-ness and white-ness would always be a barrier to 'assimilating into the culture fully'. For himself and other foreigners, Scott had concluded that dialect was unimportant and of no benefit because dialect use would not mitigate his identity as a 'white foreigner'. He hinted that dialect might play a role *if* he could assimilate but dialect was not relevant because he felt he would always be seen as a foreigner in Japan. Ultimately, Scott felt that using dialect was pointless because it would not change his identity or improve his membership in Japanese society.

Scott's perception of his membership and identity as limited by his foreigner-ness is paradoxical: although Scott did not see himself as an insider, based on my observations, he appeared to be a core member and valued participant in numerous communities and groups. Scott had a large network of friends that included both other L2 speakers as well as numerous L1 speakers. In other words, his membership concerns, and the restriction he felt due to being a white foreigner, did not stem from being unsuccessful at participating in local communities. Nevertheless, Scott's connections and acceptance in the community did not mitigate his feeling that his status as a white foreigner could not be transcended. Scott's rejection of dialect was unequivocal.

Dialect ambivalence

Many L2 participants were confident in their decisions about whether to use dialect; however, some L2 participants struggled with this question. Branden expressed strong beliefs about the correctness of Standard Japanese and a preference to avoid dialect. However, he was also concerned that his decision to avoid dialect might have negative impacts on interpersonal relationships. Branden suspected that if he used dialect, it could play a positive role in strengthening those relationships. Consequently, Branden was ambivalent about dialect's place in his Japanese linguistic repertoire. Branden's preference for himself, as well as for his future professional plans, was to prioritize politeness and Standard Japanese. At the same time, he saw the potential for dialect to play a facilitative role in memberships and be beneficial for interpersonal relationships. Branden was similar to Scott in this regard, in that Scott also saw a possibility for dialect as a membership resource. However, Scott believed that being a foreigner outweighed any benefits of dialect use, whereas Branden wanted to avoid dialect because dialect did not fit his identity or voice. Branden struggled to reconcile these competing concerns.

At the time of the study, Branden lived near Liam, and they were friends. Branden was completing his first year in the JET Program and planning to stay for another year. When I asked how he learned about dialect, Branden talked about various experiences, including exposure to dialect through manga and anime as well as learning about it from L1 speakers. Branden also described his knowledge of the local dialect, and I asked if he used it himself:

Branden: sometimes, like *ya-ken* ((it's because, JD)) will, like, slip out, um but other than that I try and just stay with my, or, I think it's gone already, but stay to that standard dialect,
Jae: so you mentioned that *ya-ken* will just slip out, does that mean you try not to use it?
Branden: aaa, yeah, I think so, I think one thing is I know that that's me sort of absorbing influence from other people, and, so I think I have resistance to like that, *ya-ken*, that's not my voice

Branden characterized his use of dialect as unintentional, and he preferred Standard Japanese. He also explained that dialect phrases such as *ya-ken* did not fit with his image of his 'voice'. I asked more about how Branden envisioned his Japanese voice, and he said that he had conflicting views about Japanese and had a difficult time reconciling them. Branden described how he believed he *should* sound, that his voice in Japanese was based on his perception of 'what should come out naturally', and, he added, 'this is how I speak Japanese'. These comments were similar to participants who talked about wanting to speak Japanese naturally, for example, Liam's explanation of his dialect use, 'because that's how I speak Japanese'.

Branden was clear that dialect did not fit his voice and he had strong feelings about what constituted correct and appropriate Japanese, which reinforced his desire to avoid dialect. In the next excerpt, Branden described his experience with formal Japanese instruction before coming to Japan. He explained his preference for polite speech, and I asked him to tell me more:

Branden: I think it's partly how I was taught, we used [the textbook] JSL, you know, so you get that emphasis on, you know, using polite expressions, and that's sort of like the first Japanese that I was able to really use and really like call my own, is all those formal expressions, and so that is sort of what comes out first, and then, towards older adults, the same things that I do in English

Branden described the textbook he used in university, which emphasized politeness. His description of polite Japanese as the 'first Japanese I could call my own' conveys language ownership, as well. Branden also explained that he valued politeness and showing respect in English, and showing respect was something he felt 'the need to do'. Thus, we might imagine that Branden's view of his English as being polite carried over into a desire to have his Japanese speech also be polite. For Branden, notions of identity and what Japanese speech styles fit his voice were closely entwined with beliefs about politeness and formal expressions, which were the most familiar and perceived as the most correct.

If we only examined the above excerpts, we would conclude that Branden did not want to use dialect and we could see his stance as similar to participants who reject dialect. However, Branden also made comments that showed uncertainty about whether dialect non-use was the right choice. He shared a positive view of dialect as part of the Japanese repertoire when I asked if he thought there were any benefits or drawbacks to living in a dialect-using region:

Branden: so, a benefit [of dialect], I think if you pay attention, I think your sort of, language tapestry maybe has more colors to it, there's a lot more nuance that you'll hear, one, and then I think that that same sort of, I think with Standard Japanese you can take that like vagueness or that wishy-washy kind of feeling to like an extreme, and dialect, at least the ones that I've come into contact with, there's a lot less of that, and then maybe drawback? I think I'm pulled towards grabbing it but at the same time I want to distance myself away from getting that, getting the dialect, so I think if you're worried about sort of, you know, your Japanese, like absorbing it too much to the point to where maybe you can't separate it anymore or something, like if you're worried about that, then I think that would be a drawback

Branden described a 'language tapestry' with dialect as adding colors to that tapestry. His comments affirm that correctness or appropriateness are not the only qualities speakers consider when making choices about languages or speech styles. Another benefit, according to Branden, was that dialect is less 'vague or wishy-washy' than Standard Japanese and might be a better resource than Standard Japanese for straightforward communication. Finally, Branden described being pulled toward dialect while simultaneously wanting to distance himself from it and he echoed the concern that dialect use might lead to an inability to separate it from Standard Japanese.

Branden also acknowledged benefits that dialect could confer on speakers' relationships. Branden's ideas came partly from his observations of Liam and his perception that Liam's dialect use strengthened his membership in the local community and deepened relationships Liam had with L1 speakers. I also asked Branden if he thought dialect was important for L2 speakers in Ehime:

Branden: oh, I think it [dialect] is [important], I think it makes a big, huh. Maybe – ok, I think, maybe I'm contradicting my own actions towards this but, I think it does play a big part in your, sort of acceptance as a local inhabitant, I mean I think it's on that continuum with, can he speak Japanese, can he not speak Japanese, but then you get that level of, can he speak our Japanese, you know, and so I found like, when I hang out with Liam, like he gets respect from the Japanese people that we're with for using the dialect, you know, and – like, not respect like *me-ue* ((senior status)) kind of respect, but he gets that acknowledgement, I think, an extra bit of acknowledgement from using the Asahi-*ben* [Asahi Dialect]. And there's also like the, I mean I don't know how much of it is just Liam being Liam, but the way he speaks, I know it breaks down those sort of barriers, that, like for our supervisors and the rest of the people in the BOE ((Board of Education)), it breaks down the barriers that I sort of like, will be constructing in my own speech. I find myself yearning for the types of interactions that Liam has, and, yeah, I mean I've wondered too, how much of that is just a reflection of his situation. But yeah, I do find that he's got a lot of, from what I see, he has deeper connections with these same people than I do, and you know, I know a lot of it is his own cheerfulness, and talking, like, I mean, you know how he talks and I think you've seen how he interacts with people, I think there's that, and then, you know I do wonder like, oh, how much, you know if I changed my speech, would that have an effect on these relationships with people as well

Branden began by saying that dialect was important for L2 speakers in Ehime, but he quickly followed up by remarking that he was contradicting earlier comments about wanting to avoid dialect. Despite the contradictions he expressed, Branden described dialect as important and as playing a role in being accepted as a local inhabitant. Branden gave the example of a continuum of Japanese ability in which L2 speakers were judged not only according to whether they could speak Japanese, but also with regard to dialect ability, which L1 speakers viewed as 'our Japanese'. While similar to Scott's comments about dialect as an insider's code, Scott saw his foreigner status as a barrier to insider status, but Branden did not see such a barrier. In fact, Branden suggested that Liam benefitted directly from using dialect. Ultimately, Branden feared that the barrier was himself and his linguistic choices. Branden described Liam as getting 'respect and acknowledgement' from L1 speakers for using dialect and he saw Liam's way of speaking, in particular Liam's dialect use, as 'breaking down barriers'. Finally, Branden described his feelings about the kinds of interactions Liam had. Branden 'yearned' for those connections and he wondered whether changing his speech would have a positive effect on his own relationships.

What we see in Branden is the tension between his desire to avoid dialect use and his fear that he was suffering negative consequences by prioritizing how he wanted to sound over adopting the dialect in use around him. Branden's inability to reconcile these conflicting views resulted in ambivalence about whether to include dialect in his Japanese linguistic repertoire.

Melissa shared Branden's ambivalence about dialect, and she also struggled with mixed messages about dialect. She did not like having her speech scrutinized by L1 speakers, especially because she noticed that such scrutiny was not similarly directed at L1 speakers, even when they made linguistic choices similar to her own. Melissa, like Branden, was ambivalent about whether to use dialect but, unlike Branden, she held predominantly positive views about dialect, and she oriented toward dialect as a resource for self-expression and friendliness. In addition, her ambivalence toward dialect use was closely related to experiences she had when her dialect use became the focus of conversation. Melissa found comments about her use of dialect troublesome because it distracted from the topic of conversation and highlighted her status as a foreigner.

Melissa was completing her third year in Japan at the time of the interview. She contrasted her motivation for studying Japanese with both Daniel, a friend, and Scott, a friend and coworker. When I asked Melissa about the local dialect, she explained that she was only learning Japanese as a hobby and, as such, she felt that dialect use was 'perfectly acceptable'. She also liked the idea that learning the local dialect was special because it could only be learned by going to that place. I asked if she heard dialect a lot?

Melissa: I'm definitely conscious of it. And I love it, I think it's really fun. And I love to learn new little bits, I don't know why, there's something about learning a dialect which is… it holds a lot more interest for me rather than just learning the textbook Japanese because it's something I can only learn, when you're in a certain place, you can only learn it when you're in that place, and so it's unique and I suppose, then, more special

Dialect offered Melissa a way to display her connection to the place where she lived in Japan, and her comments show how important having that unique, special connection was to her. Melissa shared her enthusiasm, explaining that she 'loved' dialect, it was 'really fun', and was more interesting than 'textbook Japanese'. Melissa's enthusiasm can be seen in her use of affective language to describe dialect, which contrasted with her depiction of 'textbook Japanese'. Dialect appealed to Melissa because it connected her to the local area and dialect's uniqueness seems to be a resource both for self-expression and for displaying her connection to and, by extension, membership in that place.

In addition to describing dialect as unique, Melissa also described positive things an L1 speaker told her about the benefits of using dialect:

Melissa: I think [dialect] is of interest to know, and it's fun to know, and sometimes it can help you feel a little bit closer to the people, in fact that's what [my coworker] told me one time, when I asked about Koyama-*ben* [Koyama Dialect], and they said to me, if you speak some Koyama-*ben* people will be happy that you are wanting to know about their culture and it will help you feel more like a friend to them, if you use it

Thus, Melissa was encouraged to use dialect because doing so would display friendliness and interest in the local culture. Melissa also shared advice she received from L1 speakers about specific dialect words:

Melissa: one of my [coworkers] had said at one point, when I was talking about dialect, I think I came with a word which I wasn't sure of and it turned out to be a word from, maybe it was *hiyai* ((cold, JD)), I wanted to know what *hiyai* meant, and they said, oh, and I said, should I use it, because I've been, I'll just double-check with these words, and they're like definitely, definitely use it, because it'll make it easier to communicate with the kids because it will feel more friendly, and she said those exact words to me

In addition to being an account of L1 beliefs, Melissa's description of being aware of a dialect word and seeking out the opinion of L1 speakers about whether to use it herself, shows her desire to make informed choices about her language use, as well as the importance she placed on receiving advice from L1 speakers. Together, these two excerpts from my interviews with Melissa show how dialect's benefits were perceived by some L1 speakers, and also that some L1 speakers felt that Melissa should take advantage of those benefits by using dialect herself.

Melissa showed a similar commitment to making intentional linguistic choices in terms of actively avoiding what she felt was feminine or 'cutesy' speech, as discussed in Chapter 4. Although she reported that she did not want to use 'girly girl talk', Melissa explained that using dialect would be fine and was not at odds with other qualities she favored, including being relatable, approachable and respectful. Melissa had a positive affective response to dialect as a resource for both membership and identity. However, Melissa also had reservations about dialect use and wondered whether it might be better to avoid using it. Her concerns resulted both from conflicting advice from L1 speakers who advised her not to use dialect, and also from the reactions of some L1 interlocutors when she used dialect.

Melissa: so in a way [dialect is] kind of like a fun thing I think and also, I dunno, [dialect] helps you connect to the people here, but then sometimes [other] teachers will be like Melissa-*sensei* ((teacher)) that's not so cute, you should say it like this. And so yeah it's balancing it, I think it might have been like I was talking about something and I said *shittoru* ((I know, JD)), it was like a one-on-one class ... and she [the teacher] said oh you should say *shitteiru shitteiru* ((I know, SJ)) it's more cute for you Melissa

Melissa was told that dialect was 'not so cute' for her and to use Standard Japanese instead. It should be noted here that the dialect form *toru* which is used for the present progressive tense (SJ: *te-iru*) is not considered masculine *per se* and is regularly used by both male and female dialect speakers. It may be the case that this L1 speaker was influenced by stereotypes about how Western women should sound when they speak Japanese. It is somewhat paradoxical that, although Melissa described not wanting to sound 'cutesy', she received advice from an L1 speaker that she should use Standard Japanese *because* it was cuter than dialect. Because Melissa valued the input of L1 speakers, she found such advice confusing.

In addition to conflicting advice about dialect, Melissa described some experiences in which her dialect use triggered unwanted reactions from L1 speakers. I asked whether Melissa thought dialect was easy or difficult:

Melissa: it is what it is ... but I can talk to somebody and ask them, and there's plenty of people to ask, and it's a fun thing to talk about with the kids, the kids love it when you speak a bit of Koyama-*ben* [Koyama Dialect]. You can't really continue too much of a conversation if you've just spoken Koyama-*ben* because the entire time they'd be like wahhhhhh ((exclaiming surprise))

Melissa began by saying that dialect 'is what it is' without directly addressing the question of difficulty, but she indicated that she actively sought advice from L1 speakers if she needed help with a dialect phrase. Melissa also described dialect as fun to use with schoolchildren because they loved it. Melissa's experience with both adults and children suggests her dialect use was perceived as unusual or unexpected and she felt that their surprised reactions detracted from the conversation. Melissa elaborated in the next excerpt:

Melissa: sometimes just for fun, or if I know a word or something like that, I'll use it [dialect], but often if I use it, because I'm not using it all the time, it's then seen as a novelty, which then diverts from the conversation we're having into, oh wow you're speaking Koyama-*ben*, and so if I want to just be having a conversation about something, I can't really use it because it just, you know, branches off

Although earlier excerpts suggest that Melissa saw dialect as a resource for membership, when her dialect use was perceived as surprising or unusual, it had a negative impact on the interaction. For Melissa, L1 reactions to her dialect use became a reason to avoid using dialect. Melissa explained more about why her dialect use was treated as novelty:

Melissa: I feel like, if you're a Japanese person and you've got like, I don't know, your speech has a certain type of character, because you're Japanese, the emphasis is still on the words, but when you're foreign, people are quite interested in how you speak Japanese, and so as soon as you kind of deviate from what's considered standard or normal Japanese, all of a sudden, the focus isn't on your words anymore but on how you're speaking it. And that's fun with kids or people sometimes, but if you're just in everyday communication, if I just want to communicate a point, it's easier to stick with the standard

Melissa explained that a Japanese person's use of different speech styles did not detract from the conversation at hand *because* the speaker was

Japanese. But Japanese people were 'quite interested' in how foreigners speak, and Melissa felt she could not deviate from Standard Japanese by using dialect, because if she did, the focus would become how she was speaking. Thus, she had decided that, while dialect use might be fun 'sometimes', communication was more effective when she used Standard Japanese. Melissa's experiences with dialect demonstrate how L2 speakers may be judged by different criteria from L1 speakers, which gave them fewer linguistic resources than L1 speakers.

Discussion

The interview excerpts examined in this chapter demonstrate the diversity of beliefs that L1 and L2 participants had with regard to dialect and its use by L2 speakers. Most L1 participants expressed positive feelings about dialect, describing it as warm and nostalgic. Most reported using dialect and many saw it as a useful tool for strengthening interpersonal relationships. There was also broad agreement among L1 participants that dialect cannot be used just anytime or with just anyone and, instead, speakers should make distinctions about when and with whom to speak dialect. L1 participants agreed that L2 speakers should be encouraged to understand dialect but there was little expectation that L2 speakers would use dialect. However, for those L2 speakers who did use dialect, there was a general expectation that L1 speakers would be pleased.

L2 participants' beliefs and perspectives were much more complicated and nuanced. Similar to the L1 participants, the L2 participants felt that being able to understand the local dialect was important for L2 speakers in Japan, but there was less agreement about whether L2 speakers should use dialect. Some L2 participants enthusiastically incorporated dialect into their Japanese language repertoire. These participants regarded dialect as a way to fit into the local community and a means to escape the role of perpetual foreigner. L2 participants also described dialect use as a natural result of hearing it. In addition, some L2 participants found that dialect use permitted them to express their personalities and identities as speakers of Japanese.

There were also L2 participants who rejected or resisted dialect. These participants often focused on their professional goals as reasons for avoiding dialect use. They shared a common concern that using dialect would become a bad habit and make it harder to control their use of Standard Japanese. In addition, one L2 participant felt that using dialect was not relevant for a 'white foreigner' who would always be seen as not Japanese. Finally, some L2 participants struggled with how to approach dialect use. One participant was concerned that dialect did not match his sense of his own voice. Another concern was that, when an L2 speaker used dialect, it had the paradoxical effect of shifting attention away from the topic at hand and onto their foreigner status.

Conclusion

The studies reviewed at the beginning of this chapter, along with the findings from L1 participants, underscore the ways that dialect can function as a resource within the larger Japanese language repertoire. Using dialect allows speakers to display warmth and fondness for hometown and express aspects of their identity differently than can be done in Standard Japanese. Some L2 participants recognized this aspect of Japanese Dialect and desired to incorporate it into their own linguistic repertoires. However, the experiences of L2 participants show that L2 speakers are constrained in ways that L1 speakers are not. Indeed, L2 participants' experiences suggest that dialect is not as available for use by L2 speakers in the way that it is available to L1 speakers. When L2 participants received unwanted attention because of dialect use or were told explicitly that their language use did not fit their foreigner-ness, it sent the message that dialect was off-limits to them. And when an L2 participant's dialect use attracted attention, it highlighted the ways in which L2 speakers are vulnerable to comment and sometimes even censure by L1 speakers.

Many of the L2 participants saw dialect as an important part of Japanese language and recognized its usefulness as a resource for identity and community membership. However, dialect presented them with a paradox, in that they were forced to choose between using it and risking unwanted attention, or not using it and risking lost opportunities for strengthening connections to L1 speakers. Thus, dialect presents an example of how L2 speakers lack speaker legitimacy and are unable to take ownership of the Japanese language they use.

Notes

(1) Okamoto (2008b) argues that neither *tsukaiwake* nor 'code-switching' is an accurate way to describe speakers' practices when using Standard Japanese and Japanese Dialect in the same conversation, because standard and dialect are not treated as discrete codes. At the same time, Okamoto and Shibamoto-Smith (2016: 55) observe that 'at the level of language norms and awareness, [standard and dialect] tend to be understood as two separate categories'. And indeed, participants in my study often used the term *tsukaiwake* to describe their own practices of using both standard and dialect when speaking Japanese. For this reason, while I recognize that the term code-switching has limitations, I use it as the closest English approximation to *tsukaiwake*.
(2) NHK is the government-owned public broadcasting company in Japan. NHK newscasters are often presented as ideal models for spoken Japanese.

6 'His Japanese Makes No Sense'

Introduction

Researchers have long advocated rejection of the practice of measuring second language (L2) competence against biased and idealized conceptions of 'native speakers' (e.g. Cook, 1999; Firth & Wagner, 1997; Rampton, 1990). More recent research highlights the impacts of native speaker bias on non-native speaker teachers of Japanese (Nomura & Mochizuki, 2018). However, these discussions remain limited to research settings and educational contexts and whether L2 speakers in target language contexts benefit from such advocacy is an open question. Findings introduced in Chapters 3–5 demonstrate ways that first language (L1)-Japanese speakers viewed L2 speakers' use of Japanese speech styles. Although some L1 speakers may encourage L2 speakers to use these speech styles, often the message to L2 speakers emphasizes that they can get by with Standard Japanese because using the full range of speech styles is beyond them. There are various reasons underlying L1 speakers' beliefs and opinions about how L2 speakers should speak, but often native speaker bias plays a key role. In this chapter, I review findings that show how native speaker bias emerges in L1 speakers' depictions of L2 speakers' Japanese competence, with particular attention to how L1-Japanese speakers display their beliefs and how those beliefs impact L2 speakers. I also consider how language ideologies manifest into language ownership and how claims of language ownership are used when L1 speakers judge L2 competence. As discussion in this chapter will demonstrate, ideologies of native speaker bias have negative impacts on L2 speaker legitimacy.

This chapter begins with an introduction to research about language ideologies of correctness and their impact on L2 speakers. Next, ideologies of Japanese language are reconsidered, along with the ways that these ideologies feature in displays of language ownership. I also pay specific attention to beliefs about the difficulty and uniqueness of the Japanese language. I conclude the literature review with a consideration of ideologies of Japanese language's uniqueness, which tie into a popular notion that competent L2-Japanese speakers are 'more Japanese than the Japanese'.

Against this backdrop, I introduce findings from this study that highlight participants' experiences with L1 depictions of L2-Japanese language use. I also introduce two participants with whom I conducted multiple interviews and observations: Peter, an L2-Japanese speaker with advanced competency, and Kazuki, his L1-Japanese husband. In addition to semi-structured interviews conducted separately with each spouse, I conducted participant observations with them together and apart, and those observations informed my understanding of the dynamics at play. I detail how Kazuki's stance toward Peter's Japanese is simultaneously supportive and othering; although Kazuki recognizes Peter's Japanese competence, Kazuki nevertheless denies Peter's speaker legitimacy. My analysis demonstrates how beliefs about language ownership and speaker legitimacy emerge at the level of individual speakers. Specifically, L1 speakers' beliefs about language ownership and speaker legitimacy become visible in their depictions of L2 competence, depictions which in effect reject L2 speakers as legitimate speakers of Japanese.

Previous Studies of Native Speaker Bias

Native speaker bias is often described as depicting the 'native speaker' as an idealized, perfect speaker, someone who speaks the standard, prestige variety of the language. Such depictions overlook the diversity and variation that are found from one so-called native speaker to another (e.g. Davies, 2003, 2007; Holliday, 2008; Rampton, 1990). Ideological notions of the native speaker are criticized for 'conflating linguistic and non-linguistic features' (Liddicoat, 2016: 410), which are based on race, ethnicity and nationality rather than on linguistic output (e.g. Higgins, 2003; Holliday, 2018; Pennycook, 2012). When the native speaker is posited as an ideal, perfect speaker, the non-native speaker is correspondingly depicted as a deficient communicator, a notion that has been repeatedly criticized and rejected by researchers in L2 acquisition (e.g. Cook, 1999, 2016; Davies, 2003; Doerr, 2009a; Firth & Wagner, 1997, 2007; Holliday, 2006, 2018; Rampton, 1990). The presumed deficiency of the non-native speaker is further highlighted when native speaker competence is used as the criteria against which L2 learners are judged and evaluated. Examples of this include assessment standards such as the American Council on the Teaching of Foreign Languages (ACTFL) Proficiency Guidelines (ACTFL, 2012; also cf. Doerr & Kumagai, 2009). Another example can be seen in instructional materials for English as a second language (ESL) in which Western and often white characters are put forth as the ideal toward which L2-English learners should aspire (e.g. the American Headway textbook series, Soars & Soars, 2001). Doerr (2009b) describes how instruction in an ESL classroom focused on pronunciation in ways that reinforced stereotypes of correct and incorrect pronunciation and gave L2-English learners the message that their pronunciation will always be subject to the judgment of others. As a result, learners believed their pronunciation was inherently deficient and must be corrected by a 'native speaker'. Another effect of overemphasis on meeting an idealized native speaker standard is that it shifts attention away from communication and toward students' identities as non-native speakers.

Alternative approaches for evaluating linguistic ability and affirming L2 speaker identity have been proposed as a way to avoid idealizing speaking like a native speaker. For example, Rampton (1990) suggests shifting the focus from native speaker/non-native speaker to emphasizing a speaker's connection to the language, connections he called expertise, affiliation and inheritance. Rampton argues that language competence and proficiency would be more accurately conveyed by replacing the term 'native speaker' with 'expert speaker'. Rampton (1990: 99) also proposes the terms 'language affiliation' and 'language inheritance' to express the different ways that language also functions 'as a symbol of social group identification'. Rampton argues that these terms make it possible to describe the different ways that language connects people, while avoiding the problematic association of the term 'native speaker'.

Other researchers concur with Rampton's position about changing how speakers and speaking ability are characterized. With regard to a speaker's linguistic competence, Cook (1999: 195) argues that L2 speakers should be viewed not as 'imitation native speakers' but as legitimate speakers regardless of their competence. Davies (2003) advocates for evaluating a speaker's communicative competence. Recommendations by Rampton, Cook and Davies have been well received in some circles; for example, academic conferences have problematized issues related to native speak bias. However, both Doerr (2009a) and Lowe and Pinner (2016) point out that, outside of recommendations by scholars and researchers, normative assumptions about native speakers are still common in the daily lives of teachers, learners and L2 speakers.

The pervasiveness of native speaker bias may be due in part to its origins in taken-for-granted ideologies about languages and speakers, ideologies which are so deeply embedded in popular understandings of language that they rarely rise to the level of consciousness (cf. Heinrich, 2012). Among the research and studies that examine the ideological underpinnings of native speaker bias, two findings have particular relevance for my research. First, it has been argued that native speaker bias assumes a connection between citizenship and native speaker status (e.g. Doerr, 2009a; Pennycook, 1994), with a corresponding link between ethnicity and native speaker status (e.g. Okubo, 2009). Second, native speaker discourse implies that language is homogeneous and fixed and recognizes only one standard, correct version of the language (Doerr, 2009a; Pennycook, 1994).

Although most research on native speaker bias focuses on L2-English speakers, researchers have also examined language ideologies and native speaker bias with regard to Japanese. Of particular interest is Doerr's (2009a) edited volume, which brings together ethnographic studies conducted in heretofore understudied contexts, including Japanese language learners using Japanese in internet activities (Sato, 2009), public schools in Japan (Okubo, 2009; Takato, 2009), a comparison of standardization processes in Japanese and English (Doerr, 2009a) and hiring practices for Japanese language programs in the United States (Kubota, 2009). I introduce three of these studies below.

Sato (2009) uses an ethnographic case study of a Japanese language learner, 'Yan', to analyze L2-Japanese language use in a Japanese blog project. Sato (2009: 283) focuses on Yan's construction of a textual identity and analyzes 'how texts are composed and used to represent identity in CMC [computer-meditated communication]'. Sato argues that Yan's identity as a 'non-native speaker' was only one of the identities he negotiated online, and other identities, for example, blog writer, became more salient as Yan actively engaged in online interactions. Sato finds that Yan's non-native speaker status was rarely foregrounded and, crucially, blog readers did not treat Yan as a foreign language learner. Examining Yan's online activities in terms of traditional foreign language teaching, Sato (2009: 291) problematizes the idea of 'smooth communication' as a goal, arguing that instead of stressing the value of 'correct, appropriate and accurate' language use, teachers should attend more closely to how well learners accomplish interactional tasks. Sato (2009: 277) also advocates for treating 'foreign language learners as creative designers as well as agents of "meaningful" communication', for which online activities are particularly well-suited. Sato (2009: 291) suggests a new way of conceptualizing foreign language learners, one that recognizes that they 'are not only consumers of linguistic and cultural knowledge but are also the producers of linguistic and cultural knowledge'. Sato's work offers important examples of ways to acknowledge and validate L2 learners as first and foremost language users and producers, rather than as passive consumers.

Using ethnographic observation and interviews, Takato (2009) examines the practices in a public elementary school in Japan that was attempting to meet the linguistic needs of children labeled as 'non-native speakers of Japanese'. To accomplish this goal, the school implemented special classes and extracurricular activities for this group of students. Included in the group were children whose families were reverse migrants of Japanese descent, who came to Japan from Latin America. The group also included Japan-born Korean nationals who were ineligible for Japanese nationality. The children's complex linguistic and familial backgrounds meant that some children had been born and raised in Japan and spoke Japanese as their L1, but they were not Japanese citizens. Conversely, children whose families were reverse immigrants did not speak Japanese as their L1, but these children were citizens, i.e. Japanese nationals. Students' diverse backgrounds were made invisible by official discourse and school policy that linked language competence to nationality. Takato (2009: 91) reports that 'any Japanese national was assumed to be fluent in Japanese while any foreign national was [assumed to be] not fluent in the language', despite the fact that 'often there was no match between the students' nationality and language fluency'. An additional concern was the fact that the children's spoken fluency in Japanese often did not correspond to their Japanese reading ability. However, because the official policy did not adequately account for the children's linguistic diversity, the school was not equipped to meet the children's linguistic and educational needs, and discrepancies between spoken fluency and literacy went unnoticed. The programs implemented by the school were based on highly limited conceptualizations of native speaker/non-native speaker competence. In addition to these challenges experienced by the children, many of their parents or grandparents who had migrated from Japan to Latin America were from Okinawa and spoke Okinawan. Children of migrant families had grown up being told they were speaking 'Japanese', not realizing there were significant differences between Standard Japanese and the Okinawan spoken in their homes. It was only after they migrated to Japan that they discovered the language of their childhood was Okinawan-Japanese. Japan's school-based program for non-native speakers of Japanese is an example of how the official discourse of 'one nation, one language' (Doerr, 2009a: 81) informed everyday beliefs about language and resulted in linguistic struggles, especially when transnational migrants settled in areas of Japan different from those their parents or grandparents had left years ago. Takato's (2009) study reveals how linguistic ideologies that equate native speakerhood, nationality and a homogenized standard language fail to account for the linguistic diversity within families of reverse migrants.

Similar to Takato's (2009) school-based research, Okubo (2009) examines after-school Japanese language programs in a public school in Japan which attempted to incorporate US-style multicultural educational programming. She finds that children there were taught Japanese as a second language (JSL) 'based on the fact that their parents [were] not Japanese, despite the children's fluency in the Japanese language' (Okubo, 2009: 101). Okubo observes that there is a tendency in Japan to connect native speaker status to both Japanese ethnicity and citizenship. These preconceptions resulted in the program's failure to take account of the children's language ability or inability. Okubo (2009: 102) describes various activities that resulted in positioning children in the program as 'cultural others' and served to 'reproduc[e] the ethnicized "native speaker" concept in Japan' (Okubo, 2009: 109). As a result, some children were denied opportunities to express their hybrid identities as Japanese speakers who were not ethnically Japanese.

In their review of the studies introduced above, along with the other studies included in the Doerr (2009b) volume, Doerr and Kumagai (2009) highlight the important pedagogical implications from the findings of such studies. In particular, they argue that teachers should not aim to prepare their students to 'join the "imagined" target community of "native speakers"' (Doerr & Kumagai, 2009: 305). Rather, teachers should focus on developing students' understandings of linguistic diversity and should encourage them to critically evaluate the possible consequences of various linguistic choices available to them.

The research discussed above shares a common focus on participants who are either language teachers or learners in instructional settings. Few studies focus on non-instructional contexts and L2 speakers as language *users* rather than language *learners*. As noted previously, how native speaker bias manifests in languages other than English remains understudied. As a result, numerous questions remain, especially with regard to native speaker bias that persists in unexamined, taken-for-granted understandings held by speakers in settings that are not educational contexts in which such biases might be called into question. Further, while applied linguists may agree that joining an 'imagined target community' need not be a goal for all foreign language learners, many L2 speakers find themselves in communities where native speaker ideologies are taken for granted and conveyed as unproblematic truths.

Language ownership: More Japanese than the Japanese?

One way that native speaker bias emerges in interactions occurs when language ownership is treated as available only to L1 speakers. Language ownership refers not only to a speaker's right to use a language, but also includes such concerns as control over how the language is used (Wee, 2002). Similar to research about native speaker bias, language ownership has most often been studied with regard to L2 English, including English as a lingua franca and World Englishes, and researchers find that ownership of English has grown far beyond traditional 'native speakers', particularly in the context of an increasingly globalized world (e.g. Norton, 1997; Wee, 2002; Widdowson, 1994). Wee (2002) has argued that English is owned by all those who speak it. Researchers' assertions about ownership notwithstanding, native speaker bias persists and is so ubiquitous that sometimes L2 speakers regard themselves as not owning their L2, as Parmegiani (2014) finds. At the same time, Parmegiani (2014: 691) describes other L2-English speakers who treated English as 'everybody's language', presenting a model for how an L2 can be owned by any speaker of that language, including those who speak it as a second or 'non-native' language. As these studies attest, research about L2 speakers finds diverse sentiments and opinions about who can claim ownership of a language, with such sentiments ranging from denial of language ownership by L1 speakers to L2 speakers who deny themselves language ownership and, on the other hand, to L2 speakers who treat English as a language that can be owned by all who speak it.

With regard to Japanese, Burgess (2012) looks at historical as well as contemporary features of Japanese society and culture that inform attitudes and beliefs about L2-Japanese speakers. Burgess (2012) argues that ideologies that posit connections between the Japanese language and 'Japanese-ness' have negative impacts on migrants and L2 speakers in Japan. Although Burgess does not use the term 'language ownership', his work demonstrates some of the ways that ideologies of language ownership emerge with regard to Japanese. For example, Burgess (2012: 37) criticizes the tendency to view the Japanese language as 'for Japanese only', pointing out connections between Japan's reluctance to be accepting of foreign workers and ways that attitudes toward foreigners are based on a sense of exclusive ownership of the Japanese language. Burgess also points to popular beliefs that non-Japanese are unable to become fluent in Japanese; such beliefs are often reinforced in *nihonjinron* works. Burgess explains that such beliefs can also be seen in attitudes of exclusionism directed at migrants, migration and foreigners more generally. Burgess argues that connections between beliefs about language and exclusionism are particularly important since language plays a crucial role in being able to participate in local communities.

With regard to contemporary spoken Japanese, Burgess (2012) discusses *kokusaika*, Japan's push to internationalize, and argues that Japan's aim in promoting internationalization is not concerned with integrating foreigners into Japan, but rather is more interested in how Japan is perceived abroad. It is within this broader historical and contemporary context, Burgess (2012: 45–46) argues, that Japanese language education should be understood, because language instruction for non-native Japanese speakers has been 'less about "opening up" the country—accepting and integrating migrants—than about maintaining boundaries'. Burgess further criticizes JSL and Japanese as a foreign language (JFL) education for being more concerned with Japanese learners abroad than those living in Japan. According to Burgess (2012: 46), JFL/JSL is focused on imparting 'an ideological worldview that is at base homogeneous, conservative, and closed'.

Burgess also calls into question the aims of *yasashii nihongo* (discussed in Chapter 1). Certainly, it is easy to agree that emergency information should be made linguistically accessible. However, as Burgess (2012: 46) and others have argued, the *yasashii nihongo* movement further promotes the belief that Japanese is too difficult for foreigners and this belief creates and reinforces beliefs that foreigners 'should not understand Japanese'. Burgess observes that L2 speakers are more likely to study and learn the L2 when they are welcomed into the local community. Conversely, when they are not welcomed, and when linguistic ideologies promote the belief that 'foreigners cannot learn Japanese', the effect is doubly negative: not only does L2 speakers' motivation decrease, but L2 speakers are also denied opportunities to learn and use the language. Consequently, under these conditions, Burgess (2012) argues, L2-Japanese speakers' use of 'broken Japanese' is perceived as both acceptable and expected.

Burgess presents powerful arguments about how ideologies contribute to reinforcing and maintaining an exclusionary stance toward foreigners. As he observes, Japanese language ability, which would otherwise be a resource for integration, is paradoxically an additional tool for the perpetuation of the othering of L2-Japanese speakers. Burgess (2012: 52) concludes that 'the Japanese language remains more of an obstacle than a pathway to citizenship: a barrier to being accepted as a member—a citizen—of Japanese society with the full range of rights and obligations that status implies'.

Burgess's research focuses on the sources of ideologies that portray foreigners as outsiders. Other researchers focus on specific groups of foreign nationals living in Japan. Carlson (2018) questions what it's like to be a foreigner in Japan and she looks at the experiences of Americans who lived and worked in Japan and were fans of Japanese pop culture. She considers what it means to be a 'foreigner' in Japan, taking a critical look at how her American participants experienced othering. Many of Carlson's (2018: 6) participants reported that they 'dreamed of being accepted as a native in Japan', but they also believed that such acceptance was impossible. Carlson reports that her American participants were continually reminded of their status as others, outsiders, as seen in the tendency for L2-Japanese speakers to be told '*nihongo ga jōzu*' (their Japanese skills are good) or that they are 'more Japanese than a Japanese person'. Carlson explains that her participants did not like receiving such compliments because it was a continual reminder of the assumption that foreigners cannot speak Japanese. I have reported on the frequency of such interactions (Takeuchi, 2020a), and a search online reveals numerous online blogs and YouTube videos in which L2-Japanese speakers describe their experiences of being on the receiving end of such comments (e.g. O'Donnell, 2016). Carlson (2018) discusses the frustration such comments can cause, particularly because they underscore how often L2 speakers feel excluded and othered in Japan. Carlson's findings, along with studies described above by Burgess, provide evidence of *nihonjin-ron*-style beliefs that only 'Japanese people' can master the Japanese language, and only 'Japanese people' can truly understand Japanese culture.

Another important issue Carlson raises is the situation of English speakers who come to Japan to teach English. Through the JET

Program, the Japanese government recruits English teachers from English-speaking countries. However, there are no provisions for JET Program participants to transition into long-term employment after their JET Program contracts are complete. Many JET Program participants acquire advanced Japanese proficiency, and because of their experience as assistant English teachers, JET participants could become a resource for teaching English or could serve as bilingual workers in various fields. However, the assumption is that L2 speakers are only temporary residents of Japan, a belief, Carlson points out, that television shows and other media products reinforce with their regular presentation of 'foreigners in Japan' as primarily tourists and short-term residents. Carlson (2018: 189) explains that such media depictions present 'a consumable Western, always white, foreigner who is non-threatening but misguided, interested in cliché Japanese traditions, and most importantly, just visiting'. As a result, Carlson (2018: 222) argues, for many foreigners in Japan 'their non-Japanese status is fixed', and she notes that the physical appearance of non-Asian foreigners in Japan 'marks them persistently, in every new encounter, as both non-speakers and non-citizens' (Carlson, 2018: 223) such that ultimately, being a foreigner in Japan is to be excluded, othered.

Study Participants and Depictions of L2 Speakers

The studies introduced above are suggestive of ways that language ideologies can impact L2 speakers. In previous chapters, I demonstrated how L2 speakers' choices about the use of *keigo*, Japanese gendered language and dialect point to ideologies about Japanese and L2 speakers that both L1 and L2 speakers expressed in their interviews. In the following discussion, I foreground L1 participants' depictions and evaluations of L2 speakers' language use more generally, and consider how L2 participants respond to L1 observations. Both L1 and L2 participants express beliefs and opinions, sometimes explicit, but more often implicit, that convey native speaker bias, which was also common in interactions between L1- and L2-Japanese speakers.

The excerpts introduced below come from portions of the interview protocol which sought to elicit comments about the participants' beliefs about Japanese language in general, their beliefs about Japanese language as it relates to L2 speakers and their experiences using Japanese in L1/L2 interactions. Topics addressed in the protocol include (1) beliefs and opinions about Japanese language, (2) experiences studying languages, (3) linguistic daily life and habits, (4) experiences working or socializing in L1/L2 contexts, (5) experiences of language-related troubles and (6) opinions about what kinds of Japanese skills L2 speakers need. Follow-up questions were based on participants' comments and on the stories and opinions they shared with me.

Like a native speaker?

David and Megumi

Many L2 participants shared their experiences of how L1 speakers reacted to their Japanese language use. For example, participants described being told their Japanese was '*jōzu*' (skillful or excellent) after only saying a simple greeting. Others reported being told that their Japanese language or their Japanese manners were better than those of a Japanese person. It seems common for L1 speakers to draw on native speaker stereotypes in both assessments and compliments of L2 speakers' Japanese use, as seen in a portion of the recording where David, Megumi and I were casually chatting together. I asked them whether they used Japanese or English when speaking to each other. Megumi said they mostly used Japanese, but David said they tended to use 'half and half'. This portion of the recording was in English, with the exception of Megumi saying *hontō* (really), as seen here:

Jae:	do you speak English together, Japanese, a mix?
David:	both
Megumi:	no, mostly Japanese
David:	I don't know, half and half
Megumi:	no no no, mostly Japanese
David:	(that's not)
Megumi:	because my English level is much lower than his Japanese. His Japanese like a native level
David:	no, no no
Megumi:	when we, if I talk on the phone, we cannot tell if he's native Japanese or not
David:	That's, that's not true ((Jae laughs))
Megumi:	*hontō*, *hontō* ((it's true, it's true))
David:	no, this is not true
Megumi:	I was [((overlap, inaudible))] I was saying that Takeuchi-san and you are seriously native Japanese level
David:	(shaking his head) nah...

At this point, the topic shifted to another L2 speaker's speech habits, and later Megumi added that she modulated her Japanese language use with other L2 speakers, but she did not do that with David. Several points can be made here. First, this kind of exchange is almost canonical, in that most L2 speakers in Japan have experienced similar interactions, in which an L1 speaker uses the 'native speaker' as the benchmark for Japanese linguistic and cultural competence, and then L2 speakers reject the compliment, drawing on Japanese cultural norms of self-deprecation. In the exchange above, Megumi downplays her ability as an English speaker and praises two L2 speakers' Japanese ability (both David's and mine). In response, David is self-deprecating and explicitly downplays his Japanese and implicitly compliments Megumi's English. Secondly, Megumi deploys the native speaker benchmark, and refers to the anonymity of talking on the phone, suggesting that 'when we can't see your non-Japanese face, you can pass for a Japanese person', with the additional implication that passing for a Japanese person is a compliment.

James

When I asked James if he had given any thought to how he wanted to sound in Japanese, he talked about the many Japanese people who had influenced his Japanese. His comments are notable because they are suggestive of the restrictive influence L1 speakers had on his Japanese use in the past:

Jae: have you ever given any thought to how you want to sound in Japanese?

James: yeah definitely. At first, you're just struggling to make yourself understood. … I always say my Japanese is like a patchwork of ghosts, old friends, old teachers, A-*sensei*, B-*sensei*, ex-girlfriends, they're all in there… for a long time I felt like I was almost controlled by that, they had paved a road for me, and I couldn't change it. … but nowadays I'm more comfortable with expressing myself through language …

Here, we can see a trajectory for speaking Japanese in which James moved from feeling linguistically constrained by the input and expectations of L1 speakers, to arriving at a place where he felt more comfortable expressing himself. James's description of feeling controlled is further elaborated in the next comments, which came after I asked him if there was anyone or anything that influenced his Japanese:

James: you know, when you're learning Japanese, especially with, um like [my college Japanese] *sensei*, she is a very traditional teacher and there's definitely a sense in her class that you are a foreigner speaking Japanese language, take your shoes off, you know what I mean, it's not yours, um, which always bothered me a little bit. You know, that's just her style, I don't think she's conscious of it, but it was only when I got to Japan and I started reading authors and I thought, I have a right to use [Japanese] however I want, right. And if I'm wrong, I'm just going to use it that way. [emphasis added]

James continued the discussion of the unwanted influence of others on his language use and linguistic choices and he articulated quite eloquently how the influence of other speakers emerged in his speech, 'like a patchwork of old ghosts'. His comments about his college Japanese teacher clearly depict a stance of language ownership that she asserted over Japanese, and especially over the Japanese used by learners. Crucially, the teacher's ownership of Japanese was not manifested as a denial of the right to use Japanese, but rather as a denial of the right to use Japanese the way James wanted to. As a foreigner and 'non-native' speaker, James received the message that he had no intrinsic right to use Japanese and, in particular, he had no right to be intentionally 'wrong'. In other words, as a foreigner speaking Japanese, James had no right to take creative liberties with the Japanese language. For James, the process of becoming able to express himself through Japanese was more salient than attending to the process of improving his Japanese skills. While other participants talked about how their speech was depicted by L1 speakers, James talked not about 'depictions' of his speech by L1 speakers, but about 'restrictions' that L1 speakers (perhaps unconsciously) placed on his speech.

Liam

Liam also shared concerns about the freedom to use Japanese that were similar to concerns James had about being able to express himself. For example, as discussed in Chapter 5, Liam was aware of having an unexpected accent when he spoke Japanese, and he described how L1 speakers responded to his accent. Liam had commented previously about being careful when he spoke because his students would make fun of him.

Jae:	so if you use dialect, do they make fun of you for using dialect?
Liam:	yes, or that would be more like laughing, and adults do that a lot, and really much more now than earlier, because now that I'm speaking so much and I'm using dialect so much, now it's getting very amusing of, look at the foreigner, he's speaking [Asahi]-*ben*, foreigners aren't supposed to speak Japanese like that, so that's happening a lot, and it might also be that I'm speaking with a particularly heavy accent, I'm probably not sounding like a 25 year old Japanese man sounds like, I maybe sound like what a 25 year old fisherman shipbuilder sounds like, I maybe sound like what a 60-year-old old man sounds like, but my Japanese doesn't really match people's expectations, and then coupled with that that I have an accent, I have an

American accent when speaking Japanese which causes me to stress vowels and consonants in Japanese words more than a Japanese person would, so therefore my accent might sound even a bit more kind of silly, cuz it's not only a heavy accent but it's also a heavy accent thrown in with an American accent

Liam's comments here suggest several things about his dialect use: first, that over time, he began to use dialect more, especially compared to when he first moved to Japan. Second, Liam received clear messages that 'foreigners aren't supposed to' use dialect and, if they do, it is 'amusing'. Next, Liam highlighted the fact that the way he spoke and, presumably, the way he used dialect, may be more fitting for a much older man. Lastly, Liam described his accent as sounding American, which meant that not only did he have a 'heavy' accent in terms of Japanese Dialect, but he also spoke Japanese with an American accent. The result, he said, might sound silly and might be the cause of L1 speakers laughing or making fun of him. In the next excerpt, I asked a follow-up question about his accent:

Jae: are you conscious of having an American accent when you speak Japanese?
Liam: I wish I didn't, I would like to speak unaccented Japanese, and I'm conscious of what a Japanese feels is an American accent, of accented Japanese, and I'm conscious of what other foreigners' accents sound like. I know I have an accent and I would like to not have an accent
Jae: do you think your accent is going away the longer you're here or
Liam: I think I'm discovering what my normal accent is ... I'm just now arriving at the place where I have a natural accent. Because I'm American, I'm a first language English speaker who started learning Japanese, who started learning when he was 22, so I have an unavoidable accent and I'm discovering what that is. Every once in a while, I'll try a new word or just from the way I get worked up when speaking and boom, I say something extra special, with an American accent, and it's like ah! That was, I'll notice that, but then I do know that when I'm just speaking normal Japanese, I probably am dropping a western speaker, English speaking tones in there

In this excerpt, we see Liam's desire to not speak with an American accent – in other words, a 'non-native' accent or an accent that differs from the Japanese spoken around him, and it is clear that he paid attention to accents in the speech of others, both L1 and L2 speakers. He seems at once both resigned to having an American accent and, at the same time, wanting to be able to get rid of that accent. Near the end of the interview, Liam talked about his efforts to use more natural Japanese, which he described as 'noticing the way things are done around here'. This allowed him to start using expressions and speech styles (including politeness and dialect) in ways that were more similar to how he heard Japanese people speaking. Liam explained that he knew his Japanese was getting better when people stopped telling him *'nihongo ga jōzu'* (your Japanese is good) and instead started asking him *'nihon, nagai desu ka?'* (have you been in Japan long?). As with participants in my study and in Carlson (2018), Liam saw *'nihongo ga jōzu'* as an empty compliment based upon the assumption of low Japanese ability – but to be asked if he had been in Japan long was, for Liam, a clearer sign of linguistic competence.

Melissa

Melissa shared Liam's and James's awareness that status as a foreigner routinely resulted in assumptions about how one should or should not speak. As we saw in earlier chapters, Melissa was very conscious of the judgments L1 speakers made about L2 speech, and she was aware that being perceived to be a 'foreigner' created restrictions on the speech style options for herself and other L2 speakers. Melissa discussed these concerns in the context of talking about both dialect and gendered Japanese. The following excerpt occurred during a discussion about what Melissa aimed for when speaking Japanese:

Melissa: everyday Japanese, not like that really manly one or really girly girl, just something relatable and easy, easy to communicate, and that way, more of the focus is on the words rather than how I'm saying it, and I feel like, if you're a Japanese person and you've got a kind of a, you've got like, I don't know, your speech has a certain type of character, because you're Japanese, the emphasis is still on the words. But when you're foreign, people are quite interested in how you speak Japanese, and so as soon as you kind of deviate from what's considered standard or normal Japanese, all of a sudden, the focus isn't on your words anymore but on how you're speaking it. And that's fun with kids or people sometimes, but if you're just in everyday communication, if I just want to communicate a point, it's easier to stick with the standard

Melissa had a clear idea of what was 'standard or normal' Japanese, and she described using any other kind of Japanese as a deviation. Melissa wanted people to focus on what she was saying, not on how she was saying it, and she noticed that, while Japanese people could use a variety of speech styles, L2 speakers could not, unless they were willing to risk calling attention to their way of speaking at the expense of the content of their speech. In an earlier part of her interview, Melissa had described how interested she was in the local dialect, and how she saw it as a unique and important connection to the area where she lived in Japan. However, her desire to communicate successfully meant that anything other than 'standard or normal' Japanese was off-limits to her, including the local dialect.

L1 participants

While L2 participants were often concerned about how Japanese people would react when they spoke Japanese, L1 participants noted that Japanese people were sometimes afraid to speak to those who were visibly foreign. There was also a tendency for L1 participants to link Japanese ability with Japanese-ness. During my interview with Nakamura, although I was asking him about foreigners in general, in his response, he made a comment about me and my Japanese skills:

Jae:	外国人はここにいる上で、どんな日本語のスキルが必要だと思われますか。
Nakamura:	ん、そうですね、やっぱ、あのう、日常会話、ん、やっぱりそれが一番やろうと思うんです。ま、どうしてかというとやっぱ日本人の場合は、その外国語に対するそのコンプレックスというか、も、あのう、初めの第一声、も、外国語だと、どうしてもひいてしまうよね。そ<u>や</u>から、あのう、Jaeさんのように、こう、日本語が<u>堪能</u>で、うん、日本人より日本人らしい日本語を<u>つこう</u>てもらうと日本人はすごく安心するんです。((underlined is dialect))
Jae:	what kind of Japanese skills do you think foreigners need if they are going to live here?
Nakamura:	hmm, well, of course daily conversation skills, I think that's the most important. Well, because after all, when it comes to the Japanese, they have a complex about foreigners and if the first thing they hear is a foreign language, well, they will be hesitant. So, if it's someone like you, who's fluent in Japanese and who uses Japanese that's more Japanese-like than the Japanese, Japanese people will be very relieved

In this excerpt, Nakamura referred to the 'complex' that Japanese people are often said to have with regard to speaking to foreigners. Nakamura said that for L1 speakers who were apprehensive about speaking with someone who might speak in a foreign language, hearing a visibly non-Japanese person use fluent Japanese would put the L1 speaker at ease. Here, Nakamura described my Japanese language as being 'more Japanese-like than the Japanese spoken by Japanese people'. As we saw with the studies introduced above, this phrase is now almost a cliché, and Nakamura's comments, as with Yoshio's and Megumi's above, demonstrate the same kinds of assumptions about the difficulty of Japanese and about who can be expected to speak Japanese.

Kazuki and Peter

The final participants examined in this chapter are a married couple: Kazuki and Peter. Peter is an L2 speaker of Japanese; his L1 is English, and he is from the United Kingdom. Peter has lived in Japan for more than 15 years. Peter's husband, Kazuki, is an L1 speaker of Japanese who was born and raised in Japan and speaks L2 English. Peter and Kazuki have been a couple for more than 10 years. Some years before I began this study, they lived together in an English-speaking country for one year, and other than this year abroad, their experience as a couple has been in Japan. In interviews, both of them (separately) reported that they primarily speak Japanese with each other. I interviewed each of them separately. I also spent time with them together in restaurants around town.

Peter's Japanese ability

Peter's Japanese proficiency is not relevant to a consideration of ideologies of native speaker bias and language ownership; however, I include a brief summary of his speaking ability in order to provide context for Kazuki's depictions of Peter's Japanese. I judged Peter's Japanese level to be advanced based on a consideration of the following: Peter's self-assessments in the questionnaire and during the interviews; my observations during fieldwork of his linguistic performance in Japanese language interactions across numerous contexts; and his experience of passing the highest level of the Japanese Language Proficiency Test (JLPT, a Japanese language test for L2 speakers) and also of passing multiple levels of the *Kanji Kentei* test (a test of written Japanese designed for L1 speakers). By observing Peter interact in a variety of social and workplace situations, I saw that he could use Japanese to accomplish a range of both everyday and specialized tasks. He told me that he used Japanese almost exclusively in his daily life with Kazuki; Peter also reported watching and enjoying Japanese television programs. In my observations and in audio-recordings of Peter in interactions with various L1 speakers, he used both casual speech and slang (as appropriate for his interlocutors) as well as specialized terminology (as appropriate for the topic of talk). Although Peter told me that he lacked confidence in formal interactions, he showed advanced communicative competence, made skillful use of *aizuchi* (back-channeling and interjections) and displayed pragmatic sensitivity that allowed him to successfully navigate complex interactions in a variety of contexts. The breadth of his vocabulary knowledge, the depth of his grammar knowledge, his listening comprehension and his overall communicative skills were reflective of his more than 10 years of living in Japan and also attested to his active study of Japanese. At the same time, Peter's Japanese was not perfect and sometimes his language use could be described as demonstrating some 'disfluencies', for example in terms of intonation and grammar, and, occasionally, word choice. Some characteristics of Peter's accent could be described as sounding like a 'non-native speaker', although it should also be noted that this did not affect comprehensibility. In sum, Peter's advanced Japanese abilities allowed him to live and work in a non-urban setting in Japan without relying on English, and his Japanese ability continued to progress over the years I knew him. When hearing Peter speak Japanese, whether one came away with the impression of communicative competence or of non-native disfluencies is ultimately dependent upon one's beliefs about what counts as Japanese competence, as demonstrated below.

Depictions of L2 competence

I focused my analysis of Kazuki's interview on the following: (1) how Kazuki described the language he and Peter spoke together; (2) Kazuki's assessments of Peter's Japanese skills; and (3) Kazuki's beliefs about Japanese language in general and about the kinds of Japanese skills L2 speakers need to live in Japan. I found that Kazuki made repeated associations of language (including language use and language skill) with nationality. Kazuki also shared negative depictions of Peter's Japanese ability and Kazuki reported that he made various adjustments to his speech when speaking with Peter and also when speaking with other L2 speakers.

Language and nationality

Kazuki made reference in a variety of ways to an association between using Japanese language and having Japanese nationality. He also said that if someone is '*nihonjin-poi*' (like a Japanese person), then it would be strange to speak English with them. Kazuki made comments to this effect several times during the interview. He also said that he and Peter spoke almost exclusively in Japanese. His justification for that was that Peter was 'like a Japanese person'.

Kazuki:	出会った時から日本人ぽい、僕よりもなんか日本人ぽい

Kazuki:	from the first time I met (him) he was like a Japanese person, he was somehow even more like a Japanese person than me

Kazuki also explained that even when they visited an English-speaking country together, he mainly used Japanese with Peter, because Kazuki said, it would be 'strange' to speak English with Peter.

Kazuki:	[Peter]とは日本語だし、やっぱりもともと日本人として見ているから、英語で話したらヘン

Kazuki:	with Peter [it's] Japanese, after all I've seen him as a Japanese person from the beginning so, if [we] spoke English, it would be strange

In saying that he felt Peter was 'more Japanese than me', Kazuki is sharing the notion (discussed above) that the demonstration of skill in Japanese language somehow equates to 'Japanese-ness' itself. Here, Kazuki depicted his use of Japanese with Peter as something he took for granted, adding that it would be 'strange' for them to speak English because he sees Peter as 'a Japanese person'. This statement reinforces Kazuki's earlier claim that associated Japanese language use with Japanese nationality, and adds to that the idea that if someone is Japanese, then the most logical choice is to speak Japanese with them. We might imagine other, plausible explanations for the choice of Japanese, such as referring to Peter's Japanese fluency, Kazuki's English ability or preference for Japanese, or even their location in Japan. Instead, Kazuki relied on ideological associations of language and nationality to justify his reason for using only Japanese with Peter.

Depictions of Peter's Japanese

Given Kazuki's explanation that he and Peter spoke only Japanese and his stated view that it would be strange to speak English with Peter, we might expect that Kazuki would describe Peter's Japanese skills positively. But that was not the case. For example, Kazuki was highly critical of Peter's pronunciation and intonation. Popular books seeking to explain Japanese culture to Westerners often stress that self-effacement is valued in Japanese culture, and that there is an expectation that one will downplay one's abilities as well as the abilities of family members (e.g. Davies & Ikeno, 2011). Thus, we may wonder if Kazuki's criticisms of Peter's Japanese ability are merely an example of this kind of self-effacement.

However, Kazuki offered a detailed account of the problems he perceived with Peter's Japanese, which he referred to numerous times throughout the interview. Kazuki's observations led me to conclude that Kazuki's negative depictions of Peter's Japanese were not part of an attempt to be self-effacing. Rather, they are evidence of native speaker bias, which can be seen in Kazuki's answer to my question about Peter's Japanese skills:

Jae: Peterさんの日本語についてどう思いますか
Kazuki: 慣れてない人と話す時はやっぱりイントネーションが変わるし、話し方がヘンになる。訳が分からない日本語を使うし

Jae: what do you think of Peter's Japanese?
Kazuki: when he talks to [someone he's] not used to talking to, as expected, his intonation changes, his way of speaking becomes strange. [He] also uses Japanese that makes no sense

Here, Kazuki described Peter's Japanese as '*wake ga wakaranai nihongo*' or 'Japanese that makes no sense'. Later in the interview, Kazuki also describes Peter's Japanese as 'sounding off' (*iwakan*). I asked if that was because Peter had an English accent or an accent like someone from the United Kingdom, to which Kazuki replied:

Kazuki: いや、Peterの日本語、Peterが作った日本語、のイントネーション、方言かな、Peterの方言

Kazuki: no, it's Peter's Japanese, Japanese that Peter made, his intonation, or maybe it's dialect, Peter's dialect

In saying that Peter does not speak 'Japanese', he speaks 'Peter's Japanese' or 'Peter's dialect', it seems as if Kazuki was resistant to recognizing the language Peter spoke as 'Japanese'. The implication here is that Kazuki denied the legitimacy of the language Peter was using, as if it were not real Japanese. Kazuki seemed to deny the possibility of other versions of Japanese that differ from an idealized Japanese. It is also difficult to reconcile comments about 'Peter's Japanese' with Kazuki's comments shared above, in which he described Peter as like 'a Japanese person' and 'more Japanese than me'.

In a different part of the interview, I asked Kazuki what kinds of language skills are important for L2 speakers living in Ehime, and I also asked what kinds of Japanese skills he thought Peter needed. Kazuki began by saying that Peter's 'communicative competence' (*komyunikeeshon nōryoku*) in Japanese was still low. Kazuki gave examples of ways that Peter did not follow Japanese sociolinguistic norms, for example, when making telephone calls or in workplace language use. Kazuki added that while *kanji* (Japanese characters) and other skills can be acquired through studying for exams, which Peter had done, communication skills were a separate matter. If Peter could master those skills, Kazuki said, then Peter's Japanese would be '*kanpeki*' (perfect). I also asked Kazuki if he thought skills related to dialect or slang were necessary. He indicated they were not; Kazuki felt it was necessary for Peter to study only Standard Japanese. As in the above excerpts, Kazuki continued to be critical of 'Peter's Japanese' and further implied that anything other than Standard Japanese was undesirable and unnecessary.

Kazuki's speech adjustments

In addition to the way that Kazuki depicted Peter's use of Japanese, Kazuki also reported that he (Kazuki) adjusted his speech when speaking with L2 speakers. Although he did not make reference to *yasashii nihongo*, his comments offer an example of how *yasashii nihongo* might be implemented at an individual level, and in an ad hoc manner. Prior to starting the audio-recording, Kazuki told me that recording him probably would not be helpful to me because he would not be speaking 'naturally'. During the interview, I returned to this comment and asked him about it. In response, Kazuki told me that he speaks most naturally when he is with 'only Japanese' people. He said that he adjusts his Japanese when speaking with Peter, and in response to follow-up questions, Kazuki added that he makes similar speech adjustments with other L2 speakers as well, including me. When I asked for details about how he adjusts his speech, Kazuki described how he avoids sentence-final particles and avoids any expressions that might be unclear. The complete exchange follows:

Jae:	Peterさんと話す時、私と話す時には合わせると言っていたね。だから、Kazukiさんの一番自然な喋り方は何ですか。
Kazuki:	自然な話し方は、日本人だけでいる時と思う。Peterと話す時は簡単な言葉を選んで、あいまいになるべくしない、聞きたいことは簡単に聞くし、あいまいに言っちゃうと反対に彼が分からなくなるし。
Jae:	じゃあ、Peterさんと話す時に、一切合わせないで自然に喋ると
Kazuki:	無理！できない。もう慣れているから、反対に恥ずかしいかも
Jae:	何が違いますか。何を変えますか。
Kazuki:	やっぱり発音も違うし、使う語尾も違う。なんとかだよねとか使わない、じゃないと彼もあいまいのことを出したら、訳分からなくなるから。なるべく分かりやすい日本語で、それを繋げて話してる。

Jae: you said you adjust [your speech] when talking with Peter or talking with me, right, so what is your most natural way of speaking?

Kazuki: I think [my] natural way of speaking is when I'm with only Japanese people. When I talk to Peter, I choose easy words, I try as much as possible not to be vague, if I want to ask something, I ask it simply. If I say it vaguely, then conversely, he will start to not understand, so

Jae: well, what if, when talking to Peter, you didn't do any adjusting at all

Kazuki: impossible! I can't. I'm used to [talking this way] so, conversely I'd probably be embarrassed

Jae: what's different? What do you change?

Kazuki: as expected, [my] pronunciation is different, and ... something like '*da yō ne*' ((yeah it is)), something like that I don't use ... otherwise he, if [I] say something vague he'll become confused so, as much as possible [I use] easy-to-understand Japanese and speak [by] connecting [easy-to-understand Japanese]

Kazuki described these kinds of adjustments as using Japanese that is 'easy to understand'. Further, he said that if he did not make these changes, then 'Peter won't understand or will be confused'. Kazuki seemed to assume that Peter could not understand 'real' or 'regular' Japanese. Although Kazuki did not label it as such, what he was describing was a kind of foreigner talk (Ferguson, 1981; Iino, 2006) in which, similar to *yasashii nihongo*, a speaker tries to simplify their speech in a variety of ways, rather than speaking naturally.

Kazuki's descriptions of how he adjusted his speech with Peter are an example of how assumptions about competence guided his beliefs about how he should speak with Peter. Kazuki seemed to have made a preemptive decision to use 'easy-to-understand Japanese' because he believed that to do otherwise would inhibit Peter's ability to understand. Kazuki's reaction to my question about what would happen if he did not make any adjustments is telling: he forcefully said it would be impossible and he could not do it. He added that speaking this way had become an ingrained habit and it would be embarrassing to do otherwise. Kazuki's comments reveal stereotypes about what 'non-native speakers' can or cannot understand and position the L2 speaker as someone who needs to be spoken to differently from 'real' Japanese speakers or native speakers of Japanese.

An additional question relates to the degree that Kazuki actually altered his speech. It is difficult to discuss an *absence* of linguistic features; I cannot say with certainty what, if anything, is missing from Kazuki's 'easy Japanese' speech that he explained he used with L2 speakers. However, in his interview with me and in my observations of Kazuki and Peter interacting, I did not notice obvious examples of simplified speech. In addition, although Kazuki claimed he does not use sentence-final particles when speaking with L2 speakers, there were some occurrences of them in Kazuki's interview data with me. While these observations may contradict his claims of making speech adjustments, I would argue that it does not matter to what degree Kazuki actually engaged in speech adjustments. What matters is his perception that adjusting his speech is something he *must* do when speaking with L2 speakers.

Potential impacts on Peter

Thus far, I have focused on Kazuki and his beliefs about Japanese in general and about Peter's Japanese abilities in particular. Turning to Peter's interview data, we can consider what possible impacts native speaker bias had on Peter. I conducted multiple interviews and observations with Peter; these were completed before the interview with Kazuki, due to their availability and scheduling challenges. My analysis of Peter's comments in which he expressed his beliefs and opinions about speaking Japanese and about his own Japanese use reveal ideologies of native speaker bias.

Peter discussed his lack of confidence in his Japanese ability several times during our interviews. In particular, Peter reported a lack of confidence in his accent and pronunciation, and he described himself as having 'one of the strongest accents in the world'. Although Peter did not connect his lack of confidence to any influence from Kazuki, in one interview, Peter described meta-talk discussions with Kazuki, in other words, discussions about language. For example, Peter shared with me that Kazuki frequently made negative assessments of the 'non-native' accents of otherwise highly proficient L2 speakers, including L2 speakers they saw on Japanese television shows. Although Kazuki shared with me his critical view of Peter's intonation, neither Peter nor Kazuki gave any indication that Kazuki had ever shared his criticisms of Peter's accent directly with Peter. Nevertheless, it seems likely that Peter had internalized Kazuki's opinion of what spoken Japanese 'should' sound like, which did not accommodate deviation from an idealized, 'perfect' Japanese. Both Peter and Kazuki expressed the same kinds of linguistic ideologies, and both of them described these ideas without any critical reflection, which seemed to reinforce the very ideas that caused Peter to lack confidence in his Japanese ability.

Peter also shared with me his concerns about not being able to successfully choose appropriate speech styles, e.g. polite versus casual, and he worried that he was not making the correct choices about the use of Japanese honorifics. When Peter talked about polite language and honorifics, it was clear that he attended to the importance of being appropriate and correct. Peter also described his awareness of the diversity of Japanese, and he said that he was interested in slang and fond of the local dialect. Based on his experiences with L1 speakers at work and socially, Peter felt that all of these speech styles were important, because he encountered them regularly in his daily life in Japan. At the same time, he worried about whether or how he should use non-standard speech styles, such as slang. In his comments to me, Peter did not discuss anything specifically related to Kazuki's view of these diverse speech styles. However, given the frequency with which Peter encountered a diverse array of Japanese language in use, it seems reasonable to conclude that Kazuki's assumptions about Peter's linguistic needs are most likely in conflict with the linguistic realities that Peter experienced. Thus, while Peter did not connect his concerns to Kazuki's beliefs, we can consider Peter's interest in slang and dialect against a backdrop of Kazuki's dismissiveness of the relevance of these diverse speech styles. What emerges is a disconnect between Peter's daily linguistic reality and Kazuki's understandings about which aspects of spoken Japanese are important for Peter specifically and for L2 speakers in Japan more generally.

It is also important to note that Kazuki gave no indication that his beliefs about L2 speakers might have an effect on Peter as a speaker of Japanese, despite the fact that the language he and Peter spoke routinely was Japanese. Kazuki described intentionally adjusting his Japanese and using easier Japanese speaking with Peter, although he stressed that Standard Japanese was what Peter should emphasize. Kazuki was quite clear that he always took into account the fact that L2 speakers were not native speakers and he made it a point to clarify that he only spoke 'natural' Japanese when he was speaking with other L1 speakers. Kazuki seemed unaware that his beliefs about L2 speakers might be understood as biases toward L2 speakers. He also did not consider the possibility that L2 speakers might actually benefit from Kazuki speaking 'natural Japanese' with them. As he explained, Kazuki spoke 'easy' Japanese with Peter and L2 speakers generally and, in effect, Kazuki was modeling the only Japanese he thought L2 speakers were capable of using and understanding.

In a similar fashion, Peter discussed himself as a Japanese speaker. Peter shared concerns he had about using honorific language, and he explained his interest in other speech styles, as well as his interest in slang. He also conveyed that he was aware that Kazuki favored Standard Japanese. Peter discussed meta-talk about Japanese with Kazuki and explained that Kazuki made clear his preferences for native accents, for example when they heard highly proficient L2 speakers with non-native accents on television programs. However, Peter did not suggest that he was aware of any negative effects Kazuki's preference might have on his own language choices.

Peter and Kazuki had many years of speaking Japanese together, which seemed to have little to no effect on Kazuki's opinions about L2-Japanese speakers. Peter was well aware that Kazuki believed Peter should focus on speaking Standard Japanese and what Kazuki called 'communication skills'. Peter, however, never conveyed that he resented Kazuki's biases toward L2 speakers or Kazuki's recommendations that Peter improve his 'communication skills'. Rather, Kazuki's preferences for native speakers of Japanese was simply consistent with what he understood to be natural – just as Peter's efforts to improve his Japanese also seemed natural for an L2 speaker. None of the comments and opinions Peter and Kazuki shared about speaking Japanese resulted from critical examinations of each other, or of themselves, as Japanese speakers. Their observations and remarks were not systemic analyses; rather they were casual and spontaneous, simply part of living and speaking Japanese.

Discussion

This chapter has considered how native speaker bias emerges in depictions of L2-Japanese competence. The L1 participants introduced, Megumi, Nakamura and Kazuki, each relied on the idea of an idealized 'Japanese native speaker' as the model for Japanese ability. The association of language and linguistic behavior with nationality is apparent when an L2 speaker is described as 'more Japanese than a Japanese person', and we see this association of language and linguistic behavior with nationality – if someone is speaking Japanese proficiently, then they must *be* Japanese. Nakamura and Megumi used this idea as the basis of praise for L2 competence, and Kazuki began his interview in a similar fashion, saying that Peter was 'more Japanese than me'. However, this expression became ironic in light of Kazuki's later references to 'Peter's Japanese' as strange and hard to understand. In Kazuki's depictions of L2 speakers and of Peter as well, he conveyed that he was unable or unwilling to recognize L2-Japanese as a valid form of Japanese. Native speaker bias and ideologies of ownership of Japanese, as expressed by L1 participants, deny L2 legitimacy and devalue the very real language skills and capabilities of L2 speakers. Native speaker bias also ignores diversity among Japanese speakers, rejecting the possibility of a hybrid identity in which one can be both a speaker of Japanese and simultaneously not a Japanese person.

Of equal importance is the impact these ideologies have on L2 speakers in Japan. Through the interview data presented here, we can see that rejection of the possibility of a hybrid identity is at the base of experiences such as those described by the L2 participants in this chapter: Liam's awareness that 'foreigners aren't supposed to speak Japanese' the way he does and that his Japanese 'doesn't match people's expectations'.

Another example is Melissa's concern about deviating from Standard Japanese because it will shift the focus away from what she is trying to say. On the other hand, James, despite the message he received from teachers that Japanese 'is not yours', recognized that he had arrived at a place where he realized he had a right 'to use Japanese however I want'. Lastly, Peter struggled with insecurity about his accent and uncertainty about how to incorporate diverse speech styles into his Japanese repertoire. All of their experiences are inevitable when the Japanese language is posited as homogeneous and having only one 'correct' version, and when legitimate Japanese speakers are only those who are ethnically and legally Japanese. Recalling Kazuki's comments about Peter's linguistic performance declining when speaking with less well-known interlocutors, we can only wonder whether such a decline in performance was connected to insecurities that were exacerbated by linguistic ideologies that allow no room for variation or deviation.

From a pedagogical standpoint, Kazuki's claim of making speech adjustments with L2 speakers is especially troubling, because it indicates that L2 speakers may not receive the same kind of linguistic input as L1 speakers. While my study does not examine language acquisition, it is important to note that previous studies (e.g. Lipski, 2005) have shown that foreigner talk, such as that used by Kazuki, can have negative effects on L2 proficiency. In addition, Kazuki's criticisms of Peter's Japanese are paradoxical: on the one hand, Kazuki claimed that Peter would not understand if Kazuki spoke naturally but, on the other hand, by not speaking naturally, Kazuki denies Peter the opportunity to demonstrate, or develop, the kinds of linguistic skills needed to understand natural speech.

Other potential impacts relate to the fact that L1 speakers often share their linguistic beliefs with L2 speakers. For example, L2 participants recounted their experiences with meta-talk in which L1 speakers shared their ideas about how Japanese should be spoken. And indeed, Peter described meta-talk in which Kazuki was critical of the accents of other L2 speakers. This chapter underscores that, when L1 speakers share their beliefs about an idealized, homogenized Japanese language, it contributes to L2 speakers' lack of confidence in their pronunciation and speech style choices, as seen with Peter. Ideological discourse about 'correct' and 'incorrect' pronunciation is internalized by L2 speakers who come to see themselves as 'imperfect' speakers (Doerr, 2009b); the impact of such ideologies goes beyond mere pronunciation or choice of expression and denies legitimacy for L2 speakers.

Another pressing concern is how native speaker bias may have unanticipated and unintended impacts on L2 identity, which is exemplified in Kazuki's descriptions of Peter as both 'like a Japanese' and, at the same time, as using 'Japanese that makes no sense'. These two seemingly contradictory comments are based on the same underlying assumption.

In its essence, the message is that: 'if you *speak* Japanese, you must *be* Japanese. And, if you *aren't* Japanese, then you're not (really) speaking Japanese'. Assumptions like these reinforce the idea that L2 speakers inherently lack legitimacy as speakers of Japanese and, crucially, that L2 speakers cannot maintain a non-Japanese identity despite acquiring and using fluent Japanese. In short, L2 speakers are caught in a double bind.

Conclusion

This chapter explored ways that L1 speakers convey their opinions and judgments of L2 speakers' Japanese abilities. We have considered the viewpoints of L1 speakers about L2 Japanese and seen some of the ways such viewpoints are conveyed by L1 speakers and the resulting impacts on L2 speakers. What recurs in L1 depictions of L2 Japanese is native speaker bias that only recognizes as true speakers of Japanese those whose ethnicity and nationality are Japanese. Any diversity of Japanese language or hybridity of its speakers is dismissed and thereby made invisible. It is the case that native speaker bias manifests under the radar. L1 speakers are not likely to engage in critical reflection about their views of Japanese language, nor do L2 speakers often consider alternative ways to judge their own Japanese language ability. In fact, both L1 and L2 speakers tend to internalize ideas that are hiding behind comments such as 'more Japanese than the Japanese'. These comments are presented matter-of-factly, as common-sense realities about language in which the underlying ideologies are unnoticed and unexplored. Native speaker bias emerges in the comments and observations of both L1 and L2 speakers, which offer evidence of how native speaker bias primes both L1 and L2 speakers to see L2 speakers as other-than-legitimate speakers.

7 Conclusion

To Be an L2 Speaker in Japan

Language ideologies, or beliefs and assumptions about languages and speakers, are both commonplace and, most often, unnoticed. Research on language ideologies has detailed how the depiction of languages as homogeneous obscures the very real diversity of both languages and speakers. As such, language ideologies have negative impacts on speakers regardless of their status as first (L1) or second language (L2) speakers. Native speaker bias, however, refers to specific beliefs, practices and limitations that diminish the status of L2 speakers as legitimate speakers. This study has examined the beliefs, opinions and ideas that impact L2-Japanese speakers in Japan. My analysis of interviews and observations conducted with both L1 and L2 speakers of Japanese underscores the persistence and lingering effects of language ideologies in general and native speaker bias in particular as routine features of what it means to be an L2-Japanese speaker in Japan. Researchers have learned a great deal about how native speaker bias impacts L2 speakers. However, the majority of inquiry in this area has focused on L2-English speakers and L2 speakers in instructional contexts. Nevertheless, previous findings point to the effects of language ideologies on the speaker legitimacy of L2 speakers in general and challenge ideas about L2 speakers as other than legitimate speakers.

L2-Japanese speakers

Research about L2-English speakers, while a resource for studies about L2 speakers, has limitations with regard to studies about other languages, including Japanese. Research about L2-Japanese speakers has most often looked at learners and instructors in classrooms and other educational programs, including study abroad. As a matter of course, L2-Japanese students in English-speaking countries are encouraged to have immersive, in-country experiences to enhance classroom learning. Studies of L2-Japanese speakers living in Japan for extended periods of time, or as long-term residents of Japan, are fewer in comparison to studies about Japanese learners in classroom or study abroad settings.

I conducted this study in Japan with participants who were L2-Japanese, L1-English speakers, and also included L1-Japanese speaker participants. All L2 participants had lived in Japan for at least a year, although most had lived there for much longer, and some L2 participants were permanent residents. All L1 participants were counterparts of one or more of the L2 participants, in other words, they were friends, coworkers or significant others of the L2 participants. Because many of the L2 participants worked in public schools teaching English, many of the L1 participants were also schoolteachers. However, none of the L1 participants were teachers of Japanese as a foreign language (JFL) and none of them were linguists – in other words, the L1 participants were laypeople.

I interviewed L2-Japanese speakers who lived their daily lives 'in Japanese', using Japanese at home, at work and in their local communities where they interacted with L1 speakers. L2 participants' comments and observations indicate that their interactions with L1 speakers proved to be occasions in which L1 speakers conveyed messages, often implicit but sometimes explicit, that were informed by language ideologies and native speaker bias. L2 participants described conversations with L1 speakers that often shifted from the topic at hand to how they spoke Japanese. The impact of these subtle and not so subtle reminders that they were not native speakers informed decisions L2 participants made about their language use as Japanese speakers. Sometimes, L2 participants' beliefs about how they *should* speak Japanese were at odds with how they wanted to sound or how they saw themselves as speakers of Japanese. Many L2 participants described concerns and conflicted feelings, especially with regard to choices about three key speech styles in Japanese: *keigo*, Japanese gendered language and regional dialects.

Japanese speech styles

For many L2 participants, navigating choices about *keigo*, Japanese gendered language or Japanese regional dialects was one of the most challenging aspects of Japanese. Participants struggled with the complexity of *keigo*, concerns about the appropriateness of gendered language and the relevance of dialect. In navigating the range of available speech styles, they sought to strike a balance between how they wanted to sound and how L1 speakers expected them to sound. Despite these challenges, L2 participants recognized numerous benefits to incorporating Japanese speech styles into their Japanese language repertoires. Indeed, speech styles allow Japanese speakers to go beyond basic message delivery and take full advantage of the expressive possibilities of language.

L1 speakers negotiate the use of speech styles, and L2 speakers similarly must negotiate the use of *keigo*, Japanese gendered language and dialect, if they aspire to have a rich repertoire of Japanese. However, L2-Japanese learners, especially in English-speaking countries, often have limited exposure to a range of speech styles. Learners may be taught a fixed set of ideas about *keigo* and are cautioned to be polite lest they risk giving offense to native speakers. Differences in 'men's language' and 'women's language' are similarly presented as something to avoid getting wrong. Finally, dialects in Japan are often completely overlooked. Yet, when L2-Japanese speakers live and work in Japan, they encounter each of these speech styles and need to reconcile ideas about 'appropriate' language use with their own ideas about how they want to sound as speakers of Japanese.

Bearing in mind the central role of speech styles in Japanese, it is instructive to use speech styles as a lens to explore participants' experiences with language ideologies as conveyed by beliefs and opinions about how L2 speakers should speak. For the L2 participants in the study, it was clear that concerns about appropriate and correct use of speech styles mattered, but they were equally concerned about how they wanted to be and sound as speakers of Japanese. For example, some L2 participants were concerned with improving their *keigo* skills but were uninterested in dialect, while other L2 participants were less interested in *keigo* but interested in using dialect. Considering L2 participants individually, interview data indicate there were many ways to approach the challenges that Japanese speech styles present to L2 speakers. However, looking at the L2 participants as a group, they also shared many experiences in common. For all L2 speakers who participated in this study, language ideologies were unavoidable. All L2 participants had to think about and make choices about how to use Japanese in the face of native speaker bias. All L2 participants experienced being on the receiving end of messages that the Japanese language they used was not their own. At the same time, many L2 participants struggled because they lacked confidence in their Japanese language abilities. The ways they navigated linguistic choices presented by Japanese speech styles were most often informed by conflicting messages from L1 speakers. In addition, the question of how they spoke Japanese frequently became the focus of discussion, which only compounded their concerns. Looking at the L2 participants as a group, it is apparent that being an L2-Japanese speaker in Japan means being vulnerable to unwanted attention and having one's choice of words attended to. Attention might seem to be positive when it came in the form of compliments, but, at other times, attention was explicitly negative when it came in the form of teasing, correction or even censure. Thus, negative or positive, being on the receiving end of attention for *how* they spoke meant that L2 participants were too often reminded that to be an L2 speaker in Japan is to be 'other', to be not Japanese, to be an outsider.

Native speaker bias

A preference for language spoken like a 'native speaker' seems intuitive and uncontroversial. And, indeed, learners are often told that if they want to learn a language, a native speaker will be the best teacher and, if they want to speak a language, they should strive to speak like a native speaker. However, the assumptions that form the basis of native speaker bias are, as researchers consistently point out, just that – beliefs and views that are presented as commonsensical but not supported by linguistic research findings. Instead, idealized depictions of languages and native speakers overlook the linguistic diversity found from one language variety to another and from one native speaker to another. Further, ideas about native speakers are not based on purely linguistic considerations but instead tend to mix ideas about language and race, ethnicity and nationality.

Researchers who focus on L2-Japanese speakers point out that L1 speakers bring historical and cultural 'baggage' about the Japanese language to their engagement with L2 speakers. Beginning in the Meiji era as part of its nation-building efforts, Japan saw having a standard language as a way to convey to other nations that Japan was a unified country. Language standardization in Japan put forward a dialect spoken in Tokyo as the language of Japan, Standard Japanese, which continues today as the language taught both in Japan and around the world as JFL. Anyone who acquires reasonable proficiency in spoken Standard Japanese can expect to be understood throughout Japan. At the same time, assumptions about the uniqueness of the Japanese language, such as those espoused by *nihonjinron* theories, also contribute to biases in how L1 speakers think about L2 speakers. Beliefs about the Japanese language and how L2 speakers 'should' speak it reflect cultural beliefs about language that act like silent partners when L1 speakers interact with L2 speakers.

Although L1 participants expressed a range of ideas about L2 speakers in their interviews, it was common for L1 participants to express beliefs that perpetuated and reinforced ideologies of native speaker bias and language ownership of Japanese, however unintentionally. L1 participants frequently made associations between Japanese ability and Japanese nationality, and many L1 participants described standards that differed for L1 and L2 speakers. L1 participants also referred to an idealized native speaker as the model for Japanese language use, and some repeated the idea that an L2 speaker who speaks proficient Japanese is 'more Japanese than the Japanese', not recognizing possibilities for speakers to have a hybrid identity, or to speak Japanese without being Japanese. For many L1 speakers, Japanese language use and Japanese-ness go together and are inseparable. This depiction is problematic because its net effect is to equate speaking Japanese with being Japanese and implies that one cannot be a proficient speaker of Japanese without also being Japanese. L1 participants shared their observations about L2 speakers not as judgments, but as simple matters of fact. They expressed no resentment toward L2 speakers and many L1 participants had long-standing relationships with L2 speakers, as friends, partners or spouses. Yet, missing was any acknowledgement that an L2 speaker could be someone who is both non-Japanese and also a legitimate Japanese speaker. Finally, it is important to note that L1 participants often indicated that any comments they might make to L2 speakers about their Japanese language use were offered as a way to be helpful, to help L2 speakers be more successful. Recall, for example, the suggestions that an L2 speaker use dialect to be accepted or make other speakers happy – L1 speakers did not express recognition of how such commentaries might be received by L2 speakers, for example as a reminder that, even when they spoke Japanese competently, they were not 'real' Japanese speakers.

Japan and speaker legitimacy

In Japan, where foreign workers are increasingly relied upon to augment the workforce, it seems likely that the number of foreign nationals living in Japan will continue to increase. Many who travel to Japan for learning experiences or employment opportunities remain in Japan for extended periods and some of them fall in love with Japan and hope to make Japan their home. It does seem, however, that their ability to integrate into local communities is hindered by ideologies of native speaker bias and language ownership that place L2 speakers in a category separate from native speakers. Issues related to L2 speaker legitimacy are not widely known beyond academia. Nevertheless, the lack of L2 speaker legitimacy is a fundamental concern that stands as a barrier to L2-Japanese speakers being accepted as an important and growing part of Japanese society. The findings I have presented here have implications for teachers of Japanese as a second or foreign language, for Japanese policy with regard to foreign workers and for employers and others who will be a part of the lives that L2 speakers seek to build in Japan.

Japanese pedagogy and speaker legitimacy

Continued attention to speaker legitimacy and native speaker bias in Japanese language education in and beyond Japan is essential. I believe and have argued elsewhere that teachers should have as a central goal the development of speaker legitimacy in L2-Japanese students (Takeuchi, 2020a). By showing the impact of native speaker bias on L2 speakers in Japan, my research underscores the importance of that goal. Japanese language teachers should be mindful of the negative impacts that native speaker bias can have on L2 speaker legitimacy. Further, findings that both L1 and L2 participants shared beliefs that undermine L2 speakers' legitimacy suggest the importance of teachers practicing critical self-reflection to ensure that we do not unwittingly reinforce native speaker bias in teaching and classroom practices. For L2-Japanese students outside of Japan, the Japanese language teacher is often students' first exposure to Japanese language speakers, which gives Japanese language teachers an opportunity to model affirmation of L2 speaker legitimacy for students.

Another consideration relates to the role of L2 teachers in modeling language use and correcting students' mistakes. Certainly, teachers should continue to assist students in improving their language proficiency. However, I urge Japanese language teachers to remember the experiences of the L2 participants presented in this book, especially those participants who shared their worries and fears related to using Japanese. Their experiences suggest that an additional challenge for teachers is to guide students to advanced language proficiency without tying students' L2 speaker legitimacy to an idealized native speaker model. This book echoes previous works (e.g. Okamoto & Shibamoto Smith, 2016) that point to diversity of language use and of language attitudes. By selecting teaching materials that highlight the diversity of Japanese language and Japanese speakers, Japanese language teachers can begin to dismantle the model of the idealized native speaker and demonstrate for students the very real diversity of Japanese speakers. The same approach can be taken with regard to correcting students' mistakes – namely, avoiding reliance on 'native-like' conceptions of language use and instead focusing on linguistic content, communicative tasks and interactional goals.

Finally, the findings I have presented have implications with regard to teaching about Japanese speech styles. Japanese language teachers are often in a position to make decisions about what students 'should' learn. In Takeuchi (2021), I found that JFL teachers were often concerned about ensuring that Japanese was not so difficult that it would discourage students, which is a reasonable concern. At the same time, it is not an excuse for 'dumbing down' the language or glossing over the rich variety of speech styles that Japanese offers its speakers. An additional finding, both in my earlier work and in the findings presented in this book, is that there is a tendency for the acquisition of Japanese speech styles to be depicted as trying to emulate a native speaker, and some studies assert that L2 speakers do not need to endeavor to 'become' native speakers (e.g. Iino, 2006; Moody, 2014; Niyekawa, 1991). However, taking full advantage of the rich repertoire of Japanese, including *keigo*, dialects and gendered language, should not be depicted as 'trying to become a native speaker' but instead should be recognized – and encouraged – as a way to cultivate a multifaceted Japanese language repertoire, which L2 learners can then use to conduct their lives not only in Japan, but also *in Japanese*. As such, a key takeaway of this book is the importance for Japanese language teachers, and indeed for all L2 teachers, to facilitate access to not merely enough of the target language, but to all the speech style diversity that the target language has to offer.

L2 speakers in Japan and speaker legitimacy

Foreign nationals who reside in Japan receive mixed messages. On the one hand, Japan increasingly relies on foreign workers but, on the other hand, official policies and society in general are often unwelcoming of foreigners. Regardless of bias toward immigrants and treatment that fails to recognize them as residents of Japan, foreign residents will only continue to increase in number. Despite ongoing debates about immigration and foreign residents, there is broad recognition of the importance of Japanese language ability for foreigners who reside in Japan. Recent policy changes reward foreign visa applicants for advanced Japanese language skills and there is increasing recognition of the necessity to make Japanese language education available to foreign workers. The experience of L2 participants in my study, however, indicates that without taking account of the importance of speaker legitimacy for L2 speakers, it will be difficult to achieve the goal of increasing the participation and integration of L2 speakers in communities and workplaces. The persistence of native speaker bias cannot be resolved by promoting something like *yasashii nihongo*, which presumes that foreigners cannot learn 'real' Japanese. For individuals who will be residents of Japan for extended periods and who may become permanent residents, anything less than access to the full repertoire of Japanese will perpetuate native speaker bias.

My study findings point to the importance of increasing awareness of the negative impacts of language ideologies and native speaker bias in teaching Japanese as an L2, as I address above. An important step toward recognition of the speaker legitimacy of L2-speaking foreign workers and residents would be funding for in-service training for educators, especially those who teach publicly funded programs in Japan. Japanese language teachers have played a role in bringing about the current push to increase the availability of language programs for foreign residents in Japan. Their continued involvement, particularly in ensuring that L2 speakers learn in settings that convey they are legitimate speakers of Japanese, is an essential component for language learners already residing in Japan, where they live and work with L1 speakers.

Language programs that affirm L2 speaker legitimacy are an important ingredient in Japan's efforts to improve the experiences of foreign workers. In addition to in-service and related programs for language teachers, public policies and programs can support efforts by employers and local communities to ensure access to Japanese language programs. Greater awareness of diversity in Japan and of the diversity of Japanese speakers will benefit all residents of Japan. Some critics observe that resistance to immigration and foreign workers reflects fears about 'diluting' Japanese identity, and findings from my analysis of L1 participant interview data underscore the persistence of beliefs about the inseparability of speaking Japanese and being Japanese. As such, greater recognition of linguistic diversity in Japan and affirming L2-Japanese speakers as legitimate speakers is another important ingredient in promoting the integration of L2 speakers in workplaces and communities. A growing number of L2 speakers in Japan, who enjoy and use the full repertoire of Japanese, would only serve to affirm the value of speaking the Japanese language.

It is my hope that this book will be read by those who are themselves L2 speakers of Japanese or L2 speakers of other languages. I do not think L2 speakers should be discouraged by implications or claims that they are not legitimate speakers of an L2. Countless speakers of an L2 live and thrive as foreign nationals around the world. A growing number of L2 speakers have made Japan their home or, like me, have made their home in Japanese. In Takeuchi (2020a: 322), I asked: 'what would it look like for L2 speakers to be legitimate speakers of Japanese? What would the absence of native speaker bias look like?' I believe the answer can be found in the voices of my participants: Nina and Liam, who made different choices about whether to use Japanese Dialect, but who made the decision for themselves, based on how they wanted to sound. And most especially James, who said 'I have a right to use Japanese however I want'. These participants show us how L2 speakers of Japanese can simply be speakers of Japanese.

Appendix A: Sample L2 Interview Protocol

Interview Protocol for L2 Participants (Current ALT)

Background, introductory

(1) (Making reference to the background questionnaire, I will do a short 'small talk' confirming when the participant came to Japan, some details about their job placement and residence, etc.)
(2) Do you enjoy your job in Japan?
(3) Tell me more about your job, your students, your coworkers.
(4) What do you do in your free time?

Language-specific questions

(5) (I will refer to info from the questionnaire to confirm past experience studying Japanese, current Japanese study activities, etc.)
(6) How would you describe your Japanese level/ability now? How has your Japanese ability changed since you first came to Japan?
(7) (If the person has a Japanese tutor or goes to a class) Tell me about your Japanese teacher, your classmates, the class, the textbook, etc.
(8) Who do you speak Japanese with? (coworkers/neighbors/friends/shopkeepers, etc.) Tell me a little bit about that.
(9) (For people with Japanese girlfriend/boyfriend/spouse/children) What language(s) do you speak with your (boyfriend/girlfriend/spouse)? Children? In-laws?
(10) Do you like speaking Japanese? Do you like studying Japanese?
(11) What's easy/difficult about Japanese? Or: what are the best and worst things about Japanese? (about studying it, speaking it... try to be as specific as possible)
(12) Have you ever had any problems understanding (or being understood by) your Japanese coworkers/neighbors/friends? (boyfriend/girlfriend/spouse, in-laws if relevant) (can you describe a specific event or memorable episode?)
(13) Are there any language-related 'episodes', memorable stories, eye-opening moments that you'd like to share with me?

Dialect-specific questions (note that identity-specific questions are included here)

(14) Did you know that Japanese language has dialects before you came to Japan? How/when did you first learn about dialects? (If the person has lived/visited other areas of Japan, ask about their familiarity with other dialects.)
(15) Do you hear a lot of the dialect of your town? Where? When? Who uses it?
(16) Do you understand (the dialect of your town)? Examples? Is the dialect easy/hard?
(17) Do you use (the dialect of your town)? Why or why not? How much/often?
(18) (If yes to 17) In what situations do you use dialect? With whom do you use dialect?
(19) Do you think dialect is important here? Why or why not? (Try to encourage the participant to share a specific episode or event.)
(20) Do you think it's important for you to understand dialect? Do you think it's important for non-native speakers (other JETs, etc.) in general? Why or why not?
(21) Do you think it's important for you to use dialect? For other non-native speakers (other JETs, etc.) to use dialect? Why or why not? (Have you ever given any thought to how you want to sound when you speak Japanese?)
(22) (If this has not come out yet, ask) What do you think about this dialect? (or: Do you like the dialect? Why or why not?)

(If these topics have not come up previously, ask these questions)

(23) Is there anything that you are careful about when you speak Japanese? (Any specific episode?)
(24) Have you ever given any thought to how you want to sound in Japanese? Can you tell me about that? (How do you want to sound when you speak Japanese?)
(25) Is there anything (or anyone) you think has influenced how you think about Japanese? Is there someone who you want to sound like? Tell me about that.
(26) Do you like how you sound when you speak Japanese? Can you tell me about that?
(27) How do you present yourself (at work; with Japanese friends; with non-Japanese friends)?

Wrap-up

(28) How long do you think you'll stay in Japan? (On JET? In some other capacity?) What do you think you'll do when you finish JET?

(29) Do you think you'll continue to use/study Japanese after JET? Why? How? (etc.)
   Do you have any language-related goals? What are they?
(30) Do you have any language-related advice for someone coming to this area as a JET participant?
(31) Do you have any questions for me?

Appendix B: Sample L1 Interview Protocol

Interview Protocol for L1 Participants (Japanese followed by English translation)

バックグラウンド、職場について

(1) (インフォシートを参考にしながら、インタビューを受ける人の外国人交流について確認する)
(2) 職場では、外国人は何人います・いましたか。(本研究の関係者以外に外国人の職員がいる場合は、女性か男性かを聞きます)
(3) (外国人の同僚がいる人に)(その外国人)はいつから〜さんの職場に来ましたか。いつから(外国人)と仕事するようになりましたか。
(4) 〜さんの仕事は、(外国人)と関係がありますか。一緒に仕事をしますか。それとも仕事内容が(外国人)と関係がない仕事ですか。
(5) 職場にいる(外国人)とどれぐらい交流しますか。仕事以外に会うことがありますか。

言語についての質問　(職場)

(6) (その外国人)は職場で日本語を話しますか。コミュニケーションのトラブルを見たことや経験したことがありますか。それはその人の日本語能力が原因だったと思いますか。
(7) 〜さんの職場では、外国人はどんな日本語のスキルが必要だと思いますか。それはどうしてですか。(今話していただいた意見は、〜さんの職場に限っているのでしょうか。それとも、どんな職場にでも当てはまるものですか。)

言語についての質問　(職場以外)

(8) (インフォシートを参考にしながら)(外国人の友達、恋人、配偶者がいる人)(その外国人と話す時)

何語で話しますか。（配偶者・恋人）のご両親と話す時はどうですか。
(9) （その外国人と話す時）コミュニケーションのトラブルを経験したことがあります。(その人の)日本語能力が原因だったと思いますか。
(10) ～さんの町に住んでいる外国人は、生活していく上で、どんな日本語のスキルが必要だと思いますか。（どうしてですか。）
(11) 今まで、面白いことや印象に残った言語が係るハプニングなどがありますか。それについて教えていただけないでしょう。

方言についての質問

(12) 方言についてどう思いますか。（方言が好きですか。どうしてですか）
(13) ～さんは、方言を使いますか。どうしてですか。
(14) （１３番に「はい」と答えた人に）いつ、どこで方言を使いますか。誰と話す時に使いますか。
(15) 意図的に方言を使わないように気を付けることはありますか。（いつ・どこで・だれと）どうしてこのような（場合・時・相手）に方言を使わないようにしますか。
(16) （一般的な外国人、特定の外国人）が方言を理解することは大切だと思いますか。
(職場で？町で？レジャー？友達とのお付き合いなどで)
(17) （一般的な外国人、特定の外国人）が方言を使うことは大切だと思いますか。
(職場で？町で？レジャー？友達とのお付き合いなどで)
(18) （知り合いや関係者の外国人・同僚・友達・恋人・配偶者）が方言を使っているのを聞いたことがありますか。それについて教えていただけないでしょうか。（どう思いましたか。など）
(19) (まだ男女について話していないなら) 外国人が男性か女性によって、言葉遣いや方言使用に対しての意見・考え方が変わりますか。～さんは「外国人女性の日本語の話し方、外国人男性の日本語の話し方」に対して、どういうイメージを持っていますか。

最後に

(20) （この町）に生活しに来る外国人にどんなアドバイスをしますか。
(21) 私に聞きたいことはありますか

English Translation

Background, introductory – workplace specific

(1) (Making reference to the background questionnaire, I will do short 'small talk' confirming details about their interactions with foreigners/non-native speakers of Japanese)
(2) (For people with foreign coworkers) How long have you worked with your foreign coworker(s)? How many foreigners are there now in your workplace? (If there is more than the person who introduced the interviewee to me, ask if they are male or female.)
(3) How long have (the foreigners) been in your workplace?
(4) Does your job require you to work with them, or is your job not related to their work?
(5) How often do you interact with the foreigners in your workplace? Do you interact with them outside of the workplace?

Language-specific questions – workplace specific

(6) Does (the foreign coworker) use Japanese in your workplace? Have you ever experienced or witnessed any communication troubles related to their Japanese language ability?
(7) What kind of Japanese language skills do you think are necessary for foreigners in your workplace? Why? (Try to ascertain if the interviewee's comments are specific to their workplace, or views held generally.)

Language-specific questions – non-workplace specific

(8) (For people with foreign friends/partner/girlfriend/boyfriend/spouse.) What language(s) do you speak with your (friend/partner/boyfriend/girlfriend/spouse)? In-laws?
(9) Have you ever experienced or witnessed any communication troubles related to their Japanese language ability?
(10) What kind of Japanese language skills do you think are necessary for foreigners in your area (in your town, etc.)?
(11) Are there any language-related 'episodes', memorable stories, eye-opening moments that you'd like to share with me?

Dialect-specific questions

(12) What do you think about Japanese dialect? (Or: Do you like dialect? Why or why not?)
(13) Do you use Japanese dialect? (If no, ask why not.)
(14) (If they answered yes to Question 11) When/where do you use dialect? With whom do you use dialect?

(15) Do you ever make an effort to avoid using dialect? When/where/with whom? Why do you avoid using dialect in these situations?
(16) Do you think it's important for (foreigners) to be able to understand Japanese dialect? (Ask specifically about: In workplace? Around town? In social activities?)
(17) Do you think it's important for (foreigners) to be able to use Japanese dialect? (Ask specifically about: In workplace? Around town? In social activities?)
(18) Have you ever heard (your coworker/friend/partner/spouse) use dialect? Please tell me about it.
(19) (If the topic of gender has not come up, ask) Does it make a difference if the foreign speaker is male? Female? Is there a difference in your expectations/opinions about dialect use based on whether the speaker is male or female?

Wrap-up

(20) Do you have any language-related advice for a non-native speaker of Japanese coming to this area to live and work?
(21) Do you have any questions for me?

Appendix C: Transcription Conventions

…	Represents talk omitted from the excerpt. This includes fillers and continuers such as 'yeah, uh huh' as well as side sequence or off-topic talk omitted to keep excerpts short.
[ ]	Represents a word or phrase added to the excerpt for clarity, including translation information or something specified in an earlier part of the interview which is not included in the excerpt. Also represents words changed in order to protect participants' anonymity. In English translations of Japanese language excerpts, brackets may also indicate a word that is left out of the Japanese original, but understood by context.
( )	Represents portions of the interview that were difficult to hear.
(( ))	Represents information added to explain or supplement something in the excerpt, including non-linguistic details like laughter or gestures.
Fem.	Represents feminine speech
JD	Represents speech in Japanese Dialect.
SJ	Represents speech in Standard Japanese

Appendix D: Sample Questionnaires

Background Information Questionnaire (Current ALT)

(1) Age (please circle one)
    (a) 20–29   (b) 30–39   (c) 40–49   (d) 50–59   (e) 60 and over
(2) What year did you start your ALT position?
(3) How long do you plan to stay in the JET Program in total?
    (a) 1 year
    (b) 2 years
    (c) 3 years
    (d) 4 years
    (e) 5 years
    (f) I'm not sure but a few more years
    (g) I'm not sure but I'll probably end my contract soon
(4) How long do you plan to stay in Japan after JET?
    (a) I'll leave Japan within three months after my JET contract ends
    (b) Less than 1 year
    (c) 1–2 years
    (d) 3–4 years
    (e) 5–7 years
    (f) 8–10 years
    (g) Indefinitely
(5) Had you been to Japan before starting the JET Program? (if yes, circle all that apply)
    (a) No
    (b) Study abroad (if yes, please circle elementary, junior high, high school, college)
    (c) Vacation
    (d) Work purposes
    (e) Lived here with family as a child
    (f) Other (please explain)
(6) Where is your JET placement?
    (a) Elementary school only
    (b) Junior high school only

- (c) High school only
- (d) Combination elementary school and junior high school
- (e) Combination junior high school and high school
- (f) Combination elementary, junior high and high school
- (g) BOE (board of education)
- (h) Other (please explain)

(7) How many schools do you visit?

(8) How well do you speak Japanese? (circle all that apply)
- (a) I can't really speak Japanese very much
- (b) I can do simple greetings and introduce myself in Japanese
- (c) I can use Japanese for grocery shopping and buying bus and train tickets
- (d) I can have simple conversations in Japanese about everyday topics with people I know well
- (e) I can have extended conversations in Japanese about everyday topics with people I know well
- (f) I can have simple conversations in Japanese about a variety of topics with people I don't know well
- (g) I can have extended conversations in Japanese about a variety of topics with people I don't know well
- (h) I can speak with my coworkers about simple topics in Japanese
- (i) I can speak with my coworkers about complicated topics in Japanese
- (j) I can understand half or less of the discussion in office meetings in Japanese
- (k) I can understand almost all of the discussion in office meetings in Japanese
- (l) I can watch Japanese television dramas and movies and understand some of them
- (m) I can watch Japanese television dramas and movies and understand almost all of them
- (n) I can watch Japanese television news and understand some of it
- (o) I can watch Japanese television news and understand almost all of it
- (p) I can complete (pass) the Japanese Language Proficiency Test (JLPT) level N5
- (q) I can complete (pass) the JLPT level N4
- (r) I can complete (pass) the JLPT level N3
- (s) I can complete (pass) the JLPT level N2
- (t) I can complete (pass) the JLPT level N1

(9) When did you start studying Japanese?
- (a) I've never studied Japanese
- (b) In elementary school
- (c) In junior high or middle school

        (d) In high school
        (e) In college
        (f) When I joined JET
        (g) Other (please explain)
(10) Did you study Japanese before coming to Japan? (if yes, circle all that apply)
        (a) No
        (b) Self-study
        (c) High school classes
        (d) College courses (if yes, how many years of college study?)
        (e) Other (please explain)
(11) How often do you use Japanese in your daily life? (check one)
        (a) Every day, only at work (5 days a week)
        (b) Every day, at work and outside of work (7 days a week)
        (c) Every day, outside of work
        (d) Several times a week
        (e) Several times a month
        (f) Only a few times a month
        (g) Almost never
(12) Are you actively studying Japanese now? (if yes, circle all that apply)
        (a) I'm taking a course in town
        (b) I'm studying with a tutor
        (c) I'm using the JET correspondence course (which course?)
        (d) I study on my own using textbooks
        (e) I study on my own without textbooks
        (f) I'm studying for the JLPT (which level?)
        (g) No, I'm not actively studying Japanese right now
(13) Who do you speak Japanese with (in Japan)? (circle all that apply)
        (a) Japanese coworkers
        (b) Non-Japanese coworkers
        (c) Children/students at school
        (d) People in my neighborhood
        (e) Strangers (e.g. clerks at stores, post office)
        (f) Japanese friends
        (g) Non-Japanese friends
        (h) Japanese spouse or significant other
        (i) Non-Japanese spouse or significant other
        (j) Japanese in-laws or parents/relatives of Japanese significant other
        (k) My parents (one or both)
        (l) My grandparents and/or other relatives
        (m) Other (please explain)
(14) Where do you use Japanese? (circle all that apply)
        (a) At work
        (b) In social settings (with friends)

(c) In daily activities such as shopping
(d) In hobby-type activities (e.g. team sports, martial arts, craft lessons, etc.)
(e) Other (please explain)

Background Information Questionnaire (Japanese followed by English translation)

(1) 年齢　(○を付けてください)
  (a)　20–29才　(b)　30–39才　(c)　40–49才　(d)　50–59才
  (e) 60才以上
(2) 出身はどこですか。(今の居住地と違う場合、いつここに来ましたか)
(3) 職場はどこですか。
  (a) 公立の学校
  (b) 市役所・町役場
  (c) その他（記入してください）＿＿＿＿＿＿＿。
(4) 外国人と一緒に働いたことがありますか。
  (a) はい、職場に外国人が一人います（いました）
  (b) はい、職場に外国人が何人かいます（いました）
  (c) 今まで職場に外国人がいたことがありません
(5) (3番に「はい」と答えた人)その外国人と何語で話しますか・話しましたか。
  (a) (職場の外国人と) 日本語だけで話します
  (b) (職場の外国人と) 日本語と英語を交ぜながら話します
  (c) (職場の外国人と) 英語だけで話します
(6) 職場以外に、外国人の知り合いがいます・いましたか。(該当するものすべてに　○を付けてください)
  (a) はい、外国人の配偶者がいます
  (b) はい、外国人の恋人がいます
  (c) はい、外国人の友達がいます
  (d) はい、外国人の知り合いがいます
  (e) いいえ、職場以外に、外国人の知り合いがいません
(7) (5番に「はい」と答えた人) その外国人と何語で話しますか。(アルファベットとそこにある関係者に該当するすべての項目に○を付けてください)
  (a) (配偶者・恋人・友達・知り合い)と日本語だけで話します
  (b) (配偶者・恋人・友達・知り合い)と日本語と英語を交ぜて話します
  (c) (配偶者・恋人・友達・知り合い)と英語だけで話します

　　どうもありがとうございました。

English Translation

(1) Age (please circle one)
 (a) 20–29   (b) 30–39   (c) 40–49   (d) 50–59   (e) 60 and over
(2) Where are you from? (If different from current place of residence, ask when the interviewee came here)
(3) Where do you work? (circle one)
 (a) Public school
 (b) City/town office
 (c) Other (please specify)
(4) Do/did you work with any foreigners?
 (a) Yes, there is/was one person in my workplace who is a foreigner
 (b) Yes, there are/were some people in my workplace who are foreigners
 (c) No, there are/were no foreigners in my workplace
(5) If you answered 'yes' to number 3, what languages do/did you speak with the coworker(s) who are foreigners?
 (a) Only Japanese with my coworkers who are foreigners
 (b) A mixture of Japanese and English with coworkers who are foreigners
 (c) Only English with my coworkers who are foreigners
(6) Do/did you have any non-work relationships with people who are foreigners of Japanese? (circle all that apply)
 (a) Yes, I have a spouse who is a foreigners
 (b) Yes, I have a partner (boyfriend/girlfriend) who is a foreigner
 (c) Yes, I have some close friends who are foreigners
 (d) Yes, I have some acquaintances who are foreigners
 (e) No, I don't know anyone (outside of my workplace) who is a foreigner
(7) If you answered 'yes' to number 5, what languages do/did you speak with the foreigners?
 (a) Only Japanese with my (circle: spouse partner friends) who are foreigners
 (b) A mixture of Japanese and English with my (circle: spouse partner friends) who are foreigners
 (c) Only English with my (circle: spouse partner friends) who are foreigners

References

ACTFL (2012) ACTFL proficiency guidelines 2012. See https://www.actfl.org/resources/actfl-proficiency-guidelines-2012 (accessed 11 September 2018).
Arimoto, M. (2006) 「しまなみ海道」地域諸方言における母音融合現象 [Vowel coalescence phenomenon in the dialects of the Shimanami-Kaido region]. 音声研究 [*Journal of Phonetic Society of Japan*] 10 (1), 39–48.
Armour, W.S. (2011) Learning Japanese by reading 'manga': The rise of 'soft power pedagogy'. *RELC Journal* 42 (2), 125–140.
Arudou, D. (2012) Guestists, haters, the vested: Apologists take many forms. *The Japan Times*, June 5. See https://www.japantimes.co.jp/community/2012/06/05/issues/guestists-haters-the-vestedapologists-take-many-forms.
Ball, C. (2004) Repertoires of registers: Dialect in Japanese discourse. *Language and Communication* 24 (4), 355–380.
Banno, E., Ikeda, Y., Ohno, Y., Shinagawa, C. and Tokashiki, K. (2011) *Genki I: An Integrated Course in Elementary Japanese* (2nd edn). Tokyo: Japan Times.
Banno, E., Ikeda, Y., Ohno, Y., Shinagawa, C. and Tokashiki, K. (2020) *Genki I: An Integrated Course in Elementary Japanese* (3rd edn). Tokyo: Japan Times.
Barešova, I. (2015) On the categorization of the Japanese honorific system keigo. *Topics in Linguistics* 15 (1), 1–15.
Barke, A. (2010) Manipulating honorifics in the construction of social identities in Japanese television drama. *Journal of Sociolinguistics* 14 (4), 456–476.
Barke, A. (2011) Situated functions of addressee honorifics in Japanese television drama. In B.L. Davies, M. Haugh and A.J. Merrison (eds) *Situated Politeness* (pp. 111–128). London: Continuum International Publishing Co.
Barke, A. (2018) Constructing identity in the Japanese workplace through dialectal and honorific shifts. In H.M. Cook and J.S. Shibamoto-Smith (eds) *Japanese at Work: Politeness, Power, and Personae in Japanese Workplace Discourse* (pp. 123–149). Cham: Palgrave Macmillan.
Blackledge, A. and Pavlenko, A. (2002) Ideologies of language in multilingual contexts. *Multilingua* 21 (2/3), 121–326.
Bohn, M.T. (2015) Pedagogical perspectives on gendered speech styles in the teaching and learning of Japanese as a foreign language. *Applied Language Learning* 25, 41–70.
Bourdieu, P. (1991) *Language and Symbolic Power*. Cambridge, MA: Harvard University Press.
Brown, L. and Cheek, E. (2017) Gender identity in a second language: The use of first person pronouns by male learners of Japanese. *Journal of Language, Identity & Education* 16 (2), 94–108.
Bunkacho (2019) 令和元年度「国語に関する世論調査」の結果の概要 [Summary of the results of the 'Public Opinion Survey regarding the Japanese Language' Reiwa 1]. See https://www.bunka.go.jp/tokei_hakusho_shuppan/tokeichosa/kokugo_yoronchosa/index.html (accessed 26 September 2020).

Burgess, C. (2012) 'It's better if they speak broken Japanese': Language as a pathway or an obstacle to citizenship in Japan? In N. Gottlieb (ed.) *Language and Citizenship in Japan* (pp. 37–57). New York: Routledge.

Burgess, C. (2020) Keeping the door closed: The 2018 revisions to the 'Immigration' Control Act as a continuation of Japan's 'no-immigration' principle. *Electronic Journal of Contemporary Japanese Studies*. See http://japanesestudies.org.uk/ejcjs/index.html (accessed 31 August 2022).

Burgess, C. (2021) The impact of COVID-19 on foreign residents in 'no immigration' Japan: Structural inequity, Japanese-style multiculturalism, and diminishing social capital. *IRiS Working Paper Series* (48/2021), 3–22. See https://www.birmingham.ac.uk/documents/college-social-sciences/social-policy/iris/2021/iris-node-wp-7-2021-final.pdf (accessed 31 August 2022).

Carlson, R.L. (2018) 'More Japanese than Japanese': Subjectivation in the age of brand nationalism and the internet. PhD thesis, University of Pittsburgh.

Carroll, T. (2001a) Changing attitudes: Dialects versus the standard language in Japan. In T.E. McAuley (ed.) *Language Change in East Asia* (pp. 7–26). New York: Routledge.

Carroll, T. (2001b) *Language Planning and Language Change in Japan*. New York: Routledge.

Carroll, T. (2005) Beyond keigo: Smooth communication and the expression of respect in Japanese as a foreign language. *International Journal of the Sociology of Language* 1, 233–247.

Cook, H.M. (2006) Joint construction of folk beliefs by JFL learners and Japanese host families. In M.A. DuFon and E. Churchill (eds) *Language Learners in Study Abroad Contexts* (pp. 120–150). Clevedon: Multilingual Matters.

Cook, H.M. (2008) *Socializing Identities through Speech Style: Learners of Japanese as a Foreign Language*. Bristol: Multilingual Matters.

Cook, V. (1999) Going beyond the native speaker in language teaching. *TESOL Quarterly* 33 (2), 185–209.

Cook, V. (2016) Where is the native speaker now? *TESOL Quarterly* 50 (1), 186–189.

Coulmas, F. (2005) Linguistic etiquette in Japanese society. In R.J. Watts, S. Ide and K. Ehlich (eds) *Politeness in Language: Studies in History, Theory and Practice* (pp. 299–323). Berlin: Mouton de Gruyter.

Creswell, J.W. (2007) *Qualitative Inquiry & Research Design: Choosing among Five Approaches*. Thousand Oaks, CA: Sage Publications.

Davies, A. (2003) *The Native Speaker: Myth and Reality*. Clevedon: Multilingual Matters.

Davies, A. (2007) *An Introduction to Applied Linguistics: From Practice to Theory*. Edinburgh: Edinburgh University Press.

Davies, R.J. and Ikeno, O. (2011) *Japanese Mind: Understanding Contemporary Japanese Culture*. Tokyo: Tuttle Publishing.

Doerr, N.M. (ed.) (2009a) *The Native Speaker Concept: Ethnographic Investigations of Native Speaker Effects*. Berlin: Mouton de Gruyter.

Doerr, N.M. (2009b) Uncovering another 'native speaker myth': Juxtaposing standardization processes in first and second languages of English-as-a-second-language learners. In N.M. Doerr (ed.) *The Native Speaker Concept: Ethnographic Investigations of Native Speaker Effects* (pp. 185–208). Berlin: Mouton de Gruyter.

Doerr, N.M. and Kumagai, Y. (2009) Towards a critical orientation in second language education. In N.M. Doerr (ed.) *The Native Speaker Concept: Ethnographic Investigations of Native Speaker Effects* (pp. 299–317). Berlin: Mouton de Gruyter.

Doinaka, A. (2005) 愛媛ことば図鑑：マンガで読み解く愛媛の方言 [*Ehime Language Encyclopedia: Understanding Ehime Dialect through Manga*]. Matsuyama: Atorasu Shuppan.

Duff, P.A. (2007) Qualitative approaches to classroom research with English language learners. In C. Davison and J. Cummins (eds) *International Handbook of English Language Teaching* (pp. 973–986). Boston, MA: Springer.

Duff, P.A. (2008) *Case Study Research in Applied Linguistics*. New York: Lawrence Erlbaum Associates.

Dunn, C.D. (1999) Coming of age in Japan: Language ideology and the acquisition of formal speech registers. In J. Verschueren (ed.) *Language and Ideology: Selected Papers from the Sixth International Pragmatics Conference* (pp. 89–97). Antwerp: International Pragmatics Association.

Dunn, C.D. (2011) Formal forms or verbal strategies? Politeness theory and Japanese business etiquette training. *Journal of Pragmatics* 43 (15), 3643–3654.

Dunn, C.D. (2013) Speaking politely, kindly, and beautifully: Ideologies of politeness in Japanese business etiquette training. *Multilingua* 32 (2), 225–245.

Ebuchi, T. (2019) Foreign workforce of 2.2m helps Japan ease labor crunch. *Nikkei Asia*, July 11. See https://asia.nikkei.com/ (accessed 25 January 2021).

Ehime Prefectural Website (2021) https://www.pref.ehime.jp/index-e.html (accessed 8 September 2022).

Erickson, F. (1992) Ethnographic microanalysis of interaction. In M.D. LeCompte, W.L. Millroy and J. Preissle (eds) *The Handbook of Qualitative Research in Education* (pp. 201–225). San Diego, CA: Academic Press Inc.

eStat.go.jp (2014) 政府統計の総合窓口 [Portal site of official statistics of Japan]. https://www.e-stat.go.jp/ (accessed 16 March 2021).

Facchini, G., Margalit, Y. and Nakata, H. (2016) Countering public opposition to immigration: The impact of information campaigns. *IZA Discussion Papers*, No. 10420, http://hdl.handle.net/10419/161043.

Fairbrother, L. (2020) Native-speakerism and nihonjinron in Japanese higher education policy and related hiring practices: A focus on the Japanese 'top global universities' project. In S.A. Houghton and J. Bouchard (eds) *Native-Speakerism: Its Resilience and Undoing* (pp. 47–68). Singapore: Springer.

Ferguson, C.A. (1981) 'Foreigner talk' as the name of a simplified register. *International Journal of the Sociology of Language* 1981 (28), 9–18. https://doi.org/10.1515/ijsl.1981.28.9.

Firth, A. and Wagner, J. (1997) On discourse, communication, and (some) fundamental concepts in SLA research. *Modern Language Journal* 81 (3), 285–300.

Firth, A. and Wagner, J. (2007) Second/foreign language learning as a social accomplishment: Elaborations on a reconceptualized SLA. *The Modern Language Journal* 91, 800–819.

Fukuda, C. (2014) Identities and linguistic varieties in Japanese: An analysis of language ideologies as participants' accomplishments. *Pragmatics* 24 (1), 35–62.

Geertz, C. (1973) Thick description: Toward an interpretive theory of culture. In. C. Geertz (ed.) *The Interpretation of Cultures: Selected Essays* (pp. 3–30). New York: Basic Books.

Gelin, M. (2020) Japan radically increased immigration—and no one protested. *Foreign Policy*. See https://foreignpolicy.com/2020/06/23/japan-immigration-policy-xenophobia-migration/ (accessed 19 March 2021).

Gordon, C. and Kraut, J. (2018) Interactional sociolinguistics. In B. Vine (ed.) *The Routledge Handbook of Language in the Workplace* (pp. 3–14). New York: Routledge.

Gottlieb, N. (2005) *Language and Society in Japan*. Cambridge: Cambridge University Press.

Gottlieb, N. (2012) Language, citizenship, and identity in Japan. In N. Gottlieb (ed.) *Language and Citizenship in Japan* (pp. 1–18). New York: Routledge.

Grenfell, M. (2011) *Bourdieu, Language and Linguistics*. London: Continuum.

Gumperz, J.J. (2015) Interactional sociolinguistics: A personal perspective. In D. Tannen, H.E. Hamilton and D. Schiffrin (eds) *The Handbook of Discourse Analysis* (pp. 309–323). Malden, MA: Wiley Blackwell.

Hammersley, M. and Gomm, R. (2008) Assessing the radical critique of interviews. In M. Hammersley (ed.) *Questioning Qualitative Inquiry: Critical Essays* (pp. 89–100). London: Sage.

Harrison, G. (2009) Language politics, linguistic capital and bilingual practitioners in social work. *British Journal of Social Work* 39 (6), 1082–1100.

Hasegawa, A. (2022) The past, present, and future of second language acquisition of Japanese research. In C. Shei and S. Li (eds) *The Routledge Handbook of Asian Linguistics* (pp. 637–649). New York: Routledge. https://doi.org/10.4324/9781003090205-43.

Hashimoto, N. (2018) 「移民政策はとらない」としつつ外国人受入れを拡大し続ける、という最悪の移民政策 [Maintaining a 'no immigration policy' stance while continuing to expand the acceptance of foreigners – The worst possible immigration policy]. *Huffington Post*, Japan Edition, 5 March. See https://www.huffingtonpost.jp/naoko-hashimoto/gastarbeiter_a_23376626/ (accessed 7 November 2022).

Heinrich, P. (2005) Language ideology in JFL textbooks. *International Journal of the Sociology of Language* 2005 (175–176), 213–232.

Heinrich, P. (2012) *The Making of Monolingual Japan: Language Ideology and Japanese Modernity*. Bristol: Multilingual Matters.

Heinrich, P. (2017) New presentations of self in everyday life: Linguistic transgressions in England, Germany, and Japan. In R. Bassiouney (ed.) *Identity and Dialect Performance* (pp. 210–225). London: Routledge.

Heinrich, P. (2018) Dialect cosplay: Language use by the young generation. In P. Heinrich and C. Galan (eds) *Being Young in Super-Aging Japan: Formative Events and Cultural Reactions* (1st edn). New York: Routledge. https://doi.org/10.4324/9781351025065.

Heinrich, P. (2022) After language standardization: Dialect cosplay in Japan. In N. McLelland and H. Zhao (eds) *Language Standardization and Language Variation in Multilingual Contexts: Asian Perspectives* (pp. 281–297). Bristol: Multilingual Matters.

Higgins, C. (2003) 'Ownership' of English in the outer circle: An alternative to the NS-NNS dichotomy. *TESOL Quarterly* 37 (4), 615–644.

Holliday, A. (2006) Native-speakerism. *ELT Journal* 60 (4), 385–387. https://doi.org/10.1093/elt/ccl030.

Holliday, A. (2008) Standards of English and politics of inclusion. *Language Teaching* 41 (1), 119–130.

Holliday, A. (2014) Native speakerism. See http://adrianholliday.com/wp-content/uploads/2014/01/nismencyc16plain-submitted.pdf (accessed 10 April 2018).

Holliday, A. (2018) Native speakerism. In J.I. Liontas and M. DelliCarpini (eds) *The TESOL Encyclopedia of English Language Teaching* (pp. 1–9). Hoboken, NJ: John Wiley & Sons.

Houghton, S.A. and Rivers, D.J. (eds) (2013) *Native-Speakerism in Japan: Intergroup Dynamics in Foreign Language Education*. Bristol: Multilingual Matters.

Houghton, S.A. and Hashimoto, K. (eds) (2018) *Towards Post-Native-Speakerism: Dynamics and Shifts*. Singapore: Springer.

Houghton, S.A., Rivers, D.J. and Hashimoto, K. (2018) *Beyond Native-Speakerism: Current Explorations and Future Visions*. New York: Routledge.

Iino, M. (2006) Norms of interaction in a Japanese homestay setting: Toward a two-way flow of linguistic and cultural resources. In M.A. DuFon and E. Churchill (eds) *Language Learners in Study Abroad Contexts* (pp. 151–173). Clevedon: Multilingual Matters.

Inoue, F. (2011) Standardization and de-standardization in spoken Japanese. In P. Heinrich and C. Galan (eds) *Language Life in Japan: Transformation and Prospects*. (pp. 109-123). London: Routledge.

Inoue, M. (2006) *Vicarious Language: Gender and Linguistic Modernity in Japan*. Berkeley, CA: University of California Press.

Inoue, T. and Kurata, Y. (2020) 移民政策なき外国人労働者政策を擁護する知識人たち (2): やさしい日本語 日本語学校 [The intellectuals who defend the foreign workers policy neglecting the existence of migrants(2): Plain Japanese and Japanese language schools]. 一橋社会科学, 12, 37–68. https://doi.org/10.15057/31042.

Iori, I. (2016) The enterprise of Yasashii Nihongo: For a sustainable multicultural society in Japan. *Humanities and Natural Studies* 10, 4–19.

Iori, I. (2019) やさしい日本語を用いた分かりやすい情報発信 [Easy-to-understand information dissemination using Easy Japanese]. See https://www.2020games.metro.tokyo.lg.jp/multilingual/references/pdf/1707forum/a-2.pdf (accessed 19 July 2022).

Iori, I. (2021) An interdisciplinary study for the development of integral Japanese textbooks for foreign-rooted children using Yasashii-Nihongo (Easy Japanese). *Impact* 2021 (4), 24–26. See https://www.ingentaconnect.com/content/sil/impact/2021/00002021/00000004/art00010?crawler=true&mimetype=application/pdf (accessed 26 July 2022).

Ishihara, N. and Tarone, E. (2009) Subjectivity and pragmatic choice in L2 Japanese: Emulating and resisting pragmatic norms. In N. Taguchi (ed.) *Pragmatic Competence* (pp. 101–128). Berlin: Mouton de Gruyter.

Itabashi, H. (2020) Foreign population in Japan reaches record 2.93 million at end of December. *Asahi Shimbum*, 30 March. See https://www.asahi.com/ajw/articles/photo/29196706 (accessed 16 March 2021).

Itakura, H. (2008) Attitudes towards masculine Japanese speech in multilingual professional contexts of Hong Kong: Gender, identity, and native-speaker status. *Journal of Multilingual and Multicultural Development* 29 (6), 467–482.

Ito, H. and Tokarev, A. (2021) From Yasashii Nihongo in non-disaster times towards a plurilingual language education approach: An outlook from the perspective of 'reasonable accommodation'. *F1000Research* 10, 1–16. https://doi.org/10.12688/f1000research.36372.2.

Japan Agency for Cultural Affairs (2010) 平成22年度国語に関する世論調査の結果について [Results of the 2010 survey concerning Japanese language]. See http://www.bunka.go.jp/kokugo_nihongo/yoronchousa/h22/pdf/h22_chosa_kekka.pdf (accessed 7 June 2018).

Japan Ministry of Justice (2021) 令和3年6月末現在における在留外国人数について【第4表】都道府県別在留外国人数の推移 [Number of foreign residents as of the end of June 2021 [Table 4] Changes in the number of foreign residents by prefecture]. See https://www.moj.go.jp/isa/publications/press/13_00017.html

Japan Ministry of Justice, Immigration Bureau (2017) Points-based preferential immigration control and residency management treatment for highly skilled foreign professionals [leaflet]. See http://www.immi-moj.go.jp/newimmiact_3/en/index.html (accessed 25 January 2021).

JET Program (n.d., a) The JET Program USA. See https://jetprogramusa.org/ (accessed 6 July 2021).

JET Program (n.d., b) Eligibility criteria. See https://jetprogramusa.org/eligibility-criteria/ (accessed 6 July 2021).

Jinnouchi, M. (2007) Dialect boom in Japan. *Dialectologia et Geolinguistica* 2007 (15), 44–51.

Jones, M. (2003) An argument for the teaching and learning of non-standard Japanese. *JALT Conference Proceedings*. See http://jalt-publications.org/archive/proceedings/2003/E054.pdf (accessed 17 December 2012).

Kamiyoshi, U. (2020) Japan's new 'immigration' policy and the society's responses. In N.M. Doerr (ed.) *The Global Education Effect and Japan: Constructing New Borders and Identification Practices* (pp. 61–74). New York: Routledge.

Kamiyoshi, U. (2022) Japan's immigration policy and Japanese language requirements. In T. Endoh (ed.) *Open Borders, Open Society? Immigration and Social Integration in Japan.* (pp. 169–190). Opladen: Verlag Barbara Budrich.

Kasper, G. and Omori, M. (2010) Language and culture. *Sociolinguistics and Language Education* 18, 455–491.

Kimura, G.C. (2022) Does easy language promote integration? - Japanese and German perspectives [Conference presentation]. *Attractive for Immigrants? Migrants' Life Satisfaction in Host Countries in Comparison*, Japanisch-Deutsches Zentrum, Berlin.

Kinsui, S. (2003) ヴァーチャル日本語：役割語の謎 [*Virtual Japanese: The Mystery of Role Language*]. Tokyo: Iwanami Shoten.

Kobayashi, T. (2004) アクセサリーとしての現代方言 [Contemporary dialect as accessory]. 社会言語科学 7 (1), 105–107.

Kobayashi, T. (2007) 方言機能論への誘い [An invitation to the study of functional dialectology.] In 方言の機能 [*The Function of Dialect*] (pp. v–xiii). Tokyo: Iwanami Shoten.

Kodama, N. (2019) 無核ノ付き形のピッチアクセント方言への継承 [Inherited unaccented genitives in Japanese pitch accent dialects]. ありあけ 熊本大学言語学論集 18, 29–80. See http://lg.let.kumamoto-u.ac.jp/ariake/19-02.pdf (accessed 8 September 2022).

Kramsch, C. and Zhang, L. (2018) *The Multilingual Instructor*. Oxford: Oxford University Press.

Kroo, J. (2014) Alternative masculinities: Soshokukei-danshi 'herbivore men' and first person pronoun usage. *Journal and Proceedings of the Gender Awareness in Language Education* 7, 5–28.

Kroo, J. (2018) Gentle masculinity in East Asia: 'Herbivore Men' and interlocutor constructed language. *Journal of Asian Pacific Communication* 28 (2), 251–280.

Kroo, J. and Satoh, K. (eds) (2021) *Linguistic Tactics and Strategies of Marginalization in Japanese*. New York: Palgrave McMillan.

Kroskrity, P.V. (2004) Language ideologies. In A. Duranti (ed.) *A Companion to Linguistic Anthropology* (pp. 496–517). Malden, MA: Blackwell.

Kubo, H. (2018) 愛媛県松山市方言における命令表現の使用差 [A study of the difference in the uses of imperative expressions in Ehime Matsuyama dialect]. 言語文化研究38巻1–2号, 397–416. See http://id.nii.ac.jp/1249/00002607/ (accessed 8 September 2022).

Kubota, R. (2009) Rethinking the superiority of the native speaker: Toward a relational understanding of power. In N.M. Doerr (ed.) *The Native Speaker Concept: Ethnographic Investigations of Native Speaker Effects* (pp. 233–248). Berlin: Mouton de Gruyter.

Kubota, R. (2014) Standardization of language and culture. In S. Sato and N.M. Doerr (eds) *Rethinking Language and Culture in Japanese Education: Beyond the Standard* (pp. 19–34). Bristol: Multilingual Matters.

Kusaka, L.L. (2014) Negotiating identities: An interview study and autoethnography of six Japanese American TESOL professionals in Japan. Thesis, Temple University.

Kusunoki, R. (2018) Japanese co-workers' view of their communication with EPA foreign nurse trainees. PhD thesis, University of Queensland, Australia.

Kusunoki, R. and Hashimoto, K. (2022) Is 'Easy Japanese' a language option? Local responses to the increasing foreign resident population from Southeast Asia. *Asian Studies Review* 1–18. https://doi.org/10.1080/10357823.2022.2075322.

Kvale, S. and Brinkmann, S. (2009) *InterViews: Learning the Craft of Qualitative Research Interviewing*. Los Angeles, CA: Sage Publications.

Liddicoat, A. (2016) Native and non-native speaker identities in interaction: Trajectories of power. *Applied Linguistics Review* 7 (4), 409–429.

Lipski, J.M. (2005) 'Me want cookie': Foreigner talk as monster talk. Invited lecture, 29 March, Shippensburg University, Pennsylvania.

Long, D. (1996) Quasi-standard as a linguistic concept. *American Speech* 71 (2), 118–135.

Lowe, R.J. and Pinner, R. (2016) Finding the connections between native-speakerism and authenticity. *Applied Linguistics Review* 7 (1), 27–52.

Matsumoto, Y. (2002) Gender identity and the presentation of self in Japanese. In S. Benor, M. Rose, D. Sharma, J. Sweetland and Q. Zhang (eds) *Gendered Practices in Language* (pp. 339–352). Stanford, CA: CSLI Publications.

Menard-Warwick, J. and Leung, G. (2017) Translingual practice in L2 Japanese: Workplace narratives. *Language and Intercultural Communication* 17 (3), 270–287.

Metzgar, E.T. (2012) Promoting Japan: One JET at a time. *The CPD Blog*, University of Southern California Center on Public Diplomacy. See https://uscpublicdiplomacy.org/blog/promoting-"journalism-purpose" (accessed 17 March 2015).

Miller, L. (2015) Linguistic folk theories and foreign celebrities of the past. *Japanese Language and Literature* 49 (2), 405–428.

Mishler, E.G. (1991) *Research Interviewing: Context and Narrative*. Cambridge, MA: Harvard University Press.

Miyamoto Caltabiano, Y. (2008) Consequences of shifting styles in Japanese: L2 style-shifting and L1 listeners' attitudes. In *Selected Proceedings of the 2007 Second Language Research Forum* (pp. 131–143). Somerville, MA: Cascadilla Proceedings Project.

Miyazaki, A. (2004) Japanese junior high school girls' and boys' first-person pronoun use and their social world. In S. Okamoto and J. Shibamoto-Smith (eds) *Japanese Language, Gender, and Ideology: Cultural Models and Real People* (pp. 256–274). Oxford: Oxford University Press.

Moody, S.J. (2014) 'Well, I'm a Gaijin': Constructing identity through English and humor in the international workplace. *Journal of Pragmatics* 60, 75–88.

Moody, S.J. (2018) Fitting in or standing out? A conflict of belonging and identity in intercultural polite talk at work. *Applied Linguistics* 39 (6), 775–798.

Mori, J. (2012) *Social and Interactive Perspectives on Japanese Language Proficiency: Learning through Listening towards Advanced Japanese*. University Park, PA: CALPER Publications.

Morris-Suzuki, T. (1998) *Re-Inventing Japan: Time, Space, Nation*. Armonk, NY: M.E. Sharpe.

Mukai, R. (2003) 松山における外国人留学生の方言認識と方言教育のあり方--アンケート及び聞き取りテストの結果に基づいて [An analysis of foreign students' listening comprehension of Japanese regional dialects (Research Notes)]. 松山東雲女子大学人文学部紀要, 107–119.

Nakagawa, H. (2019) 愛媛県宇和島市の方言文末詞 [Sentence-final dialect expressions in Uwajima City Ehime Prefecture.] In M. Hidaka (ed.) 全国方言文法辞典資料集, (5) 活用体系 (4), 109–178. See http://hougen.sakura.ne.jp/shuppan/2019a/5-11.pdf (accessed 8 September 2022).

Nakamura, M. (2008) Masculinity and national language: The silent construction of a dominant language ideology. *Gender & Language* 2 (1), 25–50.

Nakamura, M. (2011) Theorizing the constructive-ideological approach to Japanese women's language. 自然 人間 社会 50, 1–25.

Nakao, Y. (2020) Plain Japanese, please: Amid tourism boom, easy form of language could help ease. *The Japan Times*, 13 January. See https://www.japantimes.co.jp/news/2020/01/13/national/plain-japanese-tourism-language/ (accessed 18 January 2020).

NHK (Nihon Hoso Kyokai Hoso Bunka Kenkyujo) (2005) *NHK21 世紀に残したいふるさと日本のことば. 5(中国 四国地方) [Hometown Japan Language to Leave Behind for the 21st Century: 5 (Chūgoku, Shikoku Region)]*. Tokyo: Gakushu Kenkyusha.

Nishizaka, A. (1999) Doing interpreting within interaction: The interactive accomplishment of a 'henna gaijin' or 'strange foreigner'. *Human Studies* 22 (2), 235–251.

Niyekawa, A.M. (1991) *Minimum Essential Politeness: A Guide to the Japanese Honorific Language*. Tokyo: Kodansha.

Nomura, K. and Mochizuki, T. (2018) Native-speakerism perceived by 'non-native-speaking' teachers of Japanese in Hong Kong. In S.A. Houghton and K. Hashimoto (eds) *Towards Post-Native-Speakerism: Dynamics and Shifts* (pp. 79–95). Singapore: Springer.

Norton, B. (1997) Language, identity, and the ownership of English. *TESOL Quarterly* 31 (3), 409–429.

Norton, B. (2000) *Identity and Language Learning: Gender, Ethnicity and Educational Change*. Harlow: Pearson Education ESL.

Norton, B. (2006) Identity: Second language. In E.K. Brown and A. Anderson (eds) *Encyclopedia of Language & Linguistics* (2nd edn, pp. 502–508). Boston, MA: Elsevier.

Norton, B. (2013) *Identity and Language Learning: Extending the Conversation* (2nd edn). Bristol: Multilingual Matters.

Occhi, D. (2008) Dialect speakers on dialect speech. In M. Amano, M. O'Toole and Z. Goebel (eds) *Identity in Text Interpretation and Everyday Life: Proceedings of the Third International Conference Hermeneutic Study and Education of Textual Configuration* (pp. 99–111). Nagoya: Graduate School of Letters, Nagoya University.

O'Donnell, K. [Dogen] (2016, Sept. 26) Advanced Japanese lesson #15: 'The Conversation' / 上級日本語：レッスン 15「例の会話」[Video]. See https://www.youtube.com/watch?v=lIH6vjyHKxM.

Ohara, Y. (2001) Finding one's voice in Japanese: A study of the pitch levels of L2 users. In A. Pavlenko, A. Blackledge, I. Piller and M. Teutsch-Dwyer (eds) *Multilingualism, Second Language Learning, and Gender* (pp. 239–256). Berlin: Mouton de Gruyter.

Ohara, Y. (2019) Gendered speech. In P. Heinrich and Y. Ohara (eds) *Routledge Handbook of Japanese Sociolinguistics* (pp. 279–295). New York: Routledge.

Ohuchi, N. (2014) 臨時災害放送局における方言利用の意義に関する考察：福島県富岡町「おだがいさま FM」を事例として [A study of the meaning of dialect use in an extraordinary disaster FM station: The example of Odagaisama Radio]. 現代社会文化研究 59, 1–18.

Oka, M., Tsutsui, M., Kondo, J., Emori, S., Hanai, Y. and Ishikawa, S. (2009) *Tobira: Gateway to Advanced Japanese Learning Through Content and Multimedia*. Tokyo: Kuroshio Publishers.

Okamoto, S. (1995) 'Tasteless' Japanese: Less 'feminine' speech among young Japanese women. In K. Hall and M. Bucholtz (eds) *Gender Articulated: Language and the Socially Constructed Self* (pp. 297–325). New York: Routledge.

Okamoto, S. (2008a) Speech style and the use of regional (Yamaguchi) and standard Japanese in conversations. In K. Jones and T. Ono (eds) *Style Shifting in Japanese* (pp. 229–250). Amsterdam: John Benjamins.

Okamoto, S. (2008b) The use of 'regional' and 'standard' Japanese in conversations: A case study from Osaka. In J. Mori and A.S. Ohta (eds) *Japanese Applied Linguistics: Discourse and Social Perspectives* (pp. 132–159). London: Continuum.

Okamoto, S. (2018) Metapragmatic discourse in self-help books on Japanese women's speech: An indexical approach to social meanings. In M.E. Hudson, Y. Matsumoto and J. Mori (eds) *Pragmatics of Japanese: Perspectives on Grammar, Interaction and Culture* (pp. 246–266). Amsterdam: John Benjamins.

Okamoto, S. (2021) Japanese language and gender research: The last thirty years and beyond. *Gender & Language* 15 (2), 277–288.

Okamoto, S. and Shibamoto-Smith, J.S. (eds) (2004) *Japanese Language, Gender, and Ideology: Cultural Models and Real People*. Oxford: Oxford University Press.

Okamoto, S. and Shibamoto-Smith, J.S. (2008) Constructing linguistic femininity in contemporary Japan: Scholarly and popular representations. *Gender & Language* 2 (1), 87–112.

Okamoto, S. and Shibamoto-Smith, J.S. (2016) *The Social Life of the Japanese Language: Cultural Discourse and Situated Practice*. Cambridge: Cambridge University Press.

Okubo, Y. (2009) Localization of multicultural education and the reproduction of native speaker concept in Japan. In N.M. Doerr (ed.) *The Native Speaker Concept: Ethnographic Investigations of Native Speaker Effects* (pp. 101–131). Berlin: Mouton de Gruyter.

O'Rourke, B. and Ramallo, F.F. (2011) The native-non-native dichotomy in minority language contexts: Comparisons between Irish and Galician. *Language Problems and Language Planning* 35 (2), 139–159.

Otomo, R. (2019) Language and migration in Japan. In P. Heinrich and Y. Ohara (eds) *Routledge Handbook of Japanese Sociolinguistics* (pp. 91–109). New York: Routledge.

Otomo, R. (2020) Healthcare, language and a free-trade agreement: Institutional logics of on-the-job Japanese language training for migrant healthcare workers. *Multilingua* 39 (3), 343–367.

Parmegiani, A. (2014) The (dis)ownership of English: Language and identity construction among Zulu students at the University of KwaZulu-Natal. *International Journal of Bilingual Education and Bilingualism* 17 (6), 683–694.

Pennycook, A. (1994) *The Cultural Politics of English as an International Language*. New York: Routledge.

Pennycook, A. (2012) Lingua francas as language ideologies. In A. Kirkpatrick and R. Sussex (eds) *English as an International Language in Asia: Implications for Language Education* (pp. 137–154). Dordrecht: Springer.

Phillipson, R., Skutnabb-Kangas, T. and Rannut, M. (1995) Introduction. In T. Skutnabb-Kangas, R. Phillipson and M. Rannut (eds) *Linguistic Human Rights: Overcoming Linguistic Discrimination* (pp. 1–24). Berlin: Mouton de Gruyter.

Rampton, M.B.H. (1990) Displacing the 'native speaker': Expertise, affiliation, and inheritance. *ELT Journal* 44 (2), 97–101.

Ramsey, S.R. (2004) The Japanese language and the making of tradition. *Japanese Language and Literature* 38 (1), 81–110.

Reagan, T. (2019) *Linguistic Legitimacy and Social Justice*. Cham: Springer.

Rumsey, A. (1990) Wording, meaning, and linguistic ideology. *American Anthropologist* 92 (2), 346–361.

Saldaña, J. (2013) *The Coding Manual for Qualitative Researchers*. Thousand Oaks, CA: Sage Publications.

Sanada, S. (2019) Japanese dialects. In P. Heinrich and Y. Ohara (eds) *Routledge Handbook of Japanese Sociolinguistics* (pp. 63–77). New York: Routledge.

Soars, J. and Soars, L. (2002) *American Headway: Student Book 1*. Oxford: Oxford University Press.

Sato, S. (2009) Communication as an intersubjective and collaborative activity: When the native/non-native speaker's identity appears in computer-mediated communication. In N.M. Doerr (ed.) *The Native Speaker Concept: Ethnographic Investigations of Native Speaker Effects* (pp. 277–294). Berlin: Mouton De Gruyter.

Seidman, I. (2006) *Interviewing as Qualitative Research: A Guide for Researchers in Education and the Social Sciences*. New York: Teachers College Press.

Shibamoto-Smith, J.S. and Occhi, D.J. (2009) The green leaves of love: Japanese romantic heroines, authentic femininity, and dialect. *Journal of Sociolinguistics* 13 (4), 524–546.

Shibatani, M. (1990) *The Languages of Japan*. Cambridge: Cambridge University Press.

Shimizu M. and Akiyama, E. (1999) 愛媛県青島方言のアクセント [The accent of Aoshima dialect in Ehime prefecture]. 日本語科学 6, 49–70. http://doi.org/10.15084/00002019.

Shinkai, M. (director) (2016) *Kimi no na wa* [*Your Name*] [film]. Toho Corporation, CoMix Wave Films Inc.

Siegal, M.S. (1994) Looking East: Learning Japanese as a second language in Japan and the interaction of race, gender and social context. PhD thesis, University of California, Berkeley.

Siegal, M. (1995) Individual differences and study abroad. In B.F. Freed (ed.) *Second Language Acquisition in a Study Abroad Context* (pp. 225–244). Amsterdam: John Benjamins Publishing.

Siegal, M. (1996) The role of learner subjectivity in second language sociolinguistic competency: Western women learning Japanese. *Applied Linguistics* 17 (3), 356–382.

Silver, R.E. (2005) The discourse of linguistic capital: Language and economic policy planning in Singapore. *Language Policy* 4 (1), 47–66.

Silverstein, M. (1979) Language structure and linguistic ideology. In P.R. Clyne, W.F. Hanks and C.L. Hofbauer (eds) *The Elements: A Parasession on Linguistic Units and Levels* (pp. 193–247). Chicago, IL: Chicago Linguistic Society.

Smith, M.A. (2015) Who is a legitimate French speaker? The Senegalese in Paris and the crossing of linguistic and social borders. *French Cultural Studies* 26 (3), 317–329.

Strausz, M. (2019) *Help (Not) Wanted: Immigration Politics in Japan*. Albany, NY: SUNY Press.

Stroud, C. (2002) Framing Bourdieu socioculturally: Alternative forms of linguistic legitimacy in postcolonial Mozambique. *Multilingua* 21, 247–273.

SturtzSreetharan, C.L. (2009) *Ore* and *omae*: Japanese men's uses of first-and second-person pronouns. *Pragmatics* 19 (2), 253–278.

SturtzSreetharan, C. (2015) '*Na (a) n ya nen*': Negotiating language and identity in the Kansai Region. *Japanese Language and Literature* 49 (2), 429–452.

SturtzSreetharan, C. (2017) Language and masculinity: The role of Osaka dialect in contemporary ideals of fatherhood. *Gender & Language* 11 (4), 552–574.

Sunaoshi, Y. (2004) Farm women's professional discourse in Ibaraki. In S. Okamoto and J.S. Shibamoto Smith (eds) *Japanese Language, Gender, and Ideology: Cultural Models and Real People* (pp. 187–204). Oxford: Oxford University Press.

Suzuki, A. (2009) When gaijin matters: Theory-building in Japanese multiparty interaction. In H. Nguyen and G. Kasper (eds) *Talk-in-Interaction: Multilingual Perspectives* (pp. 89–110). Honolulu, HI: University of Hawai'i Press.

Suzuki, S. (2015) Nationalism lite? The commodification of non-Japanese speech in Japanese media. *Japanese Language and Literature* 49 (2), 509–529.

Suzuki, S. (2018) Nationalism and gender in the representation of non-Japanese characters' speech in contemporary Japanese novels. *Pragmatics* 28 (2), 271–302.

Suzuki, S. (2020) Masculinity, race and national identity: Representations of non-Japanese men's speech in contemporary Japanese novels. *Gender & Language* 14 (3), 226–243.

Takato, M. (2009) 'Native speaker' status on border-crossing: The Okinawan Nikkei diaspora, national language, and heterogeneity. In N.M. Doerr (ed.) *The Native Speaker Concept: Ethnographic Investigations of Native Speaker Effects* (pp. 17–28). Berlin: Mouton de Gruyter.

Takatori, Y. (2015) More Japanese than the Japanese: Translations of interviews with foreigners. *Perspectives* 23 (3), 475–488.

Takeuchi, J.D. (2020a) Diversity, inclusivity, and the importance of L2 speaker legitimacy. *Japanese Language and Literature* 54 (2), 317–325.

Takeuchi, J.D. (2020b) Our language: Linguistic ideologies and Japanese dialect use in L1/L2 interaction. *Japanese Language and Literature* 54 (2), 167–198.

Takeuchi, J.D. (2021) Language ideologies among Japanese foreign language teachers: Keigo and L2 speakers. *Foreign Language Annals* 54 (3), 589–606.

Tanaka, Y. (2007) 「方言コスプレ」にみる「方言おもちゃ化」の時代 [The era of dialect as dialect as plaything, as seen through dialect cosplay]. 文学 8 (6), 123–133.

Tanaka, Y. (2014) 「方言」が価値をもつ時代: StigmaからPrestige、そして…. [When dialect has value: From stigma to prestige, then…]. 都市問題 105–108, 9–17.

Taniguchi, S. and McMahill, C. (2015) Assimilation versus multiculturalism: Struggles over the meaning of 'tabunka kyōsei' in education for language minority children in Japan. In I. Nakane, E. Otsuji and W.S. Armour (eds) *Languages and Identities in a Transitional Japan* (pp. 167–188). New York/London: Routledge.

Teshigawara, M. and Kinsui, S. (2011) Modern Japanese 'role language' (yakuwarigo): Fictionalised orality in Japanese literature and popular culture. *Sociolinguistic Studies* 5 (1), 37–58.

Ueda, K. and Yamashita, H. (eds) (2006) 「共生」の内実：批判的社会言語学からの問いかけ [*The Hidden Reality of 'kyōsei' – Inquiries from Critical Sociolinguistics*]. Tokyo: Sangensha.

Vaish, V. and Tan, T.K. (2008) Language and social class: Linguistic capital in Singapore. Conference presentation at the Annual Meeting of the American Educational Research Association, New York. See http://hdl.handle.net/10497/3339 (accessed 24 November 2012).

Watanabe, T. and Karasawa, K. (2013) 共通語と大阪方言に対する顕在的 潜在的態度の検討 [Explicit and implicit attitudes toward standard-Japanese and Osaka-dialect language use]. 心理学研究 84 (1), 20–27.

Wee, L. (2002) When English is not a mother tongue: Linguistic ownership and the Eurasian community in Singapore. *Journal of Multilingual and Multicultural Development* 23 (4), 282–295.

Wetzel, P.J. (2004) *Keigo in Modern Japan: Polite Language from Meiji to the Present*. Honolulu, HI: University of Hawaii Press.

Widdowson, H.G. (1994) The ownership of English. *TESOL Quarterly* 28 (2), 377–389.

Woolard, K.A. (1992) Language ideology: Issues and approaches. *Pragmatics* 2 (3), 235–249.

Yamada, E. (2021) 「やさしい日本語」による市民との交流を取り入れた多文化クラスの活動 [A report of Yasashii Nihongo (plain Japanese) activities with locals in multicultural classrooms]. メディア コミュニケーション研究 [*Media Communication Kenkyu*] 74, 45–57. http://hdl.handle.net/2115/80911.

Yasashii nihongo ni tsuite (2020) 「やさしい日本語」について [About easy Japanese]. Bureau of Olympic and Paralympic Games Tokyo 2020 Preparation. See https://www.2020games.metro.tokyo.lg.jp/multilingual/references/easyjpn.html (accessed 18 January 2020).

Index

accents
   –dialects 91, 100, 109, 114
   –*keigo* 51
   –native speaker bias 9, 10, 137–9, 142, 144, 147–8, 150
affect, expressions of 17, 43, 97
affiliative stance, indicating 17, 128
agency 12, 41
American Council on the Teaching of Foreign Languages (ACTFL) 127
anime 60, 63, 66, 85, 117
applied linguistics
   –language ideologies 2, 8–10
   –speaker legitimacy 10–11
appropriateness 103, 118, 154
assessment 127
assimilation 7
atashi 61, 67, 69, 71, 86
audio recordings 26, 28, 30
authenticity 65, 95

back-channelling 29, 142
Ball, C. 96
Banno, E. 60
Barešova, I. 39, 40
Barke, A. 39, 42–3, 96–7
bikago 16
Blackledge, A. 2
blogs 129, 133
Bohn, M.T. 68
boku 62, 66, 67, 69, 76, 78, 86
border control 3, 4
Bourdieu, P. 9, 10, 14, 38, 90, 91, 93, 96, 98
Brinkmann, S. 28

'broken Japanese' 133
Brown, L. 69
Bunkacho 5
Burgess, C. 3–4, 5, 7–8, 13, 132, 133
business, language for 42, 81–2, 99 *see also* workplaces

Carlson, R.L. 3, 37, 133, 134
Carroll, T. 3, 39, 43, 90, 92, 93
Cheek, E. 69
citizenship 12, 128, 130, 133
co-construction of knowledge 28
code-switching 92, 93–4, 101, 103
common language (*kyōtsūgo*) 91, 92
communicative competence 12, 128, 142, 144
community building
   –dialects 91, 103, 106
   –language ideologies 10
   –language ownership 132
   –and the need for L2 Japanese 5
competence *see also* proficiency
   –communicative competence 12, 128, 142, 144
   –and ethnicity 130
   –gendered language 69
   –Japanese competence of foreign workers 5, 7
   –*keigo* 59
   –masculine versus feminine forms as markers of 64
   –native speaker bias 12, 127, 128, 135
   –participant characteristics 30
   –speaker legitimacy 10
computer-mediated communication (CMC) 129

confidence 46, 48, 142, 147, 150, 154
Cook, H.M. 13, 41, 42–3, 127, 128
copula forms 40
'correct' language
   –dialects 91, 111, 116, 118
   –gendered language 62
   –*keigo* 42
   –native speaker bias 9, 10, 11–12, 129 *see also* Standard Japanese
   –versus 'smooth communication' 129
Covid-19 23n(2)
cultural identity/heritage 68–9, 92
cultural knowledge, need for 42, 53–4, 121
cursing 80, 110

da-tai (plain form) 39–40, 44
danseigo (men's language) 17, 60–89
data analysis 28–9
Davies, A. 127, 128
deficiency-based positionings of non-native speakers 11, 12, 127 *see also* native speaker bias
de-standardization 94–7
desu/masu-tai (polite form) 40, 44, 47, 48, 56, 58, 86, 111
dialect artefacts 28
dialect cosplay 95, 96
dialects 90–125
   –description of Japanese 17–18
   –gendered language 62, 77, 85
   –JET Program 37
   –language ideologies 9
   –language ownership 14, 15
   –native speaker bias 137–8, 139–40, 148, 154
   –rural areas 36
'difficult,' Japanese viewed as 6–7, 13, 126, 132–3, 141, 157
discrimination 7, 13, 68
diversity of Japanese 62, 67, 95, 127, 130–1, 148–9, 152, 155–8
Doerr, N.M. 12, 127–8, 129, 130, 131, 150
Dunn, C.D. 42

easy/plain Japanese *see yasashii nihongo*
Ebuchi, T. 5
education/schools *see also* JET Program
   –dialects 92, 103–4
   –for foreign residents 158
   –native speaker bias 129–30, 156
Ehime 35–6
Ehime Dialect 17, 99–102
emergency information 96, 132–3
emotion *see* affect, expressions of
employment
   –dialects 110–11, 112–13
   –Ehime area 35–6
   –English teaching in Japan 134
   –*keigo* norms 44
   –native speaker bias 156, 158
   –and the need for L2 Japanese 4–5
English
   –Ehime region 35
   –jobs in Japan 36–7
   –language ideologies 9
   –most research is about 1, 12, 131, 152
   –ownership of 131–2
   –participant characteristics 30
   –research participants 24–5, 26, 27–8, 30
English as a Second Language (ESL) 127–8
English teaching in Japan 36–7, 133–4 *see also* JET Program
errors
   –gendered language 67, 87, 88
   –*keigo* 42, 43, 46–8, 49, 56–7
   –native speaker bias 137
   –teacher correction of 157
ethnicity 12, 65, 127, 128
ethnographic methods 24, 25–7, 129
etiquette 53–4, 63
exchange students 44, 97–8
expert speaker (alternative to 'native speaker') 128

Fairbrother, L. 13
Ferguson, C.A. 146
first-person pronouns 61–2, 66, 67, 74, 76–8, 87
fluency 14, 65, 130 *see also* competence; proficiency
'foreigner talk' 97, 146, 150
formulaic expressions 42
Fukuda, C. 13–14, 15

gaijin 44
Gelin, M. 3
gender and *keigo* 16
gendered language 15–17, 60–89, 95, 104, 122, 139–40, 153–4
Genki textbooks 21, 60
globalization 131
Gottlieb, N. 6, 13, 91, 92
grammar 39–40, 100
Grenfell, M. 10

Hasegawa, A. 5
Hashimoto, K. 6, 7
Heinrich, P. 8, 9, 92, 93, 96, 128
henna gaijin 14, 97
hidden ideologies 5, 7
hierarchies of languages 9
Higgins, C. 10
hōgen bokumetsu undō (movement to eradicate or beat down the dialects) 92
Holliday, A. 127
homestay students 13, 44, 97
honorific language 39–45, 48, 58, 61, 86, 147–8 *see also keigo*
humble speech 16, 39, 40, 48, 49, 58

idealization of native speakers 11, 127–8, 147, 149, 157
identity
  –affective stance 43
  –choice of first-person pronouns 76–8
  –cultural identity/heritage 68–9, 92
  –dialects 95, 97, 103, 106, 107, 109, 115–16, 118, 125
  –fears of 'dilution' by immigration 158
  –gendered language 67–9, 87
  –hybrid 131, 149
  –*keigo* 51, 59
  –native speaker bias 12, 14
  –and the need for L2 Japanese 5
  –outsider identity 18–19, 44, 45, 98, 133, 154
Iino, M. 44, 59, 97, 98, 146, 157
immigration 3–8, 129–30, 132, 158
in vivo coding 29
in-group/insider membership 18–19, 53, 64–5, 68, 96, 116, 120
Inoue, F. 7, 60, 93, 94

interactional sociolinguistics 29
internationalization 132
internet 129 *see also* online communication
interpersonal relationships 16, 103, 113, 116, 119, 123, 124 *see also keigo*
interview methods 26–7, 160–6
intonation 55, 76, 142, 143, 144, 147
Iori, I. 6
Ishihara, N. 44
Itakura, H. 68–9
Ito, H. 7

Japanese as a foreign language (JFL)
  –dialects 98–9
  –gendered language 62, 67, 68
  –*keigo* 40, 43
  –language policies 5
  –native speaker bias 132, 155, 157
Japanese as a Second Language (JSL) 98–9, 130, 132
Japanese Language Proficiency Test (JLPT) 31, 51, 141
Japanese-only ideology 7
JET Program 18–19, 30, 36–7
Jinnouchi, M. 90, 93, 95
Jones, M. 98, 99
joseigo (women's language) 17, 60–89

Kamiyoshi, U. 3, 4, 5, 7, 23n(2)
kanji 5, 145
Kanji Kentei 141
Kansai dialect 82
Karasawa, K. 93, 94
kashira 61
keigo 15–16, 38–59, 61, 153–4
kenjōgo (humble speech) 16, 39, 40, 48, 49, 58
Kimura, G.C. 7
Kinsui, S. 63
Kobayashi, T. 95, 96
Kobe Dialect 95
kokusaika 132
Kramsch, C. 11
Kroskrity, P.V. 2, 9
Kubo, H. 100
Kubota, R. 10, 13, 92, 129
Kumagai, Y. 131
Kurata, Y. 7

Kusunoki, R. 6, 7
Kvale, S. 28
kyōsei (coexisting) 7–8
kyōtsūgo (common language) 91, 92

L1 speakers
 –adjusting speech in presence of L2 speakers 145–6
 –apprehensions about speaking to L2 speakers 141
 –dialects 102–4, 120–3
 –gendered language 61, 73–4, 84–6, 87
 –*keigo* 49–50
 –language ownership 131–4
 –native speaker bias 126–51
 –regional dialects 91
L2 speakers
 –dialects 97–9, 104–24
 –gendered language 60–1, 65, 66, 67–9, 87–9
 –*keigo* 43–5, 46–8, 49, 51, 52–9
 –language ownership 131–4
 –native speaker bias 134–49
language affiliation 17, 128
language ideologies
 –definition of 2
 –dialects 96
 –gendered language 63–4, 66, 70–84, 154
 –hidden ideologies 5, 7
 –*keigo* 41–3, 154
 –monolingual ideologies 5, 7
 –native speaker bias 126–51, 153, 154
 –*nihonjinron* ideology (uniqueness of Japanese) 7, 13–14, 132, 133, 155
 –taken-for-granted/commonsense 8, 62, 128–9, 155
 –varieties of Japanese 9
language inheritance 128
language ownership
 –gendered language 65, 88
 –*keigo* 51
 –and L2 speakers 12–15, 131–4
 –native speaker bias 137, 149, 156
 –regional dialects 90
language policies 5, 92, 130
language shift 94–7

'legitimate language' 10 *see also* 'correct' language; Standard Japanese
Leung, G. 13
LGBTQ+ 89
Liddicoat, A. 127
linguistic capital 9, 38, 90, 91, 93–4, 98
linguistic marginalization 14
linguistic resources
 –dialects 106, 123
 –gendered language 85
 –*keigo* 38, 51, 59
 –L2 speakers 157
linguistic rights 15, 131
literature 47, 60, 63, 64, 66–7
Long, D. 98
Lowe, R.J. 128

MacMahill, C. 7
manga 66, 117
martial arts 52–3, 56, 84–5
Matsumoto, Y. 60, 62
Matsuyama 35–6, 99, 100
media
 –depictions of foreigners 134
 –dialects 91, 92, 113
 –gendered language 60, 63, 66, 68, 72, 75
 –*keigo* 42
 –non-native speakers in media/literature 64
Menard-Warwick, J. 13
meta-linguistic awareness 15
meta-talk 14, 147, 148, 150
Metzgar, E.T. 36
microanalysis 29
migration *see* immigration
minority languages in Japan 7
Mishler, E.G. 28
Miyamoto Caltabiano, Y. 43
monolingual ideologies 5, 7
Moody, S.J. 44, 45, 59, 157
Mori, J. 98
morphology 100–1, 122
Mukai, R. 99
multiculturalism 7–8, 130
multilingualism 7–8

Nakagawa, H. 100

Nakamura, M. 9, 60, 61, 62
nationality 130, 142–3, 149, 155
nation-building 63, 91–2, 155
native speaker bias 1–2, 7, 8, 11–13, 18, 22–23, 38, 45, 59, 61, 65, 126–9, 131, 134, 141, 144, 147, 149–51, 152–6, 158–9
 –gendered language 65–6
 –*keigo* 44, 45, 59
neutral 'everyday' Japanese with respect to gender 72–3, 76
neutral polite language 40, 48
nihonjinron ideology (uniqueness of Japanese) 7, 13–14, 42, 63, 132, 133, 155
Nishizaka, A. 14
Niyekawa, A.M. 40, 43, 157
Norton, B. 14–15, 91, 131

observation methods 28
Occhi, D. 93, 95
Ohara, Y. 62, 63, 67–8
Ohuchi, N. 96
Oka, M. 61, 67
Okamoto, S. 15, 41, 42, 43, 60, 61, 62, 63, 90, 91, 92, 93, 95, 96, 101, 125n(1), 157
Okinawa dialect 130
Okubo, Y. 12, 128, 129, 130–1
one-nation-one-language 130
online communication 95, 129, 133
ore 62, 66, 69, 76–8, 80, 82–3, 84, 86, 87
O'Rourke, B. 11
othering 7, 8, 13, 14, 44, 45, 95, 133, 134, 154
Otomo, R. 5
outsider identity 18–19, 44, 45, 98, 133, 154

Parmegiani, A. 131
participant characteristics 29–36
participant observation methods 24, 28, 30–1
particles 61, 62, 64, 71, 86
Pavlenko, A. 2
Pennycook, A. 128
Phillipson, R. 15
phonology 101 *see also* accents
Pinner, R. 128

pitch 67–8, 85
plain speech *da-tai* ('*da*' form) 39–40, 44
politeness *see also keigo*
 –dialects 118
 –gendered language 61, 62, 64, 79–80
 –native speaker bias 147–8, 153–4
 –previous studies of *keigo* 39–45
positionality, researcher 18–20
prescriptive norms 63
prestige dialects 9, 95, 127
proficiency
 –assessment against native speaker norms 127
 –dialects 98, 104, 105–6, 119–20
 –exclusionary stances towards foreigners 132–4
 –gendered language 67–8, 79
 –JET Program 36–7
 –*keigo* 46–8, 53–7, 58
 –language ownership 13
 –native speaker bias 132–4, 157
 –*nihonjinron*, 13
 –participant characteristics 31
 –resistance to L2 speakers' 65
 –visa conditions 5
Promotion of Japanese Language Education Act (PJLEA, 2019) 5, 7
pronouns 17, 61–2, 66, 67, 69, 74, 76–8, 87
prosody 85

questionnaires 27–8, 168–72

race 127 *see also* ethnicity
racism 13
Ramallo, F.F. 11
Rampton, M.B.H. 127
Ramsey, S.R. 92, 93, 128
recruitment of study participants 24–5, 30
regional dialects *see* dialects
register 39, 43, 50
researcher positionality 18–20
rights 15, 131
role language 63–4
role models, following 75–6, 80, 83, 157
rough-sounding Japanese 62, 70, 80–4, 86, 109–10
Rumsey, A. 8
rural areas 35–6, 95

Saldaña, J. 28, 29
Sanada, S. 90, 91, 92
Sato, S. 129
schools *see* education/schools
scripted speech 63–4
second language acquisition (SLA) research 1, 2, 10–11, 127
Seidman, I. 28
self-effacement 143–4
self/identity
 –affective stance 43
 –choice of first-person pronouns 76–8
 –cultural identity/heritage 68–9, 92
 –dialects 95, 97, 103, 106, 107, 109, 115–16, 118, 125
 –fears of 'dilution' by immigration 158
 –gendered language 67–9, 87
 –hybrid 131, 149
 –*keigo* 51, 59
 –native speaker bias 12, 14
 –and the need for L2 Japanese 5
 –outsider identity 18–19, 44, 45, 98, 133, 154
sentence-final particles 17, 61–4, 71, 86, 103, 145
shakaijin 42
Shibamoto-Smith, J.S. 15, 41, 42, 43, 60, 61, 62, 63, 90, 91, 92, 93, 95, 96, 125n(1), 157
Shibatani, M. 22, 40, 90, 91
Siegal, M.S. 43, 67
Silverstein, M. 8
simplified Japanese 5, 145–7 *see also yasashii nihongo*
slang 13–14, 65, 80, 81, 142, 148
Smith, M.A. 10
social distance 40
social media 95
social mobility 93
sociocultural context 29
sociolinguistic research
 –interactional sociolinguistics 29
 –politeness, gender and locality in Japanese 15
sonkeigo 40, 48, 49
stance, speaker 41, 97
speaker legitimacy 1–2, 10–11, 12, 14, 18, 20, 23, 38, 39, 44–5, 46, 59, 60, 90, 125, 126, 127, 152, 156–8
Standard Japanese *see also* 'correct' language
 –choosing over dialects 110–12, 114, 117, 118, 122, 150
 –dialects measured against 17, 91–7, 99, 101
 –gendered language 63, 65
 –hierarchies of languages 9
 –*keigo* 41–2
 –L1 speakers expect foreigners to stick to 139–40, 145, 148–9
 –standardization processes 17, 41–2, 90, 92, 99–100, 129, 155
standard language ideologies 9, 12, 129
stereotyping
 –dialects 92, 95, 114
 –foreigners 14
 –gendered language 77, 86, 87
 –*keigo* 60, 62, 63–4
 –native speaker bias 128, 135
 –non-native speakers 146
stigmatization 90, 92, 94
Strausz, M. 3, 4, 5
SturtzSreetharan, C.L. 62, 63
Sunaoshi, Y. 62, 92, 95
Suzuki, A. 13
Suzuki, S. 21, 60, 63, 64–5, 88
swearing 80, 110
symbolic capital 9, 10
tabunka-kyōsei (multicultural coexisting) 7–8

Takato, M. 129–30
Takatori, Y. 64
Takeuchi, J.D. 13, 14, 43, 133, 156, 157, 159
Tanaka, Y. 95, 101
Taniguchi, S. 7
Tarone, E. 44
teachers 6, 12, 156–7 *see also* JET Program
teineigo 40, 48
television 63, 72, 75, 80, 85, 92, 94–5, 113
textbooks 6, 60, 66–7, 118
thematic analysis 28–9

thick description 24
Tobira textbook 61, 66–7
Tokarev, A. 7
Tokyo dialect 92, 155
Toyko Olympics 6
TPO (time, place, occasion) 103
transcription conventions 29, 167
translation 64, 66
tsukaiwake 93, 103 *see also* code-switching

uchi 79
uniqueness of Japanese (*nihonjinron* ideology) 7, 13–14, 42, 63, 132, 133, 155
verb forms 100–1, 122
vernacular varieties 13–14
visa conditions 3–4, 5, 158
vocabulary
   –dialects 100
   –gendered language 62, 85
voice 67–8
vulgar language 62, 80, 81, 86–7

wa 61, 64, 67, 69, 71, 86, 87
Watanabe, T. 93, 94

watashi 17, 61, 67, 69, 76, 78, 86
Wee, L. 10, 13, 14, 131
Wetzel, P.J. 39, 40–1
Woolard, K.A. 8
workplaces
   –dialects 96–7, 98, 100, 103, 110–11, 114
   –gendered language 68, 71
   –*keigo* 40–1, 47, 48, 49–50
   –native speaker bias 156

xenophobia 3

yakuwarigo (role language) 63–4
Yamada, E. 6
yasashii nihongo 5–7, 132–3, 145, 146, 158
yo 64–5, 67
Your Name (Shinkai, 2016) 66

ze 62, 64, 67
Zhang, L. 11
zo 62, 64, 67

For Product Safety Concerns and Information please contact our EU Authorised Representative:

Easy Access System Europe

Mustamäe tee 50

10621 Tallinn

Estonia

gpsr.requests@easproject.com

www.ingramcontent.com/pod-product-compliance
Lightning Source LLC
Chambersburg PA
CBHW050327020526
44117CB00031B/1980